CHAMPI**NS**

2003/2004 PREMIERSHIP WINNERS

2003/2004 OFFICIAL YEARBOOK

hamlyn

Acknowledgements
The publisher would like to thank Julian Flanders, Joe Cohen,
Ivan Ponting, Stuart MacFarlane and Vic Ackers for their help
throughout this project.

Produced for Hamlyn by Butler and Tanner

First published in 2004 by Hamlyn,
a division of Octopus Publishing Group Ltd,
2–4 Heron Quays, London E14 4JP

ISBN 0 600 61201 5

A CIP catalogue record for this book is available from the British Library

Printed and bound in the UK by Butler & Tanner Ltd.

10 9 8 7 6 5 4 3 2 1

Executive Editor Trevor Davies
Project Editor Julian Flanders at Butler and Tanner
Design Craig Stevens, Kathie Wilson and Lyn Davies at Butler and Tanner
Production Ian Paton
All images Copyright © Arsenal Football Club Plc /Stuart MacFarlane

All statistics are complete to 31 May, 2004

Arsenal.com

CONTENTS

DIRECTORS

Peter Hill-Wood (Chairman)
David Dein (Vice-Chairman)
Sir Roger Gibbs
Richard Carr
Daniel Fiszman
Ken Friar OBE

Managing Director
Keith Edelman

Manager
Arsène Wenger

Secretary
David Miles

MAJOR HONOURS

League Champions 1930–31, 1932–33, 1933–34, 1934–35, 1937–38, 1947–48, 1952–53, 1970–71, 1988–89, 1990–91, 1997–98, 2001–02, 2003–04

FA Cup Winners 1929–30, 1935–36, 1949–50, 1970–71, 1978–79, 1992–93, 1997–98, 2001–02, 2002–03

League Cup Winners 1986–87, 1992–93

European Fairs Cup Winners 1969–70

European Cup Winners Cup Winners 1993–94

FA Youth Cup Winners 1965–66, 1970–71, 1987–88, 1993–94, 1999–2000, 2000–01

CLUB INFORMATION

Address Arsenal Stadium, Avenell Road, Highbury, London N5 1BU

Club 020-7704-4000
Box Office 020-7704-4040
Recorded ticket information 020-7704-4242
Commercial Department 020-7704-4100
Website www.arsenal.com
Information info@arsenal.co.uk

Junior Gunners 020-7704-4160/4150
Arsenal Travel Club 020-7704-4150/4160

ARSENAL IN THE COMMUNITY

t 020-7704-4140
f 020-7704-4141
e bnicholas@arsenal.co.uk

ARSENAL MERCHANDISE

The Gunners Shop 020-7704-4120
Arsenal World Of Sport 020-7272-1000
Mail Order Credit Line 020-7704-2020

Arsenal Museum contact Iain Cook on 020-7704-4100

MANAGER'S MESSAGE

What we have achieved at Arsenal during the 2003/2004 season will live with the players and the Club forever. To win the championship is tremendous, because it is not easy to do in this country. But to do it without losing a match, and then to remain undefeated for the whole season, is almost beyond belief. It is a feat which has earned the team a place among the immortals of sporting history, and I am proud to have been a part of it.

We have played magnificent football at times, with everyone in the squad making a significant contribution. For example, you take a player like Kolo Toure who has played his first year in the Premiership. He will improve. Also at the back you have Sol Campbell, who is getting better and better every year and then up front Thierry Henry in whom I believe we have the finest striker in the world.

It is not just that we have played beautifully, but we have shown spirit, too. Combine those two attributes and you have a wonderful team.

Of course, we had our disappointments in Europe and in the FA Cup, but I am convinced that topping the English League table is the truest measure of a team's ability.

Now is the time to enjoy Arsenal's remarkable triumph, but also to look forward to reaching new heights. Next year there will be a challenge to win honours again and we will go for it.

ARSÈNE WENGER

AUGUST

FA Community Shield
Sunday 10 August 2003 at the Millennium Stadium, Cardiff 2.00 p.m.
Attendance: 59,293 Referee: Steve Bennett

FORM GUIDE
W D L W W W [17 goals scored, 6 conceded]   D W W W W W [17 goals scored, 8 conceded]

ARSENAL 1
Henry 20

MANCHESTER UNITED 1
Silvestre 15

Substitutes		Jens **LEHMANN**	1	14	Tim **HOWARD**		Substitutes
Stuart **TAYLOR**	13	**LAUREN**	12	3	Phil **NEVILLE** ▪	13	Roy **CARROLL**
Pascal **CYGAN**	18	Sol **CAMPBELL**	23	5	Rio **FERDINAND**	22	John **O'SHEA** ▶
▶ Giovanni **VAN**		Kolo **TOURE**	28	27	Mikael **SILVESTRE**		(Fortune) 69 ◀
BRONCKHORST	16	▪ Ashley **COLE**	3	25	Quinton **FORTUNE** ▪	12	David **BELLION**
◀ (Ljungberg) 65		Ray **PARLOUR**	15	20	Ole **GUNNAR SOLSKJAER**	19	Eric **DJEMBA-DJEMBA** ▶
▶ **EDU**	17	▪ Patrick **VIEIRA**	4	8	Nicky **BUTT**		(Butt) 61 ◀
◀ (Gilberto) 60		**GILBERTO**	19	16	Roy **KEANE**	21	Diego **FORLAN** ▶
▶ Robert **PIRES**	7	Fredrik **LJUNGBERG**	8	18	Paul **SCHOLES**		(Neville) 78 ◀
◀ (Parlour) 46		Dennis **BERGKAMP**	10	11	Ryan **GIGGS** ▪	23	Kieran **RICHARDSON**
▶ Sylvain **WILTORD**	11	Thierry **HENRY**	14	10	Ruud **VAN NISTELROOY**	24	Darren **FLETCHER**
◀ (Henry) 46							
▪ ▶ Francis **JEFFERS**	9						
◀ (Bergkamp) 60							

MANCHESTER UNITED won 4-3 on penalties
MANCHESTER UNITED penalties:
Scholes scored, **Ferdinand** scored, **van Nistelrooy** missed, **Solskjaer** scored, **Forlan** scored
ARSENAL penalties: **Edu** scored, **van Bronckhorst** missed, **Wiltord** scored, **Lauren** scored, **Pires** missed

| MATCH REPORT

On the hottest day ever recorded in Britain, Arsenal lost the Community Shield in a penalty shoot-out. Given the sweltering conditions, both the Gunners and Manchester United performed creditably in a tight contest, which was more important as a workout for the coming campaign than for the result.

Arsenal's preparation had been hampered by the late return of several key players from Confederations Cup duty, and open spaces in the stands at the north Londoners' end of the stadium suggested that travel problems during the holiday period had taken a toll on public enthusiasm. The players, though, remained fiercely committed and the game began at such a furious tempo that men from each side, Neville and Cole, were shown yellow cards inside the first two minutes.

As the action settled, the Gunners were the first to deliver a meaningful strike, but Henry's speculative 30-yarder drifted wide. However, the response from United was devastating as Keane touched on a Giggs corner and Silvestre charged forward unopposed to nod past Lehmann, who was making his debut between Arsenal's

Thierry Henry celebrates Arsenal's first goal of the season.

posts. Immediately Arsène Wenger's men attacked in search of an equaliser and they were rewarded within five minutes when Butt's foul was punished by Henry's arcing 35-yard free-kick, the Frenchman's shot breaching an inadequate defensive wall and eluding the despairing dive of Howard, the Red Devils' new goalkeeper.

Now United launched a succession of forays, and they went perilously close to regaining the advantage after 33 minutes when Giggs glanced a Solskjaer cross against the foot of an upright, then van Nistelrooy clipped the crossbar from the rebound. Silvestre and Solskjaer both went close shortly before the interval, and van Nistelrooy failed narrowly to hook home a Giggs dispatch at the start of the second period.

But gradually Pires, called from the bench to replace Parlour, grew in influence and after 55 minutes he broke clear of several trailing opponents, only to chip wide from 20 yards. Thereafter Scholes, Giggs and Djemba-Djemba threatened for United, as did Wiltord for Arsenal. With 15 minutes of the game left Jeffers was sent off following a clash with Neville.

Now the ten men were forced back in the stifling heat, but they contained United comfortably enough and deep into injury time Wiltord might have plundered a winner when he was through on Howard, only for the American to pull off a courageous block.

Thus the day was to be decided by penalties, and after a van Bronckhorst miss saw Arsenal in arrears, Lehmann's fabulous save from van Nistelrooy offered new hope. But then Howard denied Pires and the Community Shield changed hands.

Patrick Vieira and Roy Keane demonstrate the fierce commitment of both teams despite the energy-sapping heat.

Jens Lehmann plunges to his right to keep out van Nistelrooy's penalty.

FORM GUIDE

D L W W W D [16 goals scored, 7 conceded]   **W L L W L L** [7 goals scored, 12 conceded]

ARSENAL 2   EVERTON 1
Henry pen 33, Pires 57   Radzinski 83

Substitutes	Jens **LEHMANN**	1	1	Richard **WRIGHT**	**Substitutes**	
Stuart **TAYLOR** 13	**LAUREN**	12	3	Alessandro **PISTONE**	13 Steve **SIMONSEN**	
◄ Martin **KEOWN** 5	Kolo **TOURE**	28	20	Joseph **YOBO**	5 David **WEIR**	
► (Wiltord) 30	■ Sol **CAMPBELL**	23	4	Alan **STUBBS**	12 Li **TIE** ◄ ■■	
◄ Ray **PARLOUR** 15	Ashley **COLE**	3	6	David **UNSWORTH**	(Unsworth) 67 ►	
► (Pires) 70	Fredrik **LJUNGBERG**	8	2	Steve **WATSON**	15 Gary **NAYSMITH** ◄	
Dennis **BERGKAMP** 10	■ Patrick **VIEIRA**	4	22	Tobias **LINDEROTH**	(Pembridge) 67 ►	
Francis **JEFFERS** 9	**GILBERTO**	19	16	Thomas **GRAVESEN** ■	18 Wayne **ROONEY** ◄ ■	
	Robert **PIRES**	7	11	Mark **PEMBRIDGE**	(Linderoth) 57 ►	
	Sylvain **WILTORD**	11	30	Nick **CHADWICK**		
	Thierry **HENRY**	14	8	Tomasz **RADZINSKI**		

MATCH REPORT

When the going gets tough, the Gunners get going. Refusing to be fazed by the first-half dismissal of Sol Campbell before a goal was scored, Arsenal displayed spirit and flair in equal measure to triumph over Everton in a pulsating encounter on the opening day of the Premiership campaign. Star of the show was Thierry Henry, who netted once, contributed centrally to the hosts' second strike, and worked prodigiously as

Gilberto's pace takes him past Everton's Thomas Gravesen.

the sole all-out attacker after Arsène Wenger's team had been reduced to ten men.

Yet in the early stages it had been the Merseysiders who had carried the most potent threat and they might have taken the lead when Radzinski crossed from the right to Chadwick, whose close-range stab was diverted clear by Lehmann's left leg. Arsenal hit back through a 30-yard Henry free-kick which dipped on to the roof of Wright's net, but Everton continued to raid dangerously and their enterprise almost paid off in the 24th minute when Gravesen surged goalwards past Gilberto and Toure. However, Gravesen was tripped by Campbell who, as the last defender, was shown the red card. Stubbs' resultant free-kick was blocked by Ljungberg.

The Gunners reorganised with Keown joining the action in place of front-runner Wiltord, and despite their numerical disadvantage they assumed the upper hand. Claims for a penalty were refused when Pires was felled by Unsworth, but soon Stubbs handballed under pressure from Henry and the Frenchman sent Wright the wrong way with a perfect spot-kick.

Now the Gunners began to play with their customary fluency and almost doubled their lead shortly before the break when Henry intercepted a loose pass from Gravesen and set up a clear opening for Gilberto. Alas, the Brazilian miscontrolled the ball with only Wright to beat and the chance was gone.

Arsenal remained convincing at the outset of the second half and Vieira was only fractionally wide with a firm header from a Pires corner. Radzinski responded with a right-wing dash climaxed by a cross-shot which cleared Lehmann's far post, but immediately the Gunners counter-attacked to lethal effect. When the ball fell to Henry his thunderous 25-yarder was parried by Wright, who also repelled Vieira's follow-up, but the former Highbury keeper was finally beaten from six yards when Pires seized on a third rebound. Everton might have fallen even further behind after Lauren was fouled by Rooney, but Wright saved brilliantly from Vieira at point-blank range after Gilberto had touched on Henry's tempting dispatch.

Next Henry was flattened by Gravesen and Ljungberg's exquisitely curled free-kick smacked against the Toffees' bar before bouncing to safety. Still the visitors were not beaten and Radzinski revived their hopes of a comeback when he capitalised on determined work by Li Tie, Yobo and Naysmith to fire a low shot past Lehmann from 15 yards. However, Everton's renewed optimism was punctured when the Chinese midfielder was dismissed four minutes later for a second bookable offence, and Arsenal cruised through the closing stages in relative comfort.

Robert Pires seizes on a rebound to sidefoot the ball home for the Gunners' winning goal.

AUGUST

FA Barclaycard Premiership
Sunday 24 August 2003 at the Riverside Stadium, 4.05 p.m.
Attendance: 29,452 Referee: Dermot Gallagher

FORM GUIDE

L L L W L L [8 goals scored, 12 conceded]   L W W W D W [16 goals scored, 6 conceded]

MIDDLESBROUGH 0   ARSENAL 4

Henry 5, Gilberto 13, Wiltord 22, 60

Substitutes					Substitutes
Carlo **NASH**	25	Mark **SCHWARZER**	1	1 Jens **LEHMANN**	Stuart **TAYLOR** 13
◀ Andrew **DAVIES**	24	Colin **COOPER** 28	12	**LAUREN**	Martin **KEOWN** 5
▶ (Riggott) 66		Chris **RIGGOTT** 5	28	Kolo **TOURE**	Ray **PARLOUR** ◀ 15
Robbie **STOCKDALE**	2	Gareth **SOUTHGATE** 6	23	Sol **CAMPBELL**	(Ljungberg) 75 ▶
Mark **WILSON**	18	Stuart **PARNABY** 21	3	Ashley **COLE**	**EDU** ◀ 17
◀ Stewart **DOWNING**	19	Alan **WRIGHT** 22	8	Fredrik **LJUNGBERG**	(Pires) 75 ▶
▶ (Nemeth) 85		George **BOATENG** 7	19	**GILBERTO**	Dennis **BERGKAMP** ◀ 10
		Guidoni **DORIVA** 20	4	Patrick **VIEIRA**	(Wiltord) 75 ▶
		JUNINHO 10	7	Robert **PIRES**	
		Szilard **NEMETH** 8	11	Sylvain **WILTORD**	
		Malcolm **CHRISTIE** 11	14	Thierry **HENRY**	

MATCH REPORT

Arsenal put shell-shocked Middlesbrough to the sword in the Riverside sunshine and moved alongside Manchester United as early Premiership pacesetters. Three goals in the opening quarter ended the game as a meaningful contest, paving the way for a second-half cruise during which the Gunners added a fourth exquisitely crafted strike.

Yet Boro had been first into their attacking stride after only 40 seconds when a loose ball rebounded to Nemeth in the visitors' box, only for the Slovakian to fire wastefully high from a narrow angle. Arsenal's response was devastating as they engulfed Steve McClaren's men in a tidal wave of fluent assaults, which began when Vieira threaded a delightful pass to Ljungberg, who shrugged off a challenge on the right flank before unleashing a low cross-shot. Schwarzer plunged to his right but could only parry into the path of the onrushing Henry, who tapped home from six yards.

Soon the Australian keeper was in action again, tipping away a rasping 25-yarder from Wiltord. Ljungberg volleyed high from a similar distance before the Gunners doubled their lead. Cole and

Middlesborough's George Boateng fails to stop Lauren's surging run.

Henry exchanged passes with slick precision near the left touchline before the Frenchman checked

It's a team game. Pires, Ljungberg, Henry and two-goal Sylvain Wiltord celebrate Arsenal's fourth goal.

inside a tackle and crossed for Gilberto to net with a fabulous 15-yard volley. It was the Brazilian's first Premiership goal and it left Middlesbrough in a state of defensive disarray.

Still the tidal wave of Arsenal pressure did not abate and after a Ljungberg cross had been scrambled behind by Southgate, Pires' corner was met by a thunderous Campbell header, which shaved an upright. Next it was the turn of Henry, who saw his long-distance drive held by Schwarzer, and then a Lauren surge was foiled by a last-ditch intervention before the third goal arrived in a truly majestic manner. Pires sent Henry forward on the left and Thierry cut inside before to passing to Wiltord, who directed the ball inside the far post with a cushioned side-foot from six yards.

At last Boro hit back, only for Lehmann to pull off a courageous block at the feet of the charging Nemeth, then Juninho miskicked in front of goal following smart work by the Slovakian.

Before half-time Henry went close with a bending shot and a looping header, then the start of the second period signalled the hosts' most menacing spell to date, with Lehmann being forced to save from both Nemeth and Juninho.

Any faint Middlesbrough hope was squashed, however, when Campbell speared an incisive through-ball to Ljungberg, who produced a neat cut-back from the right for Wiltord to sweep in from five yards. Henry threatened further grief when he sprinted through the home rearguard, but his cross was cleared by Wright, after which Juninho attempted to raise the spirits of Riverside regulars with a flurry of enterprising dribbles. Lehmann was never unduly troubled, though, and Arsène Wenger made a triple substitution as his men coasted comfortably towards the finishing line. As a demonstration of intent for the coming season, Arsenal's display had been impressive.

FORM GUIDE
W W W D W W [18 goals scored, 3 conceded]   D L W L L D [5 goals scored, 8 conceded]

ARSENAL 2   ASTON VILLA 0
Campbell 57, Henry 90

Substitutes				Substitutes
	Jens **LEHMANN**	1	1	Thomas **SORENSEN**	
Stuart **TAYLOR** 13	**LAUREN**	12	2	Mark **DELANEY** ■	
Martin **KEOWN** 5	■ Kolo **TOURE**	28	4	Olof **MELLBERG**	Stefan **POSTMA** 13
◀ Ray **PARLOUR** 15	Sol **CAMPBELL**	23	27	Ronny **JOHNSEN**	Ozalan **ALPAY** 5
▶ (Ljungberg) 78	Ashley **COLE**	3	3	J Lloyd **SAMUEL**	Thomas **HITZLSPERGER** 12
EDU 17	Fredrik **LJUNGBERG**	8	15	Ulises **DE LA CRUZ**	Hassan **KACHLOUL** 22
■ ◀ Dennis **BERGKAMP** 10	**GILBERTO**	19	7	Lee **HENDRIE** ■	Darius **VASSELL** ◀ 10
▶ (Wiltord) 67	■ Patrick **VIEIRA**	4	26	Mark **KINSELLA**	(Kinsella) 59 ▶
	Robert **PIRES**	7	6	Gareth **BARRY**	
	Sylvain **WILTORD**	11	17	Pete **WHITTINGHAM** ■	
	Thierry **HENRY**	14	18	Juan Pablo **ANGEL** ■	

MATCH REPORT

Arsenal suffered long periods of frustration against David O'Leary's hard-working Villains, and were indebted to a slickly poached goal from Sol Campbell for breaking the deadlock nearly an hour into the action. There seemed to be little danger from a Pires corner until Samuel, well placed to clear, miskicked with an inexplicable backpass; Hendrie's desperate lunge deflected the ball on to the crossbar and Campbell was on hand to nod home the rebound from six yards.

Earlier there had seemed little prospect of such a close encounter as the Gunners had dominated the opening stages. Henry led the charge as usual, speeding past Delaney and cutting in from the left,

Sol Campbell points the way after heading the Gunners into the lead.

Patrick Vieira bursts through the Villa defence despite the attentions of Hendrie and De La Cruz.

only to be halted by a messy but effective joint clearance by Sorensen and Samuel. From the resultant corner, Pires fired a cross-shot marginally beyond the far post. Moments later Toure found Henry with a beautiful pass but the Frenchman's lob from the edge of the area bounced narrowly wide.

Soon Ljungberg went even closer when he was set up by Vieira and Henry, and though the Swede's curling chip evaded Sorensen, the ball bounced back off the crossbar before skewing awkwardly to the onrushing Wiltord, whose header was just wide.

At last Villa, who were doing their best to stifle their hosts with a five-man midfield, offered an attacking threat of their own, but Lehmann moved smartly to clutch a 30-yard drive by Kinsella following a half-clearance from Whittingham's cross, and the lively Angel was off-target with a toe-poke after turning neatly past Lauren.

After the interval the visitors showed further signs of enterprise, but offside decisions against Hendrie and Barry halted their progress before Campbell's opportunism changed the picture. But Villa refused to lie down and with the speedy Vassell rising from the bench to increase their offensive options, they pushed forward in search of an equaliser. Angel went close with a savage free-kick which brushed Lehmann's upright, but the Midlanders' enter-prise was exposing

gaps at the back and gradually Arsenal began to re-assert their authority.

Henry exchanged passes with Parlour on the right before chipping sweetly to Pires, who glanced a header wide from six yards when a second goal seemed inevitable. The same trio was involved again when Parlour's miscued nod from Henry's dispatch fell to Pires, whose low drive was saved by the diving Sorensen.

Still Highbury could not relax with only a single-goal margin and there was a collective sigh of relief when Henry put the issue beyond doubt in the final minute. Bergkamp pressurised Mellberg on the left and as the ball squirmed clear of the Swedish defender, Sorensen raced from his goal to claim it. However, Henry reached it first, rounded the keeper and bent home an unerring shot from a narrow angle.

The Gunners' speed on the ball and their intelligence off it, especially in the opening and closing periods of the game, had secured them a deserved victory in a far from easy match.

Thierry Henry slips the ball past Villa keeper Sorensen to wrap up the points for the Gunners.

AUGUST

FA Barclaycard Premiership
Sunday 31 August 2003 at the City of Manchester Stadium, 4.05 p.m.
Attendance: 46,436 Referee: Graham Poll

FORM GUIDE

L W W D W W [14 goals scored, 4 conceded]   W W D W W W [14 goals scored, 2 conceded]

MANCHESTER CITY 1
Lauren o.g. 10

ARSENAL 2
Wiltord 48, Ljungberg 72

Substitutes					Substitutes
Nicky **WEAVER**	12	David **SEAMAN** 1	1 Jens **LEHMANN**	13	Stuart **TAYLOR**
Richard **DUNNE**	22	Sun **JIHAI** 17	12 **LAUREN**	18	Pascal **CYGAN**
◀ Eyal **BERKOVIC**	14	David **SOMMEIL** 2	5 Martin **KEOWN**	15	Ray **PARLOUR** ◀
▶ (Bosvelt) 79		Sylvain **DISTIN** 5	28 Kolo **TOURE**		(Ljungberg) 76 ▶
◀ Danny **TIATTO**		Michael **TARNAT** 18	3 Ashley **COLE**	17	**EDU** ◀
▶ (Sibierski) 69		Shaun **WRIGHT-PHILLIPS** 29	8 Fredrik **LJUNGBERG**		(Pires) 83 ▶
◀ Robbie **FOWLER**		Paul **BOSVELT** 26	19 **GILBERTO**	10	Dennis **BERGKAMP** ◀
▶ (Wright-Phillips) 79		Joey **BARTON** 24	4 Patrick **VIEIRA**		(Wiltord) 76 ▶
		Trevor **SINCLAIR** 28	7 Robert **PIRES**		
		Antoine **SIBIERSKI** 10	11 Sylvain **WILTORD**		
		Nicolas **ANELKA** 39	14 Thierry **HENRY**		

MATCH REPORT

Arsenal maintained their 100 per cent start to the League campaign, bouncing back from a bizarre own goal to beat Manchester City and move three points clear at the top of the table. A home victory would have put Kevin Keegan's men at the top of the table so the stakes were high as the Gunners paid their first visit to the plush City of Manchester Stadium.

The encounter got off to a lacklustre start but burst into action in the tenth minute when Sky Blues' skipper Distin launched a long clearance which Lauren appeared to be shepherding comfortably into the safe custody of Lehmann. The reliable Cameroonian was shoved by Sinclair as he took an awkward first touch, and unfortunately shinned the ball into the far corner of his own net with his second contact.

Arsenal needed to raise their game, but Henry mishit a volley, then Pires fired straight at former team-mate Seaman. For the next 20 minutes it was ambitious City who called the shots. Wright-Phillips threatened havoc with a sinuous dribble before being squeezed out by Cole, Anelka sidefooted high from a Tarnat cross, then Lehmann

made two good saves, pulling off a smart catch from Sibierski's shot on the turn and plunging to his left to repel an Anelka scorcher.

As the interval approached the visitors began to look increasingly convincing and Seaman had to be at his most alert to deal with efforts from Ljungberg and Wiltord.

Ashley Cole shows the necessary commitment as he tussles with City's Shaun Wright-Phillips.

Evidently Arsène Wenger's half-time team talk was effective as Arsenal began the second period with a fresh attitude and a will to win. This was evident almost immediately when Cole eluded Wright-Phillips to reach a neat Pires dispatch on the byline, setting up a pull-back for Wiltord to equalise from six yards.

Now the Gunners exerted steady pressure as City became ragged, and Ljungberg hooked over the crossbar from close range when he might have snatched the lead.

The Sky Blues rallied midway through the second half and had two shots at goal on target in the space of a minute. First Sibierski poked tamely at Lehmann from 12 yards, and then Anelka hit a venomous 20-yard drive that demanded a sharp save from the keeper. Lehman duly obliged.

Arsenal weathered that brief storm and gradually seized the initiative, although there was an element of fortune about their decisive goal. Ljungberg darted across the City defence and found Wiltord, who passed forward for the charging Pires. Seaman and Sun Jihai appeared to have the threat covered between them, but confusion ensued and the ball bounced off the keeper's knee to the lurking Ljungberg, who slotted in clinically from ten yards.

After that the Gunners might have extended their advantage, but the ball escaped Henry after getting past Seaman, then the Frenchman skinned a post with a low shot. As for City, they never menaced seriously again, their best effort being a late Fowler header from a Tarnat corner.

Freddie Ljungberg accepts the congratulations of his team-mates after putting Arsenal ahead in the 72nd minute.

Arsenal.com PLAYER OF THE MONTH

Kolo TOURE

" Kolo has been outstanding in August and he deserves his recognition. The fact that this award would have been unexpected a month ago shows how full of surprises football can be. Also it demonstrates how well Arsenal fans know the game, quickly assessing what Kolo has done for us alongside Sol Campbell at the centre of defence. **"**

ARSÈNE WENGER

" Kolo came to the Club as a central defender and plays there for his country, so it's not new to him. But he's showed how adaptable he is by playing in other positions, where he's excelled, too, using his pace and ability. He's very willing to learn and asks lots of questions, then he takes the knowledge he's gathered into match situations, which is very encouraging to see. **"**

MARTIN KEOWN

" I am very happy for Kolo. Last year he was playing at right back or in midfield, but I think centre back is his real position and he's really enjoying his football. Kolo is one of those guys who just loves the game. **"**

PATRICK VIEIRA

ARSENAL DIARY

Monday 4 August
- Arsenal sign 18-year-old French full-back Gael Clichy from Cannes.

Friday 8 August
- The Gunners announce new long-term kit sponsorship deal with Nike.

Tuesday 12 August
- Patrick Vieira and Robert Pires agree new contracts with Arsenal.

Tuesday 26 August
- Arsenal announce children's charity 'ChildLine' as the club's first Charity of the Season.
- Giovanni van Bronckhorst departs for a season's loan with Barcelona.

Sunday 31 August
- Francis Jeffers returns to his former club, Everton, on loan for the rest of the season.

THE WIDER WORLD

Wednesday 6 August
- Chelsea announce arrival of Juan Sebastian Veron from Manchester United and Joe Cole from West Ham.

Saturday 9 August
- Death of former Blackburn Rovers manager Ray Harford after cancer battle.
- Manchester United youngster Jimmy Davis, on loan at Watford, killed in car crash.

Tuesday 12 August
- Manchester United complete the signings of Kleberson from Atletico Paranaense and Cristiano Ronaldo from Sporting Lisbon.

Wednesday 13 August
- Newcastle and Chelsea win their opening Champions League qualifiers.

Sunday 24 August
- West Ham sack manager Glenn Roeder.

Saturday 30 August
- David Beckham scores on League debut for Real Madrid.

FA CARLING PREMIERSHIP

31 August 2003

	P	HOME					AWAY					Pts
		W	D	L	F	A	W	D	L	F	A	
ARSENAL	3	2	0	0	4	1	1	0	0	4	0	9
Manchester United	3	2	0	0	5	0	1	0	0	2	1	9
Portsmouth	4	2	0	0	6	1	0	2	0	1	1	8
Manchester City	3	0	1	0	1	1	2	0	0	6	2	7
Chelsea	3	1	1	0	4	3	1	0	0	2	1	7
Birmingham City	3	1	0	0	1	0	1	1	0	1	0	7
Fulham	3	1	0	0	3	2	1	0	1	4	3	6
Blackburn Rovers	4	1	0	1	7	4	0	2	0	4	4	5
Liverpool	4	0	1	1	1	2	1	1	0	3	0	5
Charlton Athletic	4	0	1	1	2	5	1	1	0	4	0	5
Leeds United	4	0	2	0	2	2	1	0	1	4	4	5
Aston Villa	4	1	1	0	3	1	0	0	2	1	4	4
Everton	4	1	0	1	3	4	0	1	1	3	4	4
Tottenham Hotspur	4	1	0	1	2	4	0	1	1	0	1	4
Southampton	3	0	1	0	0	0	0	2	0	2	2	3
Leicester City	4	0	2	0	2	2	0	0	2	2	5	2
Bolton Wanderers	4	0	2	0	2	2	0	0	2	0	8	2
Newcastle United	3	0	0	2	1	3	0	1	0	2	2	1
Middlesbrough	4	0	0	2	2	7	0	1	1	2	3	1
Wolverhampton Wanderers	4	0	1	1	0	4	0	0	2	1	6	1

FORM GUIDE
W D W W W W [12 goals scored, 3 conceded]   W W W D W D [15 goals scored, 4 conceded]

ARSENAL 1   PORTSMOUTH 1
Henry pen 40   **Sheringham 26**

Substitutes		Arsenal			Portsmouth		Substitutes
		Jens **LEHMANN**	1	1	Shaka **HISLOP**		Substitutes
Graham **STACK**	33	**LAUREN**	12	28	Sebastien **SCHEMMEL**	25	Harald **WAPENAAR**
Martin **KEOWN**	5	Sol **CAMPBELL**	23	6	Arjan **DE ZEEUW**	5	Hayden **FOXE**
Fredrik **LJUNGBERG**	8	Kolo **TOURE**	28	3	Dejan **STEFANOVIC**	8	Tim **SHERWOOD** ◄
◄ (Edu) 69		Ashley **COLE**	3	4	Boris **ZIVKOVIC**		(Sheringham) 90 ►
► Sylvain **WILTORD**	11	Ray **PARLOUR**	15	19	Steve **STONE**	30	Alexei **SMERTIN** ◄
◄ (Bergkamp) 73		Patrick **VIEIRA**	4	15	AMDY **FAYE**		(Berger) 33 ►
► Jeremie **ALIADIERE**	30	**EDU**	17	11	Nigel **QUASHIE**	31	Jason **ROBERTS** ◄
		Robert **PIRES**	7	23	Patrik **BERGER**		(Yakubu) 71 ►
		Dennis **BERGKAMP**	10	10	Teddy **SHERINGHAM**		
		Thierry **HENRY**	14	20	YAKUBU **AIYEGBENI**		

MATCH REPORT

The Gunners dropped their first League points of the season after their best start for 56 years, but still managed to hit back from a goal down to claim the draw that kept them at the Premiership summit. In truth, Arsène Wenger's men were not at their superlative best, but immense credit should go to unbeaten Portsmouth for the verve and enterprise which maintained their own place among the early front-runners.

The visitors began purposefully, but Berger fired high and wide with a 30-yard free-kick, then Quashie was even further off target with a half-volley after Lehmann had punched out a Faye cross. Arsenal retaliated but Henry's clip was deflected to safety and Parlour was marginally high with a fierce drive from the edge of the box after bursting on to a neat pass from Lauren.

The Gunners' rearguard was sliced open twice in quick succession as Pompey counter-attacked with venom. The first assault resulted in a narrow escape as Yakubu raced on to a through-pass from Quashie, slipping away from Campbell and Cole, only to fire into Lehmann's midriff from 18 yards with the goal at his mercy. But the

second brought more serious consequences as Schemmel's deft dispatch freed Stone on the right and Sheringham, the reigning Barclaycard Premiership player of the month, converted the midfielder's whipped cross with a firm diving header.

Patrick Vieira's progress is halted painfully by Pompey's Steve Stone.

Kolo Toure shapes to shoot but a last-ditch tackle from De Zeeuw prevents a clean contact.

Stung into action, the Gunners surged forward in search of a quick equaliser, and they went close when Cole's delivery from the left was sliced on to the roof of his own net by De Zeeuw. However, parity was not long in coming. Pires exchanged passes with Edu before charging into the box, where he sprawled headlong after contesting for the ball with Stefanovic. The contact resulted in the referee awarding a penalty. Even then the tension did not end after the shot, as Henry's first conversion was disallowed for encroachment. The Frenchman remained unperturbed, though, sucessfully slotting his second effort into the opposite corner of the net.

In a frantic opening to the second half Bergkamp might have scored twice, but Hislop blocked his close-range effort after a miskick by De Zeeuw. After that the keeper pulled off a brilliant plunging parry after the Dutchman had danced past two challenges. At the other end, Yakubu might have restored Pompey's lead after a slip by Campbell, but the dashing Nigerian arced marginally wide from 18 yards.

Thereafter Arsenal exerted steady pressure, with Vieira, Pires and Henry combining sweetly, but a win was just beyond reach. Hislop beat out a high-velocity curling free-kick from Edu, Toure miscued from three yards after Wiltord had cushioned a hanging cross from Henry, and the Gunners' substitute was robbed on the point of shooting by a last-ditch block by De Zeeuw.

Despite that flurry of late chances, Harry Redknapp's men were well worthy of their point.

SEPTEMBER

UEFA Champions League, Group Phase, Group B
Wednesday 17 September 2003 at Highbury, 7.45 p.m.
Attendance: 34,393 Referee: Manuel Mejuto Gonzalez, Spain

FORM GUIDE
D W W W W D [12 goals scored, 4 conceded]   D D W D W W [9 goals scored, 4 conceded]

ARSENAL 0   ## INTERNAZIONALE 3

Cruz 21, van der Meyde 24, Martins 41

Substitutes		Jens **LEHMANN**	1	1	Francesco **TOLDO**		Substitutes
Graham **STACK**	33	**LAUREN**	12	4	Javier **ZANETTI**	12	Alberto **FONTANA**
Martin **KEOWN**	5	Sol **CAMPBELL**	23	13	Fabio **CANNAVARO**	15	Daniele **ADANI**
Pascal **CYGAN**	18	Kolo **TOURE**	28	23	Marco **MATERAZZI**	22	Okan **BURUK**
◀ Ray **PARLOUR**	15	Ashley **COLE**	3	2	Ivan **CORDOBA**	13	Thomas **HELVEG** ◀
▶ (Wiltord) 78		Fredrik **LJUNGBERG**	8	7	Andy **VAN DER MEYDE**		(van der Meyde) 70 ▶
EDU	17	**GILBERTO**	19	6	Cristiano **ZANETTI**	8	Sabri **LAMOUCHI** ◀
◀ Dennis **BERGKAMP**	10	Patrick **VIEIRA**	4	5	Belozoglu **EMRE**		(Emre) 66 ▶
▶ (Pires) 64		Robert **PIRES**	7	18	Kily **GONZALEZ**	11	Siqueira **LUCIANO**
◀ **KANU**	25	Sylvain **WILTORD**	1	9	Julio **CRUZ**	3	Mohamed **KALLON** ◀
▶ (Gilberto) 64		Thierry **HENRY**	14	30	Obafemi **MARTINS**		(Cruz) 84 ▶

MATCH REPORT

Arsenal fell heavily at the first hurdle of the new Champions League campaign, swept aside by the ruthless efficiency of Internazionale, who inflicted on the Gunners their most comprehensive home defeat in Europe's top competition.

Arsène Wenger's side endured a torrid first half in which they conceded three goals and missed a chance to hit back from the penalty spot. This was all immensely perplexing after they had started brightly, stretching the Italian rearguard with clever movement and slick passing. A free-kick by Henry was charged down, a fierce shot from Ljungberg cleared Toldo's crossbar and there were encouraging thrusts from Lauren and Wiltord. Pires set up a clear shooting opportunity for Ljungberg, who fired straight at the keeper from 15 yards.

As the first half progressed Inter began to stir, mounting sharp attacks through Martins and van der Meyde. It was not long before they transformed the contest with two goals in the space of three minutes. First Cordoba's throw-in on the left was nodded by Martins behind Lauren and Toure into the path of Cruz, who advanced on

Lehmann before dinking neatly beyond the German, the ball finishing just inside the far post. Then, with the home defence still reeling, Kily Gonzalez galloped clear on the left, his cross was

Ashley Cole keeps his eyes on the ball as he fights for possession with Inter captain Javier Zanetti.

glanced by Campbell into the path of van der Meyde and the Dutchman dispatched a rasping 15-yard volley which Lehmann reached but could not quite repel.

Soon, Arsenal were gifted a golden opportunity to reduce the arrears when Materazzi leaned on Ljungberg to concede a clear penalty. Up stepped Henry to hit a low shot which Toldo saved at full stretch. A Gilberto header from the resultant corner flashed inches wide of an upright. Still the Gunners fought, but their task took on awesome proportions shortly before the break when Emre weaved past two challenges in midfield and threaded a pass to the pacy Martins, who rode a tackle from Campbell, then hammered a 12-foot drive past Lehmann.

The second period brought plenty of Arsenal possession but their goal threat was unusually muted, though Materazzi was required to make a courageous block on Wiltord and Henry shot tamely at Toldo when well placed.

Midway through the half Inter flexed their attacking muscles again, and Cole did well to foil Cruz. A 25-yarder from Lamouchi was held by Lehmann and moments later the keeper plunged to his right to keep out a quickly-taken free-kick from Cruz.

Now the Gunners mounted a late surge, but Toldo dealt masterfully with a powerful dipper from Henry, a close-range side-foot from Kanu after adroit work from Cole and a 20-yard free-kick, also from Henry.

As time ebbed away, a Bergkamp shot and a narrow-angled effort from Kanu tested the giant Italian goalkeeper more rigorously, but it was Inter who went nearest to another goal in the 91st minute when Kallon wriggled clear, only to shoot against the inside of Lehmann's left upright. Arsenal were spared further grief as Martins skied the rebound.

There's no way through for Freddie Ljungberg as Inter's Fabio Cannavaro takes the ball off his toes.

SEPTEMBER

FA Barclaycard Premiership
Sunday 21 September 2003 at Old Trafford, 4. 05 p.m.
Attendance: 67,639 Referee: Steve Bennett

FORM GUIDE

W W W L W W [14 goals scored, 2 conceded]   W W W W D L [11 goals scored, 6 conceded]

MANCHESTER UNITED 0   ARSENAL 0

Substitutes					Substitutes
		Tim **HOWARD**	14	1	Jens **LEHMANN**	
Roy **CARROLL**	13	Gary **NEVILLE**	2	12	**LAUREN**	33	Graham **STACK**
Nicky **BUTT**	8	Rio **FERDINAND**	5	5	Martin **KEOWN** ▪	18	Pascal **CYGAN**
Eric **DJEMBA-DJEMBA**	19	Mikael **SILVESTRE**	27	28	Kolo **TOURE** ▪	17	**EDU**
Darren **FLETCHER**	24	John **O'SHEA**	22	3	Ashley **COLE**		(Bergkamp) 82
◄ Diego **FORLAN**	21	▪ Cristiano **RONALDO**	7	15	Ray **PARLOUR**	7	Robert **PIRES**
► (O'Shea) 76		Phil **NEVILLE**	3	19	**GILBERTO**	11	Sylvain **WILTORD**
		▪ Roy **KEANE**	16	4	Patrick **VIEIRA** ▪▪		
		▪ Quinton **FORTUNE**	25	8	Fredrik **LJUNGBERG**		
		Ryan **GIGGS**	11	10	Dennis **BERGKAMP**		
		▪ Ruud **VAN NISTELROOY**	10	14	Thierry **HENRY**		

MATCH REPORT

Ten-man Arsenal regained the leadership of the Premiership thanks to a spirited display at Old Trafford. Though the Gunners didn't manage a shot on target, they laboured mightily for their point and could take immense credit for their defensive organisation in the absence of Sol Campbell.

Dennis Bergkamp shields the ball from United's captain Roy Keane.

The opening passage of play was tight, with the two great rivals sparring like a pair of wary heavyweights. But then the hosts began to threaten, particularly through the tricky Ronaldo, with whom Cole enjoyed a spirited and entertaining personal duel. The closest to an early breakthrough materialised in the 14th minute when United won a free-kick on the right and Giggs' curling left-footer bounced to safety via Lehmann's far post.

The Gunners remained tight at the back, however, and showed their attacking potency when Bergkamp attempted to free Henry with an exquisitely timed through-pass, only for the Frenchman to be the victim of a harsh offside decision. United responded with their most potent pressure of the match and went close to taking the lead from another Giggs free-kick, which the unmarked van Nistelrooy met at the far post, but he directed his header on to the roof of the net.

A Lehmann punch away from a Ronaldo corner, resulted in the Gunners breaking smoothly and Cole capped a sweeping move with a low 20-yarder which flashed inches wide of Howard's post.

For the remainder of the first period, United held sway. Lehmann had to deal smartly with a Fortune header from a Gary Neville dispatch, then Ronaldo danced past two challenges before shooting high from 25 yards, and a penalty appeal was turned down after a cross from the Portuguese youngster struck Cole's arm.

The Gunners began the second half in more adventurous mode, and Ljungberg almost squirmed through following a slip by Gary Neville, a power-drive from Gilberto was deflected for a corner and Henry skewed high with an ambitious volley. The champions responded with a couple of incisive thrusts, Ronaldo cutting in from the right to fire wastefully straight at Lehmann, then van Nistelrooy also shot tamely into the arms of the German goalkeeper.

The feeling grew that Arsenal might yet snatch victory and after 75 minutes Henry and Bergkamp put together the visitors' sweetest move of the match, only for Howard to snatch the ball from the toes of the onrushing Vieira.

The atmosphere soured following the dismissal of the Arsenal skipper for a second bookable offence, and there followed a rash of yellow cards to United men.

As for the outcome, a draw seemed inevitable after Edu's 35-yard free-kick cleared the bar in the 90th minute, but then Keown was penalised for fouling Forlan. Thus van Nistelrooy was presented with a gilded opportunity to win the game, but he drove his spot-kick against the crossbar and the spoils were shared.

Ray Parlour is at full stretch as he gets in his cross despite the presence of Mikael Silvestre.

FORM GUIDE

W W W D L D [9 goals scored, 5 conceded]   L L L D D W [8 goals scored, 6 conceded]

ARSENAL 3
Henry 18, pen 80, Gilberto 67

NEWCASTLE UNITED 2
Robert 26, Bernard 71

Substitutes		Jens **LEHMANN**	1	1	Shay **GIVEN**		Substitutes
Graham **STACK**	33	**LAUREN**	12	18	Aaron **HUGHES**	24	Tony **CAIG**
◀ Pascal **CYGAN**	18	Martin **KEOWN**	5	5	Andy **O'BRIEN**	2	Andy **GRIFFIN**
▶ (Cole) 52		Kolo **TOURE**	28	19	Titus **BRAMBLE**	17	Darren **AMBROSE** ◀
◀ **EDU**	17	Ashley **COLE**	3	35	Olivier **BERNARD**		(Robert) 81 ▶
▶ (Vieira) 25		Ray **PARLOUR**	15	8	Kieron **DYER**	11	Gary **SPEED** ◀
◀ Robert **PIRES**	7	**GILBERTO**	19	29	Lee **BOWYER**		(Bowyer) 72 ▶
▶ (Parlour) 62		Patrick **VIEIRA**	4	7	Jermaine **JENAS**	23	Shola **AMEOBI** ◀
Jeremie **ALIADIERE**	30	Fredrik **LJUNGBERG**	8	32	Laurent **ROBERT** ■		(Jenas) 89 ▶
		Sylvain **WILTORD**	11	10	Craig **BELLAMY**		
		Thierry **HENRY**	14	9	Alan **SHEARER**		

MATCH REPORT

Arsenal just shaded a five-goal thriller with struggling Newcastle to stretch their overnight lead at the top of the Premiership to four points. Given that the Gunners operated with only ten fit men for the final third of the match, with Ljungberg injured after all three substitutes had been used, it was a victory which offered compelling testimony to the team's unquenchable spirit.

Heavy rain made mistakes inevitable but the hosts made a reasonably fluent start and might have taken an early advantage but for the alertness of the Magpies' keeper, Given, who cut out a sharp pull-back from Wiltord, then palmed away a sudden, savage 20-yarder from Henry after the Frenchman had danced past two challenges.

The Geordies' goal came under concerted pressure and they had narrowly survived a pinball sequence, in which efforts by Wiltord and Ljungberg rebounded clear. It wasn't long before Arsenal made a deserved breakthrough. Lauren crossed from the right, Bramble miscued his clearance and the ball fell to Henry, who volleyed in unopposed at the far post. This seemed to spur Newcastle into action and they were rewarded

with a goal from their first effort on target when a skewed pass reached Dyer, whose low cross was tapped home by Robert from close range.

That changed the tenor of the contest with Newcastle looking the more coherent unit for the remainder of the half. That said, after Lehmann had saved efficiently from Bernard, it was the Gunners who went closest to registering, with Wiltord failing to convert a Gilberto dispatch and Henry shooting high from 30 yards.

Arsène Wenger's men resumed the offensive after the break and a slip by Hughes allowed Wiltord to send in Ljungberg on the left, but the Swede's neat dink over Given bounced to safety via the near upright. Edu skimmed the crossbar with a raking free-kick and a Wiltord surge was halted by a desperate tackle from Bramble. Arsenal stepped up the pressure, which paid dividends when a Pires free-kick was turned past Given by Gilberto, who celebrated his first goal at Highbury.

Almost immediately, the Gunners' momentum was jolted by an injury to Ljungberg and although Wiltord tested Given with a fizzing 30-yard volley from a cleared free-kick, soon the scores were level when Bernard ran on to a neat Dyer through-ball to hammer a rising shot past Lehmann from 15 yards.

Having regained parity for the second time, and facing depleted opponents, Newcastle attacked briskly and Lehmann did well to fist away a Shearer cross under heavy pressure. Still Arsenal had their sights on maximum points and their tireless probing paid off when Jenas handled from a Pires corner, leaving the ultra-cool Henry to beat Given with an impudent, centrally placed chip from the penalty spot.

In the ten minutes that remained, the

Magpies strove in vain for a third equaliser, but the Gunners suffered few alarms as they held on for a richly merited win.

The Brazilian Gilberto connects with Pires' free-kick to score his first goal at Highbury.

What's all the fuss about? Thierry Henry celebrates after his impudent chip from the spot secured all three points from a hard-fought match.

SEPTEMBER

UEFA Champions League, Group Stage, Group B
Tuesday 30 September 2003 at the Lokomotiv Stadium, Moscow 8.30 p.m.
Attendance: 27,000 Referee: Jan Wegereef, Holland

FORM GUIDE
W W D L D W [8 goals scored, 7 conceded]   W W L L W W [10 goals scored, 8 conceded]

LOKOMOTIV MOSCOW 0   ## ARSENAL 0

Substitutes					Substitutes
Ruslan **NAGMATULLIN**	9	Sergei **OVCHINNIKOV**	1	1	Jens **LEHMANN**	33	Graham **STACK**

Substitutes							Substitutes
Ruslan **NAGMATULLIN**	9	Sergei **OVCHINNIKOV**	1	1	Jens **LEHMANN**		
Narvik **SIRKHAEV**	6	Dmitri **SENNIKOV**	17	12	**LAUREN**	33	Graham **STACK**
Malkhaz **ASATIANI**	30	Sergei **IGNASHEVICH**	5	5	Martin **KEOWN**	18	Pascal **CYGAN**
◀ Gennadi		Oleg **PASHININ**	14	28	Kolo **TOURE**	27	Stathis **TAVLARIDIS**
■ **NIZHEGORODOV**	2	Sergei **GURENKO**	41	3	Ashley **COLE**	42	Justin **HOYTE**
▶ (Evseev) 73		Vadim **EVSEEV**	16	15	Ray **PARLOUR**	35	David **BENTLEY**
◀ Ruslan **PIMENOV**	25	Dmitri **KHOKHLOV**	28	19	**GILBERTO**	25	**KANU**
▶ (Ashvetia) 65		Vladimir **MAMINOV**	8	17	**EDU**	30	Jeremie **ALIADIERE**
Lessa **LEANDRO**	77	Dmitri **LOSKOV**	10	7	Robert **PIRES**		
Jorge **WAGNER**	99	Marat **IZMAILOV**	7	11	Sylvain **WILTORD**		
		Mikhail **ASHVETIA**	32	14	Thierry **HENRY**		

MATCH REPORT

Depleted Arsenal garnered the opening point of their Champions League campaign, but missed several inviting chances to score the goal which would have secured their first victory in seven European outings.

Three Lokomotiv defenders combine to stop Thierry Henry as tries to pick his way towards goal.

Making light of the absence of Vieira, Campbell, Ljungberg and Bergkamp for various reasons, the Gunners began brightly and Henry brought a sharp save from Ovchinnikov with a low drive, then ran on to an exquisite through-pass from Edu, only to fire high from 15 yards.

Soon Lokomotiv settled, stroking the ball around neatly and progressively, and they fashioned a series of opportunities. Lehmann had little difficulty in gathering a Khokhlov header from a Gurenko cross, but Keown was at full stretch when he managed to block goal-bound shots from Ashvetia and the elusive Izmailov.

As the hosts' pressure mounted, Keown denied Maminov, Toure cleared his lines with a courageous header, Ashvetia's near-post nod from Loskov's whipped corner was scrambled off his line by Cole and Loskov curled a free-kick on to the roof of Lehmann's net from 25 yards.

After Ashvetia miskicked with only the goal-keeper to beat, the Gunners revived to dominate the closing ten minutes of the first period. Henry and Pires combined beautifully on the left only for Wiltord to drift offside, Parlour and Pires both tested Ovchinnikov with powerful drives from outside the box and Toure shaved the Russians' far post with a glancing header from a Pires corner.

Lokomotiv returned to the attack at the outset of the second half, with Lehmann diving athletically to palm away a fierce low cross from Khokhlov. But Arsenal remained dangerous on the break, and after Henry had nodded wide from a Lauren cross, the inspirational Frenchman set up the best chance of the match. After stepping cleverly past Pashinin, he surged through the centre before freeing Pires, who cut in from the left flank but shot tamely, allowing Ovchinnikov to beat the ball away.

Though increasingly cautious, Lokomotiv still entertained thoughts of a win and Maminov almost surprised Lehmann with a rasping 25-yarder, and then dispatched another piledriver straight at the keeper.

As the final quarter of the game approached, Arsenal looked the most convincing team and they went close to capitalising on that superiority when Parlour's cross was met by a firm right-footer from Cole, only for Ovchinnikov to save superbly before the ball was hacked clear amid appeals for handball. Nothing was given and Lokomotiv almost caught the Gunners unawares with a quickly taken free-kick at the other end. However, Toure, who underlined his recent admirable progress in the first-team's defence with another impressive display, stood firm to repel Loskov.

With the action becoming stretched as the players tired, both teams might have sealed a late triumph as several good chances went begging.

Henry cracked his 30-yard free-kick straight into the midriff of Ovchinnikov, Toure robbed Loskov in the act of shooting and Parlour half-volleyed high into the capacity crowd from the edge of the area.

It had been an intriguing contest, with Arsenal earning plaudits for their defensive discipline but kicking themselves for their wastefulness in front of goal.

Robert Pires had a fine match but both he and Thierry Henry were unable to break the deadlock despite several fine chances.

SEPTEMBER 2003

Arsenal.com PLAYER OF THE MONTH

Kolo TOURE

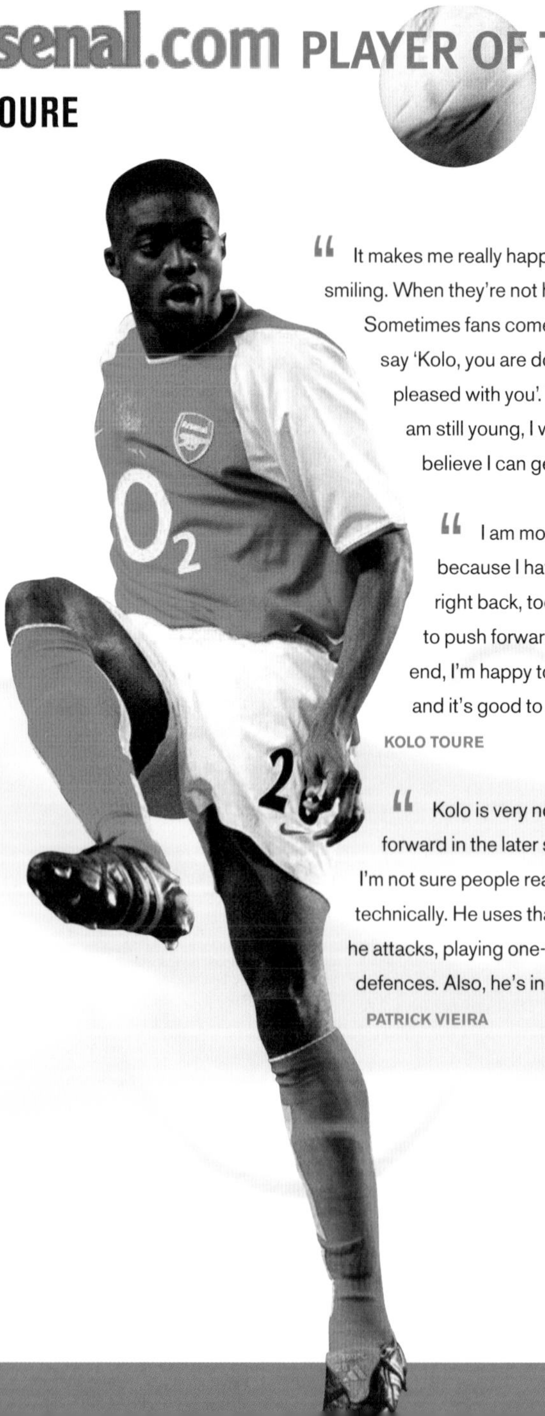

" It makes me really happy when I see the supporters smiling. When they're not happy, then neither am I. Sometimes fans come up to me in the street and say 'Kolo, you are doing so well and we are pleased with you'. This is a great feeling for me. I am still young, I will continue to learn, and I believe I can get better. "

" I am more comfortable at centre back because I have played there more. I like it at right back, too, though. It gives me a chance to push forward, which I enjoy a lot. In the end, I'm happy to play wherever I'm asked, and it's good to be able to adapt. "

KOLO TOURE

" Kolo is very noticeable when charging forward in the later stages of certain games, but I'm not sure people realise how fine a footballer he is technically. He uses that in defence and also when he attacks, playing one-twos and dribbling through defences. Also, he's incredibly strong. "

PATRICK VIEIRA

ARSENAL DIARY

Saturday 6 September
- Arsène Wenger rules out the possibility of Arsenal moving to Wembley.
- Arsenal announce record turnover of £117.8m, and operating profit of £25.3m before player dealings, for half-year ending in May 2003.

Friday 12 September
- Arsène Wenger wins Premiership manager of the month award for August.
- Arsenal's young Swiss defender Philippe Sanderos is sidelined for at least a month with a back injury.

THE WIDER WORLD

Saturday 6 September
- Wayne Rooney becomes England's youngest ever scorer during the victory in Macedonia.

Sunday 7 September
- Former England International Bill Slater advocates a Great Britain football team for the 2012 Olympics.

Wednesday 10 September
- England move closer to automatic qualification for Euro 2004 with 2–0 win over Liechtenstein.

Monday 15 September
- Manchester United deny reports of imminent £600m takeover.

Sunday 21 September
- Tottenham Hotspur sack manager Glenn Hoddle.

FA CARLING PREMIERSHIP
28 September 2003

	P	HOME					AWAY					Pts
		W	D	L	F	A	W	D	L	F	A	
ARSENAL	7	3	1	0	8	4	2	1	0	6	1	17
Chelsea	6	3	1	0	9	5	2	0	0	7	1	16
Manchester United	7	2	1	0	5	0	3	0	1	8	3	16
Birmingham City	6	2	1	0	5	2	2	1	0	3	0	14
Southampton	7	2	1	1	3	1	1	2	0	5	3	12
Manchester City	6	1	1	1	6	4	2	1	0	8	4	11
Liverpool	6	1	1	1	3	3	2	1	0	6	1	11
Portsmouth	7	2	0	1	7	3	0	3	1	2	4	9
Blackburn Rovers	6	1	0	2	8	7	1	2	0	6	5	8
Fulham	5	1	1	0	5	4	1	1	1	6	5	8
Aston Villa	7	2	1	0	5	2	0	0	4	2	9	7
Middlesbrough	7	1	0	2	3	7	1	1	2	3	5	7
Bolton Wanderers	7	1	3	0	5	3	0	1	2	0	8	7
Charlton Athletic	6	0	1	2	2	7	1	1	1	5	2	5
Leicester City	7	1	2	1	7	6	0	0	3	3	7	5
Everton	6	1	1	1	5	6	0	1	2	3	5	5
Leeds United	6	0	2	1	2	4	1	0	2	4	8	5
Tottenham Hotspur	6	1	0	2	3	7	0	1	2	2	5	4
Newcastle United	6	0	1	2	1	3	0	2	1	6	7	3
Wolverhampton Wanderers	7	0	1	2	0	9	0	1	3	2	9	2

FORM GUIDE

D W W W D L [11 goals scored, 6 conceded]   W D L D W D [6 goals scored, 7 conceded]

LIVERPOOL 1   ARSENAL 2

Kewell 14   Hyypia og 31, Pires 68

Substitutes					Substitutes
Chris **KIRKLAND** 22	Jerzy **DUDEK**	1	1	Jens **LEHMANN**	
Stephane **HENCHOZ** 2	Steve **FINNAN**	3	12	**LAUREN**	Graham **STACK** 33
◀ Anthony **LE TALLEC** 20	▨ Igor **BISCAN**	25	28	Kolo **TOURE**	Martin **KEOWN** 5
▶ (Smicer) 42	Sami **HYYPIA**	4	23	Sol **CAMPBELL**	Pascal **CYGAN** 18
▨ ◀ John **WELSH** 32	John **ARNE RIISE**	18	3	Ashley **COLE** ▨	**KANU** 25
▶ (Diao) 83	El-Hadji **DIOUF**	9	15	Ray **PARLOUR** ▨	Sylvain **WILTORD** ◀ 11
◀ Emile **HESKEY** 8	Salif **DIAO**	15	19	**GILBERTO**	(Aliadiere) 73 ▶
▶ (Owen) 72	Steven **GERRARD**	17	17	**EDU**	
	Vladimir **SMICER**	11	8	Robert **PIRES**	
	Harry **KEWELL**	7	30	Jeremie **ALIADIERE**	
	Michael **OWEN**	10	14	Thierry **HENRY**	

MATCH REPORT

A wonder goal by Robert Pires sealed a magnificent comeback by the resilient Gunners after they had been dominated by Liverpool for long spells in the first half. It was a memorable victory demonstrating both grit and polish, and it showcased Arsenal's championship credentials while cementing their pole position in the Premiership table.

Gérard Houllier's team attacked from the outset, Edu heading over his own bar from a waspish Gerrard free-kick and Lehmann making full-length saves from Owen and Smicer soon afterwards. The relentless pressure paid off when Edu's clearance from Riise's lofted cross rebounded from Owen into the path of the lurking Kewell, who buried a scorching left-foot volley from 15 yards.

Kewell later skied from a similar position before the Gunners rallied. Dudek only just managed to deflect a bouncing 25-yarder from Henry around a post. Liverpool continued to pour forward and Owen spurned two clear-cut opportunities to stretch the lead. The first chance came when Kewell glanced on a clearance from

Dudek, but Owen's scoop over the stranded Lehmann also cleared the crossbar. The second came after Gerrard delivered a free-kick from the left flank and Owen lost his marker but he headed high from six yards.

At this point there seemed only one winner, but Arsène Wenger's indomitables burst back into contention, albeit thanks to a slice of fortune when Edu's header from a Pires free-kick slid into the Liverpool net via the outstretched foot of Hyypia. Liverpool reacted by launching a fresh series of assaults, in which Kewell was prominent, but now the Gunners had regained a foothold and in the minutes before the interval it was they who carried the most threat, with Parlour and Toure both going close. In addition, Biscan appeared to foul Aliadiere as the young Frenchman advanced on goal, but the referee waved play on.

After the break Diouf and Owen might have achieved more from headed openings, but as the hour mark approached, Arsenal began to assert their authority. A dipping shot from Parlour was deflected into the arms of Dudek, Gilberto nodded

The ball eludes everyone but Edu whose header slides into the Liverpool goal via the outstretched boot of defender Sami Hyypia (far right).

wide, Lauren mishit a cross with three colleagues unmarked in the middle, and Henry fired high; so the masterpiece which followed was hardly against the run of play. A fluent passing movement culminated in neat work by Aliadiere and Edu, who turned the ball back to Pires near the left touchline. The Frenchman swerved inside, danced across a challenge from Finnan and dispatched a sublime 28-yard curler that left Dudek clutching thin air as it hit the net.

Thereafter there was an air of desperation about Liverpool as they strove to regain parity. Lehmann held a Kewell shot, an acrobatic Diouf volley was cleared off the line by Cole, Heskey outmuscled Campbell only for his pull-back to be intercepted, then Le Tallec was marginally off-target with a 20-yard clip. But throughout this hectic period, Arsenal maintained an attacking threat and twice Henry might have increased the winning margin. As it was,

though, the Gunners could feel supremely satisfied with all three points taken from potential title rivals.

Thierry Henry is the first to congratulate Robert Pires after his wonder goal that kept the Gunners at the top of the Premiership table.

FORM GUIDE

D L D W D W [6 goals scored, 7 conceded]   W W W L W D [9 goals scored, 3 conceded]

ARSENAL 2   CHELSEA 1

Edu 5, Henry 75   Crespo 8

Substitutes							Substitutes	
Graham **STACK**	33	Jens **LEHMANN**	1	23	Carlo **CUDICINI**			
◄ Pascal **CYGAN**	18	**LAUREN**	12	2	Glen **JOHNSON**	31	Marco **AMBROSIO**	
► (Pires) 90		Sol **CAMPBELL**	23	15	Mario **MELCHIOT**	12	Mario **STANIC**	
◄ Dennis **BERGKAMP**	10	Kolo **TOURE**	28	29	Robert **HUTH**	30	Jesper **GRONKJAER** ◄	
► (Wiltord) 65		Ashley **COLE**	3	18	Wayne **BRIDGE**		(Mutu) 66 ►	
◄ **KANU**	25	▨ Ray **PARLOUR**	15	8	Frank **LAMPARD**	10	Joe **COLE** ◄	
► (Parlour) 65		**GILBERTO**	19	4	Claude **MAKELELE** ▨		(Duff) 70 ►	
Jeremie **ALIADIERE**	30	**EDU**	17	14	**GÉRÉMI**	9	Jimmy Floyd	
		Robert **PIRES**	7	11	Damien **DUFF**		**HASSELBAINK** ◄ ▨	
		Sylvain **WILTORD**	11	7	Adrian **MUTU**		(Gérémi) 77 ►	
		Thierry **HENRY**	14	21	Hernan **CRESPO**			

MATCH REPORT

The Gunners shaded a pulsating contest to end Chelsea's unbeaten League record and maintain top spot in the League. The Blues, who have never won a Premiership game at Highbury, could claim to be a tad unfortunate, with Arsenal's two goals coming from a deflection and Cudicini's uncharacteristic clanger, but the hosts deserved their victory for showing greater ambition throughout the second half.

The game began in thrilling style with Wiltord surging down the left flank and crossing to Henry, who missed his shot from ten yards. But the hosts were not to be denied for long. Pires' trickery forced Johnson to handle near the edge of the box and Edu's low free-kick deflected off the leg of Parlour to leave the keeper helpless.

The Cameroon connection. Chelsea's Gérémi fails to stop Lauren's powerful run down the right flank.

Chelsea keeper Cudicini is in all sorts of trouble as he drops the ball onto the onrushing Thierry Henry's knee and from there it's into the net.

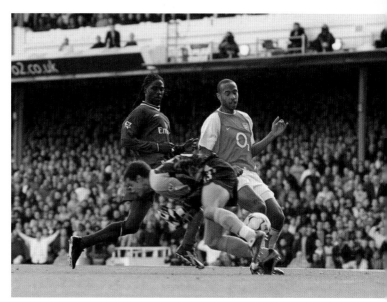

Chelsea bounced straight back with a world-class strike by Crespo, who latched on to a raking crossfield dispatch from Gérémi, he then checked inside Lauren and beat Lehmann with a ferocious long-distance curler. The Arsenal keeper protested that the Argentinian had gained an unfair advantage having left the pitch and returning without permission, but the referee was unmoved and the goal stood.

Now the visitors enjoyed their most fluent interlude and a slick interchange between Duff and Johnson created a shooting chance for the young defender, but Campbell intervened with a courageous block. Henry responded with a searing surge down the inside-left channel which took him past three challenges before the ball was squeezed to safety, but Chelsea continued to threaten, with both Lampard and Johnson forcing Lehmann to make smart saves.

The Gunners finished the half strongly, though, with Lauren charging through only to stumble in the act of shooting, Edu testing Cudicini with a crisp 15-yarder on the turn and a Pires penalty appeal being rejected.

Chelsea began the second period enterprisingly, but after Edu had made a brilliant last-ditch tackle on Lampard and a Johnson cross had narrowly eluded Crespo with the goal at his mercy, Arsenal started to dominate. Henry rose athletically to meet a Lauren centre but the Frenchman's header brushed an upright, and shots from Gilberto and Pires were gathered cleanly by Cudicini. Thereafter the pressure intensified with Edu and Kanu combining sweetly to work an opening for Henry, who pirouetted on a pass by the Brazilian and hammered goalwards from ten yards, only for Cudicini to plunge heroically and push the ball away.

Next Kanu shaved a post with a powerful header from a Pires corner and it seemed that Chelsea might escape, but then came Cudicini's calamity. Bergkamp wasted no time in stabbing a free-kick to Pires on the right, and the keeper raced from his line to scoop up the resultant low cross. However, it squirmed through the Italian's grasp and rebounded into the empty net via the knee of the onrushing Henry.

Thereafter Claudio Ranieri's men might have been expected to mount a last, desperate onslaught, but it never materialised, and Arsenal cemented their place at the top of the table.

UEFA Champions League, Group Stage, Group B
Tuesday 21 October 2003 at the Olimpiyskyi, 9.45 p.m.
Attendance: 80,000 Referee: Konrad Platz, Austria

FORM GUIDE

W W W L D W [12 goals scored, 3 conceded]   L D W D W W [7 goals scored, 7 conceded]

DYNAMO KIEV 2   ARSENAL 1

Shatskikh 27, Belkevich 63   Henry 80

Substitutes					Substitutes	
		Olexander **SHOVKOVSKYI**	1	1	Jens **LEHMANN**		
Vitaliy **REVA**	21	Yuri **DMYTRULIN**	6	12	**LAUREN**	
◀ Goran **SABLIC**	35	Sergei **FEDOROV**	3	28	Kolo **TOURE**	
▶ (Dmytrulin) 32		Goran **GAVRANCIC**	32	23	Sol **CAMPBELL**	
Badr **EL KADDOURI**	9	Andriy **NESMACHNYI**	26	3	Ashley **COLE**	
◀ Aleksander		Valentin **BELKEVICH**	8	15	Ray **PARLOUR**	
KHATSKEVITCH	2	Tiberiu **GHIOANE**	17	19	**GILBERTO**	
▶ (Ghioane) 79		Jerko **LECO**	36	17	**EDU**	
◀ Diogo **RINCON**	15	Oleg **HUSYEV**	20	7	Robert **PIRES**	
▶ (Gusev) 65		Georgi **PEEV**	11	11	Sylvain **WILTORD**	
Andrei **MILEVSKI**	25	Maksim **SHATSKIKH**	16	14	Thierry **HENRY**	
Roberto **NANNI**	18					

Graham **STACK**	33
Gael **CLICHY**	22
Patrick **CYGAN**	18
Justin **HOYTE**	42
Patrick **VIEIRA** ◀	4
(Edu) 61 ▶	
Fredrik **LJUNGBERG** ◀	8
(Parlour) 74 ▶	
KANU ◀	25
(Gilberto) 74 ▶	

MATCH REPORT

A valiant late fightback was thwarted by the width of Kiev's crossbar as the Gunners' Champions League hopes suffered a setback in the Ukraine. When Dynamo keeper Shovkovskyi spilled Henry's second-half effort in stoppage time, Toure was poised to secure Arsenal the point they deserved, but his close-range drive cannoned off the woodwork and away to safety.

It was the crowning frustration of a night on which luck abandoned the visitors, from the early moment when Henry's corner was met by a near-post header from Pires which bounced back from the bar. Roared on by a vast and wildly partisan crowd,

Despite a fine performance from Robert Pires, whose free-kicks and corners created a number of chances for the Gunners, a poor result left Arsenal at the bottom of their qualifying group.

Kiev responded swiftly when Shatskikh burst on to a long ball from the influential Belkevich and swerved wide of Toure before bringing a magnificent one-handed save from Lehmann.

Thereafter a pleasingly open game developed, with mistakes plentiful on the rain-soaked surface. By the midway point of the first half Arsenal began to get on top. They almost broke through at the climax of one sweeping move, only for Lauren's shot to be squeezed away for a corner. It was not long after this effort that Arsenal fell behind in cruel circumstances. Taking advantage of confusion between Gilberto and Edu, Leko shot from distance and the ball rebounded high into the air off the heel of Shatskikh; it could have gone anywhere, but it dropped conveniently for the striker to volley past Lehmann from 12 yards.

The end-to-end action continued with Ghioane's 25-yarder forcing the German keeper to tip over, then Henry going close and Shovkovskyi diving to clutch Edu's downward header from Pires' flighted free-kick.

Arsenal almost grabbed an equaliser at the outset of the second half, but Cole sliced his shot after being sent in by Campbell, then a Pires free-kick was headed goal-wards by Henry only for Shovkovskyi to scramble the ball away at the far post. But just as Kiev were showing signs of strain they were gifted a second goal when Lehmann struggled twice to clear, allowing Shatskikh to feed Belkevich who curled the ball into the unguarded net from 25 yards.

Now, fortified by Vieira's arrival from the substitutes' bench, the Gunners poured forward. They almost reduced the deficit after 70 minutes when a delightful inter-change of passes fashioned a clear opening for Wiltord, but the Frenchman's effort to beat Shovkovskyi at his near post proved to be fruitless.

As the pressure increased, Campbell glanced wide from a Pires corner, but ten minutes from the end Arsenal stunned the stadium into momentary silence when Kanu found Pires, whose clever clipped cross was stabbed home clinically by Henry. Now there was genuine hope of salvation. Cole fired weakly from a Lauren dispatch and a Wiltord snapshot hammered into the keeper's midriff. Shatskikh missed a chance to put the issue beyond doubt, but then came that agonising denouement, with Toure deprived of glory at the death and Arsenal marooned at the foot of their qualifying group.

Keen to get on with it, *Thierry Henry carries the ball back to the centre spot after stunning the Ukrainian crowd with his goal 10 minutes from time.*

FORM GUIDE

L L D W W W [11 goals scored, 11 conceded]   D W D W W L [8 goals scored, 6 conceded]

CHARLTON ATHLETIC 1

Di Canio pen 27

ARSENAL 1

Henry 39

Substitutes		Starting XI			Starting XI	Substitutes	
Simon **ROYCE**	25	Dean **KIELY**	1	1	Jens **LEHMANN**	Graham **STACK**	33
Jonathan **FORTUNE**	24	Radostin **KISHISHEV**	2	12	**LAUREN** ▪	Pascal **CYGAN**	18
Chris **POWELL**	3	Mark **FISH**	6	23	Sol **CAMPBELL**	**EDU**	17
◀ Jason **EUELL**	9	Chris **PERRY**	36	28	Kolo **TOURE**	Sylvain **WILTORD** ◀	11
▶ (Di Canio) 45		Hermann **HREIDARSSON**	12	3	Ashley **COLE**	(Bergkamp) 71 ▶	
◀ Jamal		Matt **HOLLAND**	8	8	Fredrik **LJUNGBERG**	**KANU** ◀	25
CAMPBELL-RYCE	22	▪ Scott **PARKER**	7	15	Ray **PARLOUR**	(Ljungberg) 71 ▶	
▶ (Johansson) 76		Claus **JENSEN**	10	19	**GILBERTO**		
		Graham **STUART**	4	7	Robert **PIRES**		
		Paolo **DI CANIO**	11	10	Dennis **BERGKAMP**		
		Jonatan **JOHANSSON**	21	14	Thierry **HENRY**		

MATCH REPORT

Yet another majestic strike by Thierry Henry, contributor of almost half the Gunners' goals in the season to date, earned the point which kept Arsène Wenger's men at the Premiership summit after they had fallen behind to a hotly disputed penalty.

Charlton started brightly and were determined to shatter Arsenal's proud record of remaining undefeated in London derbies for more than two years. A Holland cross furnished Stuart with an early opening but he nudged the ball tamely straight at Lehmann. Soon, though, the visitors settled into their customary fluent rhythm and chances began to materialise. Kishishev was required to make a saving tackle on Bergkamp, then Henry and the Dutchman over-elaborated after fine work by Ljungberg.

Next Parlour, still skipper in the absence of the injured Vieira, found Ljungberg on the right and the Swede cut inside menacingly, only to scuff his shot from the edge of the box. Now the Addicks hit back spiritedly, with Johansson's low cross being stabbed to safety and a Parker shot deflected away by Campbell. From the ensuing corner,

Holland tumbled to the ground under minimal challenge from Lauren and the referee pointed to the spot. As Di Canio stepped up, Lehmann danced along his line, but the Italian was not fazed, chipping coolly into the middle of the net as the German plunged to his left.

Fired into action, the Gunners launched a wave of potent attacks, with Cole going close before Henry swerved in from the right touchline and unleashed a curling left-footer which beat Kiely but hammered against an upright before being scrambled away.

In an isolated counter-assault Johansson latched on to a long ball before shooting narrowly wide. Arsenal continued to mount pressure which paid off when Parlour was fouled by Parker and Henry found the top corner of Kiely's net with a glorious free-kick from 22 yards. The Frenchman almost repeated the dose during first-half stoppage time, but this time his shot whistled into the side-netting.

Thus reprieved, Charlton began the second period in relatively menacing mode, but mustered little more than a dangerous cross by Johansson,

which was cut out by Campbell, and a Euell drive which was saved comfortably by Lehmann. With the Addicks working prodigiously, Arsenal fashioned few clear openings of their own, being limited to long-range efforts from Bergkamp, Parlour and Henry.

At the other end Lauren nodded over his own bar after a floated cross from Stuart had created momentary mayhem. Lehmann tipped over an awkwardly bouncing header from Hreidarsson following a Jensen corner and Euell slipped when well placed, but there was little sense of an impending breakthrough by the hosts.

Near the end Arsenal might have claimed all three points when Parlour found Kanu, who tricked two defenders inside the box but then shot straight at Kiely from a narrow angle instead of passing to either Henry or Pires, both of whom were free in the middle.

Charlton's Scott Parker can only admire as Thierry Henry unleashes a glorious 20-yard free-kick for Arsenal's equaliser.

Sol Campbell is the first to show his appreciation of Thierry Henry's magnificent strike.

OCTOBER

FORM GUIDE
W D W W L W [9 goals scored, 7 conceded]   L D D D L [4 goals scored, 8 conceded]

ARSENAL 1
Aliadiere 11

ROTHERHAM UNITED 1
Byfield 90

Substitutes					Substitutes
	Graham **STACK**	33	1	Michael **POLLITT** ■	
Craig **HOLLOWAY** 44	Justin **HOYTE**	45	16	Paul **HURST**	30 Gary **MONTGOMERY** ◄
Olafur-Ingi **SKULASON** 55	Stathis **TAVLARIDIS**	27	8	Chris **SWAILES** ▥	(Sedgwick) 101 ►
◄ John **SPICER** 52	Pascal **CYGAN**	18	15	Martin **MCINTOSH**	6 Julien **BAUDET** ◄
► (Hoyte) 117	Gael **CLICHY**	22	22	Shaun **BARKER** ▥	(Talbot) 105 ►
◄ Quincy	Francesc **FABREGAS**	57	10	Paul **WARNE**	20 Andy **MONKHOUSE**
OWUSU-ABEYIE 54	**KANU**	25	12	Stewart **TALBOT**	17 John **MULLIN** ◄
► (Fabregas) 85	**EDU**	17	19	Carl **ROBINSON**	(Robinson) 73 ►
◄ Ryan **SMITH** 56	Jerome **THOMAS**	53	24	Chris **SEDGWICK** ▥	7 Mark **ROBINS**
► (Thomas) 73	Sylvain **WILTORD**	11	23	Darren **BYFIELD**	
	▥ Jeremie **ALIADIERE**	30	29	Richard **BARKER**	

ARSENAL won 9-8 on penalties

ARSENAL penalties:
Wiltord missed, Edu scored, Aliadiere scored, Cygan scored, Owusu-Abeyie missed, Kanu scored,
Spicer scored, Smith scored, Clichy scored, Stack (GK) scored, Wiltord scored

ROTHERHAM UNITED penalties:
Swailes scored, McIntosh missed, Mullin missed, Baudet scored, Byfield missed, Hurst scored, Warne scored,
S. Barker missed, R. Barker missed, Montgomery (GK) scored, Swailes missed

| MATCH REPORT

History was made at Highbury as the Gunners triumphed in an attractively open contest which featured 22 penalties and in which Arsène Wenger blooded six debutants. At 16 years and 177 days, midfielder Francesc Fabregas became the youngest player to represent Arsenal at senior level. He acquitted himself admirably in an experimental starting line-up which showed 11 changes from the side which kicked off against Charlton Athletic two days earlier.

Also making their entrance against First Division strugglers Rotherham United were goalkeeper Graham Stack and defender Gael Clichy, with Quincy Owusu-Abeyie, Ryan Smith and John Spicer joining the action from the bench.

Rotherham's fans were perhaps inspired by the experience of their manager Ronnie Moore, who had been part of the Tranmere Rovers side which

had beaten Arsenal 1-0 at Highbury in the same competition 30 years earlier. The Millers refused to be overawed by the occasion and their 3,000 travelling fans had plenty to cheer. For all that, it was the Gunners who carried the early threat and they took the lead with a fine goal after 11 minutes. Edu found Clichy wide on the left and the young defender threaded a beautiful pass to Wiltord on the corner of Rotherham's box. The French star swivelled to shrug off a challenge, and then switched inside for Kanu to ferry on to Aliadiere, who beat Pollitt comprehensively with a low left-foot drive from ten yards. Rotherham retaliated with spirit and shortly before the break Byfield might have equalised with a clever flick, but he was foiled by an alert smother from Stack.

In the second half the play surged from end to end, with Byfield going close for Rotherham

Jeremie Aliadiere shows superb close control to keep the ball in play despite the attentions of Rotherham's Paul Hurst.

and the lively Fabregas dispatched a shot just past an upright.

Those earlier misses seemed unlikely to matter, though, until the final minute of normal time when Sedgwick broke clear on the right and his volleyed cross was headed home emphatically from six yards by the ever-menacing Byfield.

The first period of extra time produced further drama when Pollitt was judged guilty of deliberate handball after racing from his box to intercept a through-pass, and the crestfallen keeper was red-carded. Immediately Rotherham withdrew outfielder Sedgwick to bring on substitute custodian Montgomery, but the Gunners could not make the most of their numerical advantage and the valiant ten-man Millers held out until the final whistle signalled a penalty shoot-out.

Briefly the underdogs seized the upper hand, with Montgomery saving a spot-kick from Wiltord, but Arsenal regained parity after eight hits and two misses for each team. Finally Stack, who had scored himself moments earlier, plunged to his left to clutch a low side-foot from Swailes, and Wiltord settled the issue by sweeping his second effort confidently into a bottom corner.

but Arsenal creating the bulk of the scoring opportunities. However, Aliadiere couldn't capitalise on lovely approach work by skipper-for-the-night Kanu, Wiltord fired high when favourably placed

At 16 years and 177 days Francesc Febregas became the youngest player ever to represent Arsenal at senior level.

OCTOBER 2003

Arsenal.com PLAYER OF THE MONTH

Thierry HENRY

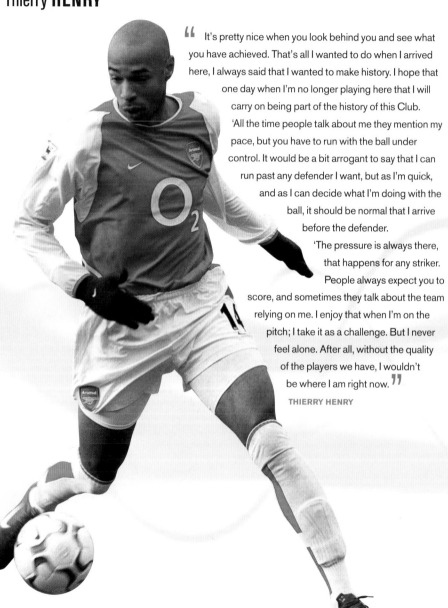

" It's pretty nice when you look behind you and see what you have achieved. That's all I wanted to do when I arrived here, I always said that I wanted to make history. I hope that one day when I'm no longer playing here that I will carry on being part of the history of this Club.

'All the time people talk about me they mention my pace, but you have to run with the ball under control. It would be a bit arrogant to say that I can run past any defender I want, but as I'm quick, and as I can decide what I'm doing with the ball, it should be normal that I arrive before the defender.

'The pressure is always there, that happens for any striker. People always expect you to score, and sometimes they talk about the team relying on me. I enjoy that when I'm on the pitch; I take it as a challenge. But I never feel alone. After all, without the quality of the players we have, I wouldn't be where I am right now. "

THIERRY HENRY

ARSENAL DIARY

Thursday 2 October
- Arsenal's AGM is told the Club hopes to start construction work at Ashburton Grove early in 2004.

Monday 6 October
- Joe Baker, a free-scoring Arsenal centre-forward of the 1960s, dies in Lanarkshire aged 63.

Friday 17 October
- Arsène Wenger calls for a major crackdown on drug taking in domestic and European football.

Tuesday 21 October
- Patrick Vieira's comeback from injury is halted by thigh damage against Dynamo Kiev.

THE WIDER WORLD

Tuesday 7 October
- The FA rules Rio Ferdinand out of contention for the Turkey match because he failed to take a routine drug test on time.

Saturday 11 October
- England's goalless draw in Istanbul earns a place at Euro 2004. Scotland join Wales in the play-offs.

Thursday 30 October
- The FA are fined £4,400 after a tunnel fracas involving England players in Istanbul.

FA CARLING PREMIERSHIP
26 October 2003

	P	HOME					AWAY					Pts
		W	D	L	F	A	W	D	L	F	A	
Chelsea	10	4	1	0	10	5	3	1	1	10	4	23
ARSENAL	9	4	1	0	10	5	3	1	0	8	2	23
Manchester United	10	3	1	1	9	3	4	0	1	9	3	22
Birmingham City	10	2	3	0	5	2	3	1	1	4	3	19
Fulham	10	2	2	1	9	7	3	1	1	11	6	18
Southampton	10	3	1	1	5	1	1	3	1	5	4	16
Manchester City	10	2	2	1	12	6	2	1	2	8	6	15
Newcastle United	10	2	1	2	5	3	2	2	1	10	9	15
Liverpool	10	2	1	2	7	6	2	1	2	8	5	14
Charlton Athletic	9	1	1	2	5	9	3	1	1	8	3	14
Portsmouth	10	3	0	2	9	5	0	3	2	2	7	12
Tottenham Hotspur	9	2	0	2	6	7	1	2	2	4	6	11
Everton	10	2	2	1	9	6	0	2	3	3	8	10
Aston Villa	10	2	3	0	6	3	0	1	4	2	9	10
Wolverhampton Wanderers	10	2	1	2	5	12	0	2	3	2	9	9
Blackburn Rovers	10	1	0	4	8	10	1	2	2	7	9	8
Bolton Wanderers	10	1	3	1	5	4	0	2	3	3	15	8
Leeds United	10	1	2	2	4	6	1	0	4	5	15	8
Middlesbrough	9	1	0	4	4	10	1	1	2	3	5	7
Leicester City	10	1	2	2	8	8	0	0	5	6	13	5

FORM GUIDE

D L W L L L [7 goals scored, 14 conceded]   D W W L D D [7 goals scored, 6 conceded]

LEEDS UNITED 1   ARSENAL 4
Smith 64   Henry 8, 33, Pires 17, Gilberto 50

Substitutes						Substitutes
Scott **CARSON**	40	Paul **ROBINSON**	1	1	Jens **LEHMANN**	
Michael **DUBERRY**	22	Gary **KELLY**	2	12	**LAUREN**	Graham **STACK** 33
Ian **HARTE**	3	Zoumara **CAMARA**	6	23	Sol **CAMPBELL**	Pascal **CYGAN** 18
▶ Aaron **LENNON**	25	Jose Vitor **ROQUE JUNIOR**	12	28	Kolo **TOURE**	**EDU** ▶ 17
■ ◀ (Sakho) 60		■ Salomon **OLEMBE**	24	3	Ashley **COLE**	(Ljungberg) 70 ◀
▶ James **MILNER**	38	Jermaine **PENNANT**	11	8	Fredrik **LJUNGBERG**	Sylvain **WILTORD** 11
◀ (Bridges) 46		Seth **JOHNSON**	20	15	Ray **PARLOUR**	Jeremie **ALIADIERE** ▶ 30
		David **BATTY**	23	19	**GILBERTO**	(Bergkamp) ◀
		Lamine **SAKHO**	10	7	Robert **PIRES**	
		Michael **BRIDGES**	8	10	Dennis **BERGKAMP**	
		Alan **SMITH**	17	14	Thierry **HENRY**	

MATCH REPORT

Man-of-the-match Thierry Henry led the way with two goals as rampant Arsenal outclassed Leeds with a stunning exhibition of sublime counter-attacking. The visitors' victory confirmed their position as the Premiership's pacesetters while deepening the gloom of the Yorkshiremen, mired at the opposite end of the table.

Yet it was Leeds who began on the front foot, with on-loan Gunner Jermaine Pennant asking early questions of his own team-mates with several enterprising touches. Indeed, it was the hosts who posed the first threat when Kelly crossed from the right, Johnson touched on and Sakho delivered a venomous 15-yard volley which demanded a diving clutch from the alert Lehmann.

Robert Pires can't resist a smile as he turns away after scoring Arsenal's second after 17 minutes.

But then the roof fell in on Peter Reid's beleaguered team, whose adventurous approach of employing two flank raiders was exploited mercilessly as Arsenal hit them on the break three times in a destructive 25-minute spell. First Cole dispatched a raking long ball down the left to Henry, who outpaced Camara before steering a precise right-footer past the advancing Robinson to put the Gunners in front. Next Parlour clipped a neat pass to Ljungberg, who advanced down the right touchline and cut inside to deliver a low cross which eluded the stretching Gilberto and Henry but found its way to Pires, who was granted all the time he needed to slot home from the corner of the six-yard box. The devastation continued when Bergkamp exchanged passes with Parlour, then poked a shot against an upright from the edge of the penalty area; the ball rebounded to Henry, whose fierce ten-yard drive deflected off Roque Junior to leave Robinson helpless.

Shortly before the interval Arsenal almost made it four when Ljungberg and Bergkamp combined enchantingly to create an opening for Henry, but the Frenchman fired high.

That proved only a fleeting reprieve for United, however. Five minutes into the second half Bergkamp floated a free-kick from the right, Pires returned the ball into a crowded goalmouth, and when Leeds failed to clear, Gilberto netted with a low first-time drive from eight yards.

At this point some distraught home fans headed for the exits, though the majority roared on their struggling side with impressive loyalty and they were rewarded by a spell of coherent pressure. Olembe struck one scorching

shot which hit Sakho, who swivelled to test Lehmann with the follow-up, but there was nothing the German could do when a Lennon centre found Smith untended six yards out and the England marksman reduced the arrears with a deft finish.

Thereafter Smith shot against a post, albeit with Lennon adjudged offside, but the result was not seriously in doubt and Arsenal spurned several opportunities to increase the margin. Edu surged through the centre to create havoc and when the ball emerged from a scramble at the feet of Henry it seemed certain that he would claim a hat-trick, only for his goalbound effort to bounce clear off Parlour.

An even more inviting chance fell to Aliadiere, but he headed over an empty net from Parlour's perfect cross.

Freddie's flying. Leeds' Cameroonian defender Salomon Olembe can't stop Freddie Ljungberg's surging run down the flank.

FORM GUIDE

W W L D D W [11 goals scored, 7 conceded]   L D W W W W [11 goals scored, 5 conceded]

ARSENAL 1   DYNAMO KIEV 0

Cole 88

Substitutes		Starting XI			Starting XI		Substitutes
Graham **STACK**	33	Jens **LEHMANN**	1	1	Olexander **SHOVKOVSKYI**		
Gael **CLICHY**	22	**LAUREN**	12	3	Sergei **FEDOROV**	21	Vitaliy **REVA**
Pascal **CYGAN**	18	Sol **CAMPBELL**	23	32	Goran **GAVRANCIC**	35	Goran **SABLIC** ▸
▸ **EDU**	17	■ Kolo **TOURE**	28	26	Andriy **NESMACHNYI**		(Onyschenko) 21 ◂
◂ (Bergkamp) 90		Ashley **COLE**	3	8	Valentin **BELKEVICH**	5	**ALESSANDRO**
▸ Sylvain **WILTORD**	11	Fredrik **LJUNGBERG**	8	17	Tiberiu **GHIOANE**	9	Badr **EL KADDOURI**
◂ (Ljungberg) 69		Ray **PARLOUR**	15	36	Jerko **LEKO** ■	15	Diogo **RINCON** ▸
▸ **KANU**	25	■ **GILBERTO**	19	22	Denys **ONYSCHENKO**		(Husyev) 60 ◂
◂ (Parlour) 75		Robert **PIRES**	7	20	Oleg **HUSYEV**	7	Olexander **MELASCHENKO**
Jeremie **ALIADIERE**	30	Dennis **BERGKAMP**	10	11	Georgi **PEEV**	18	**ROBERTO NANNI** ▸
		Thierry **HENRY**	14	16	Maksim **SHATSKIKH**		(Shatskikh) 71 ◂

MATCH REPORT

A last-gasp diving header by Ashley Cole kept alive Arsenal's dream of Champions League glory and ended nearly a year of frustration with a first European victory in nine outings. The result did not lift the Gunners off the bottom of their qualifying group, but it moved them to within only three points of leaders Internazionale with two games to play.

Only 120 seconds of normal time remained when Wiltord floated a cross from the right, Fedorov failed to clear and Cole launched himself horizontally to beat Shovkovskyi from six yards. Until then the Gunners, though creating a succession of clear-cut scoring opportunities, had appeared tense, with leading marksman Henry closely shackled by the spirited and well-organised Ukrainians.

Arsène Wenger's men had started brightly enough, with Ljungberg going close twice in the opening minutes, the Swede forcing the Kiev keeper to make a reflex save with his trailing leg, then turning another effort narrowly wide. Bergkamp probed tirelessly and he might have crafted the breakthrough with a free-kick, only for

Gilberto to head straight at Shovkovskyi, who also palmed a Pires shot into the side netting.

However, as the Arsenal manager had warned beforehand, Dynamo were not to be underrated as an attacking force, and Campbell was forced to make a timely covering tackle on the dangerous

The tireless Dennis Bergkamp did much to wrestle control of the midfield from a resolute Dynamo Kiev.

Shastkikh. Still, though, the Gunners maintained territorial mastery, and Shovkovskyi made a brave interception at the feet of Ljungberg, a Pires appeal for a spot-kick was turned down and, from the subsequent corner, a Ljungberg header was cleared off the line.

Only occasionally could Henry escape the close attentions of his markers but, soon after firing high over the crossbar, he freed Bergkamp with an astute pass. Highbury held its collective breath, fully expecting the Dutchman to shatter the deadlock, but Shovkovskyi was up to the challenge yet again, pulling off a superb block.

As time ebbed away the litany of misses continued with Pires dragging one shot across goal from a narrow angle, then miscuing with a free header when the keeper was stranded. Thus encouraged, Dynamo launched several assaults of their own and Shastkikh was repelled by desperate challenges by both Campbell and Toure, and Husyev steered a shot wide from a promising position.

Never lacking in courage or enterprise when the chips are down, Arsène Wenger increased his offensive options by throwing on Wiltord and Kanu for the closing stages. The reinforcements were prominent in the wave of attacks, which followed, but it was Toure, freed from defensive duties, who went agonisingly close after 86 minutes when he burst on to a cute backheel from Henry before being tackled heavily by Leko. The Gunners called for a penalty but the referee waved play on, setting the scene for the breathtaking finale in which Arsenal rescued their European campaign.

With two minutes left Ashley Cole launches himself at Wiltord's cross to score the goal that kept Arsenal's Champions League hopes alive.

W L D D W W [10 goals scored, 6 conceded]   D W W D W L [6 goals scored, 2 conceded]

ARSENAL 2
Pires 69, Ljungberg 79

TOTTENHAM HOTSPUR 1
Anderton 5

Substitutes		Arsenal			Tottenham	Substitutes	
		Jens **LEHMANN**	1	13	Kasey **KELLER**		
Graham **STACK**	33	**LAUREN**	12	2	Stephen **CARR**	Robert **BURCH**	24
▶ Pascal **CYGAN**	18	Sol **CAMPBELL**	23	30	Anthony **GARDNER**	Gary **DOHERTY**	12
◀ (Lauren) 60		Kolo **TOURE**	28	36	Dean **RICHARDS** ■	Mbulelo **MABIZELA** ▶	21
Justin **HOYTE**	45	Ashley **COLE**	23	3	Mauricio **TARICCO** ■	(Konchesky) 72 ◀	
▶ **EDU**	17	Fredrik **LJUNGBERG**	8	26	Ledley **KING**	Rohan **RICKETTS** ▶	27
◀ (Kanu) 80		■ Ray **PARLOUR**	15	7	Darren **ANDERTON** ■	(Dalmat) 81 ◀	
Dennis **BERGKAMP** 60	10	**GILBERTO**	19	16	Paul **KONCHESKY** ■	Bobby **ZAMORA** ▶	25
		Robert **PIRES**	7	11	Stephane **DALMAT**	(Postiga) 81 ◀	
		KANU	25	10	Robbie **KEANE**		
		Thierry **HENRY**	14	8	Helder **POSTIGA**		

MATCH REPORT

Displaying rousing resilience under fire, the Gunners stared the possibility of defeat in the face before bouncing back to emerge triumphant from the north London derby. The victory over Tottenham preserved their status as the only unbeaten side in all four divisions and stretched their Premiership lead to four points, albeit only until Chelsea trimmed the margin to a single point 26 hours later.

Although Arsenal deserved enormous credit for battling so valiantly only three days after their energy-sapping effort against Dynamo Kiev, in truth Spurs were unlucky to leave Highbury empty-handed. The visitors had snatched an early lead when King fed Keane and the ball ricocheted clear to Anderton, who dinked cleverly beyond Lehmann from six yards.

Clearly taken aback, the Gunners struggled to muster their characteristic rhythm for the remainder of the first period, although Henry was an honourable exception. The Frenchman launched a series of assaults on Keller's goal, most spectacularly in the 12th minute when he juggled a knockdown from Kanu before bringing

the best from the American with a cracking 30-yard half-volley. Soon afterwards Keller repelled a low drive from Henry, who then curled a free-kick on to the roof of the net from the edge of the box, and the keeper also denied Pires at his near post.

Still, the two best chances of the half fell to Postiga, courtesy of loose back passes from Lauren. The first time the Portuguese dithered, allowing Lehmann to save with an outstretched foot, then the German pulled off a magnificent block after the Tottenham man had fired crisply from point-blank range.

After the interval, Spurs continued to perform impressively, holding on to their advantage into the final quarter as Gardner cleared a Pires free-kick, Gilberto headed over and Henry shot high after wriggling clear of two challenges. But now the Gunners dug deep to demonstrate true championship pedigree. Deftly springing a hitherto effective offside trap, Henry raced on to a raking dispatch from Parlour to bear down on Keller, who pulled off a superb parry, only for Pires to sweep home the equaliser from close range.

Kanu's close control sees him retain possession despite the presence of Spurs' Mauricio Taricco.

Visibly jolted by the reverse, Tottenham began to wobble and Arsenal built up pressure, Henry going close with a deflected drive and Toure almost catching Keller unawares with an awkwardly bouncing volley. When the decisive thrust materialised, it was cruel, indeed. Bergkamp, whose imaginative passing had done much to revive his side since his arrival from the bench, found Kanu, who transferred the ball to Ljungberg. The Swede swerved inside from the left and hit a 20-yard shot which went high into the air off the boot of Carr before dropping into the net beyond the hopelessly stranded Keller.

Tottenham were justified in rueing their misfortune, but it was a reward for tremendous determination by Arsène Wenger's side, whose admirable capacity for never giving up augured well for the months ahead.

Ray Parlour was the Gunners' driving force in midfield in the absence of Patrick Vieira.

NOVEMBER

FA Barclaycard Premiership
Saturday 22 November 2003 at St Andrew's, 3.00 p.m.
Attendance: 29,588 Referee: Paul Durkin

FORM GUIDE
L D D W L D [3 goals scored, 6 conceded]   L D W W W W [10 goals scored, 6 conceded]

BIRMINGHAM CITY 0

ARSENAL 3
Ljungberg 4, Bergkamp 80, Pires 88

Substitutes				Starting XI						Starting XI			Substitutes
		Maik **TAYLOR**	12	1	Jens **LEHMANN**				Ian **BENNETT**	1	Damien **JOHNSON**	22	28	Kolo **TOURE** ■	33	Graham **STACK**

Substitutes								Substitutes
Ian **BENNETT**	1	Maik **TAYLOR**	12	1	Jens **LEHMANN**			
Olivier **TEBILY**	26	Damien **JOHNSON**	22	28	Kolo **TOURE** ■	33	Graham **STACK**	
▸ Bryan **HUGHES**	10	Kenny **CUNNINGHAM**	4	23	Sol **CAMPBELL**	27	Stathis **TAVLARIDIS**	
◂ (Lazaridis) 84		Matthew **UPSON**	25	18	Pascal **CYGAN**	45	Justin **HOYTE** ▸	
▸ Stern **JOHN**	14	Jamie **CLAPHAM**	23	3	Ashley **COLE**		(Pires) 90 ◂	
◂ (Cisse) 63		Stephen **CLEMENCE**	32	8	Fredrik **LJUNGBERG**	25	**KANU** ▸	
▸ Clinton **MORRISON**	19	■ Aliou **CISSE**	6	7	Robert **PIRES**		(Clichy) 58 ◂	
◂ (Forssell) 86		Robbie **SAVAGE**	8	17	**EDU** ■	30	Jeremie **ALIADIERE** ▸	
		Stan **LAZARIDIS**	11	22	Gael **CLICHY**		(Bergkamp) 89 ◂	
		David **DUNN**	16	10	Dennis **BERGKAMP**			
		Mikael **FORSSELL**	9	14	Thierry **HENRY**			

MATCH REPORT

Another day, another record for Arsenal, who became the first side to go 13 games unbeaten at the start of a Premiership season on the day that Arsène Wenger celebrated his 400th match in charge. More importantly, the victory over fifth-placed Birmingham City lifted the Gunners back above Manchester United to resume their leadership of the championship race.

With Dennis Bergkamp in ravishing form, the visitors made light of the absence of half a dozen members of their senior squad, getting off to a flying start which culminated in an early breakthrough. The Dutchman charged down a Cunningham clearance, surged inside from the left touchline and passed to Henry, whose deft dispatch sent Ljungberg scampering between two defenders to stroke past Taylor from ten yards.

Soon Henry might have doubled the advantage, but after drifting left-to-right across the face of the Birmingham rearguard, leaving three would-be tacklers in his wake, he fired a low drive which was held by Taylor.

Birmingham had mounted no meaningful assaults to that point, but now they stirred and a neat combination between Clemence and Dunn resulted in a near-post cross which Lazaridis stabbed narrowly wide. Then Dunn set up another chance for Lazaridis but Lehmann dealt competently with the Australian's cross-shot and thereafter the Gunners preserved their lead comfortably until the break.

The second period commenced with a spell of Arsenal pressure in which Henry was prominent. First he raced on to a delivery from Edu and swerved in from the left before testing Taylor with a clipped drive. Then his pull-back to Pires was almost turned into his own goal by Cunningham, who was rescued by his keeper's full-length plunge.

Lifted by the arrival of John from the bench, Birmingham responded spiritedly and Toure ended one menacing Lazaridis sortie with a beautifully timed challenge, then Forssell went close to an equaliser when he beat Lehmann to Savage's teasing cross, only for his firm header to flash outside an upright.

Any thoughts of a home revival were dispelled by a typically scintillating Arsenal counter-attack in which the ball was ferried from Toure to Kanu to Henry, who freed Bergkamp for a run on goal. Belying his veteran status, Dennis outstripped a posse of defenders before chipping exquisitely over the onrushing Taylor.

With only ten minutes remaining, the Blues threw everything into a last-ditch assault, but Cole soared high to nod out a dangerous Savage cross and when Matthew Upson outjumped Lehmann from a Lazaridis corner, the former Gunner missed the target with his header.

In ravishing form. Dennis Bergkamp shows off his ball control as he keeps Birmingham's Robbie Savage and Aliou Cisse at bay.

Arsenal's fourth goal came after Henry found space on the left before slipping the ball to Pires. The Frenchman then ghosted between two markers to steer delicately past Taylor from the corner of the six-yard box. It was a sublime goal and it completed a richly satisfying afternoon for Arsenal, for whom French teenager Gael Clichy made a promising League debut on the left of midfield.

After ghosting past two Birmingham defenders Robert Pires steers the ball home for Arsenal's third goal, two minutes from time.

51

NOVEMBER

UEFA Champions League, Group Stage, Group B
Tuesday 25 November 2003 at the San Siro, 7.45 p.m.
Attendance: 50,000 Referee: Wolfgang Stark, Germany

FORM GUIDE
L D W D W W [12 goals scored, 4 conceded]   D D W W W W [12 goals scored, 4 conceded]

INTERNAZIONALE 1
Vieri 32

ARSENAL 5
Henry 25, 85, Ljungberg 48,
Edu 87, Pires 89

Substitutes						Substitutes
	Francesco **TOLDO**	1	1	Jens **LEHMANN**		
Alberto **FONTANA** 12	Ivan **CORDOBA**	2	28	Kolo **TOURE**	33	Graham **STACK**
Daniele **ADANI** 15	Marco **MATERAZZI**	23	23	Sol **CAMPBELL**	5	Martin **KEOWN**
▶ Giovanni **PASQUALE** 26	Fabio **CANNAVARO**	17	18	Pascal **CYGAN** ▪	22	Gael **CLICHY**
◀ (Cannavaro) 59	Javier **ZANETTI**	4	3	Ashley **COLE**	45	Justin **HOYTE**
▶ Matias **ALMEYDA** 25	Cristiano **ZANETTI**	6	8	Fredrik **LJUNGBERG**	19	**GILBERTO** ▶
◀ (Lamouchi) 57	Sabri **LAMOUCHI**	8	15	Ray **PARLOUR**		(Kanu) 73 ◀
Kily **GONZALEZ** 18	Jeremie **BRECHET**	31	17	**EDU** ▪	30	Jeremie **ALIADIERE** ▶
Siqueira **LUCIANO** 11	Andy **VAN DER MEYDE**	7	7	Robert **PIRES**		(Henry) 89 ◀
▶ Julio **CRUZ** 9	Obafemi **MARTINS**	30	25	**KANU**	32	Michal **PAPADOPULOS**
◀ (van der Meyde) 69	Christian **VIERI**	32	14	Thierry **HENRY**		

MATCH REPORT

A vibrant display of breathtakingly incisive football earned Arsenal the biggest victory in their Champions League history and put them firmly in charge of their own qualification fate. The Gunners were the better team throughout, thoroughly deserving their 2-1 advantage as the closing stages of the game approached. Then Arsenal hit Inter with a devastating salvo of three strikes in four minutes, rubbing in their crushing superiority and transforming their previously poor goal difference.

Unbeaten at home by English opposition for 42 years, Inter began confidently, with pacy front-runner Martins looking a particularly worrying threat. But gradually Arsenal drew their sting and the opening goal was a just reward for the visitors' spirit and invention.

Freddie Ljungberg
converts coolly to give
the Gunners the lead
just after half-time.

Cole started the move on the left, then the ball fizzed at speed to Pires, Henry and back to the England defender, whose perfect knock-back was sidefooted home with sublime precision by Henry from the edge of the box.

After that the Gunners continued to impress and were unlucky to concede an equaliser. Van der Meyde found Vieri on the left and the Italian's wayward shot rebounded from the heel of Campbell and looped agonisingly beyond the groping Lehmann on its way into the net.

Inter sought to capitalise on their fortune, and Materazzi brought a fine diving save from Lehmann with a curving free-kick. But the Gunners regained the ascendancy shortly after the interval, and this time Henry turned provider. Cutting in from the left, he sent two defenders the wrong way before setting up Ljungberg, who converted coolly from four yards. That jolted the hosts into mounting pressure and Cristiano Zanetti shaved an upright with a snap-volley from 25 yards, and a few minutes later van der Meyde was only inches high with a fiercely struck free-kick.

With Cygan and Campbell looking solid in central defence, the Gunners remained in the ascendancy and Ljungberg almost increased their lead when he deflected a Toure header narrowly wide. Henry, the outstanding attacker on show, was stretching the Inter defence relentlessly and his darting runs created several more inviting opportunities, which went begging. At the other end Lehmann held a hooked effort from Vieri and Cole frustrated Martins with a glorious last-ditch tackle.

Then the roof fell in on the increasingly nervy Italians. First Henry ran half the length of the field, sent Javier Zanetti first one way and then another, then lashed a savage cross-shot beyond the diving Toldo. The Frenchman then roamed to the right to receive a raking crossfield pass from Cole before threading a pass to the far post, where Edu met it and scored with aplomb. Finally Aliadiere outwitted Brechet on the right, reaching the byline before pulling back for Pires to shrug off the attentions of two markers and rap home the Gunners' fifth.

The result lifted Arsenal into second place in their group, and now a home victory over Lokomotiv Moscow would guarantee them a place in the knockout stages.

After sending Javier Zanetti this way and that, Thierry Henry lashes a savage cross shot past Toldo to put Arsenal 3-1 ahead.

FORM GUIDE

D W W W W [16 goals scored, 4 conceded]   D L W L L W [9 goals scored, 9 conceded]

ARSENAL 0   FULHAM 0

Substitutes		Arsenal			Fulham	Substitutes	
		Jens **LEHMANN**	1	1	Edwin **VAN DER SAR**		
Graham **STACK**	33	Kolo **TOURE**	28	2	Moritz **VOLZ**	12	Mark **CROSSLEY**
Gael **CLICHY**	22	Sol **CAMPBELL**	23	16	Zat **KNIGHT**	17	Martin **DJETOU**
Justin **HOYTE**	45	Pascal **CYGAN**	18	4	Andy **MELVILLE**	24	Alain **GOMA**
▸ **KANU**	25	Ashley **COLE**	3	18	Jerome **BONNISSEL**	15	Barry **HAYLES** ▸
◂ (Gilberto) 67		Fredrik **LJUNGBERG**	8	6	Junichi **INAMOTO**		(Saha) 76 ◂
▸ Jeremie **ALIADIERE**	30	**GILBERTO**	19	23	Sean **DAVIS**	9	Facundo **SAVA**
◂ (Ljungberg) 79		▩ **EDU**	17	10	Lee **CLARK**		
		Robert **PIRES**	7	5	Sylvain **LEGWINSKI** ▩		
		Dennis **BERGKAMP**	10	14	Steed **MALBRANQUE**		
		Thierry **HENRY**	14	8	Louis **SAHA**		

MATCH REPORT

Here was a genuine footballing curiosity, a goalless draw which crackled with thrills and excitement from first minute to last. With Robert Pires, Thierry Henry and skipper Dennis Bergkamp all in scintillating form, Arsenal attacked incessantly and created an avalanche of scoring opportunities, only to be denied by Fulham's inspirational keeper Edwin van der Sar.

The Dutchman made at least a dozen breathtaking saves as the Gunners pounded his goal and he was supported nobly by a heroic back-four in which young Moritz Volz, on loan from Highbury,

ran himself to a standstill. The upshot was that Arsène Wenger's men were toppled from their Premiership pinnacle by Chelsea, who moved a point clear after their defeat of Manchester United at Stamford Bridge.

Freddie Ljungberg keeps his feet as he surges between Fulham's Louis Saha and Sylvain Legwinski.

You go that way, I'll go this way. Ashley Cole dazzles Fulham defender Moritz Volz with his deft footwork, but Arsenal couldn't quite break through.

Robert Pires was in fine form during this London derby but resolute defending and a brilliant performance from van der Sar in Fulham's goal kept the scoresheet blank.

The visitors, seeking their first ever win at Arsenal, made a misleadingly positive start, with Saha forcing a free-kick on the edge of Lehmann's box only 20 seconds into the action. But after Ljungberg had blocked Knight's explosive free-kick, the game settled into a rhythm of rampant Gunners pressure.

The first clear chance fell to Toure, who stabbed high from six yards after Cygan glanced on a corner by Henry, and then Ljungberg strode forward to stretch van der Sar from 25 yards. Now Bergkamp threatened to take charge, and twice he set up Ljungberg with exquisitely subtle passes. First the Swede was foiled at point-blank range by the flying Fulham keeper, then he shot high over the crossbar. Efforts from Henry, Edu and Pires all fizzed wide, then the keeper took centre-stage again. He repelled a powerful side-foot and a long-range drive from Henry, a mishit clip from the World Player of the Year nominee after Pires had brilliantly nutmegged the overworked Volz, and a rasping volley from Bergkamp. As the first half closed, the Dutch custodian stood firm against yet another Ljungberg screamer.

The second period began in similar vein with Henry bamboozling two defenders before setting up Bergkamp, whose fierce shot was saved. Next van der Sar caught a deflection from Knight, plunged unerringly at the feet of Pires, and rose to new heights with a blinding save from Bergkamp following a magnificent crossfield set-up by Cole.

As the three-quarter mark approached, the home crowd began to wonder if it was to be one of those days when the gods were plotting against them. Right on cue Fulham launched two threatening breakaways, Volz firing high when well placed, then Malbranque nodding marginally wide from a Davis cross.

In truth a goal for Fulham would have represented a grave injustice, but that possibility subsided as the hosts launched a renewed onslaught. Henry hurled himself horizontally but just failed to connect with a Toure delivery, Kanu danced through but was crowded out, Bergkamp volleyed off-target from a deflected Cole centre and there were two more near misses by Henry.

Near the end the elastic van der Sar pulled off yet another superb stop, this time from Kanu, and so condemning Arsenal to a blank scoresheet at Highbury for the first time in 47 Premiership games.

NOVEMBER 2003

Arsenal.com PLAYER OF THE MONTH

Thierry HENRY

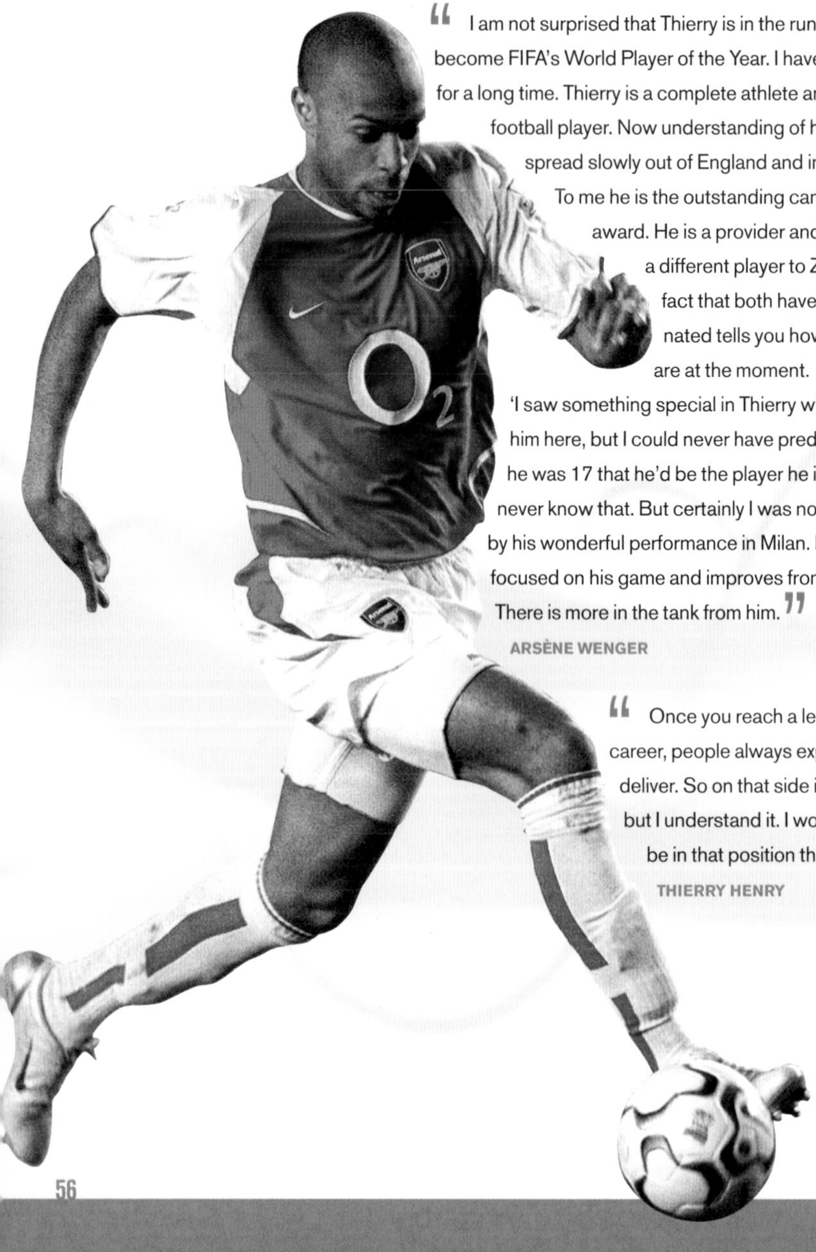

" I am not surprised that Thierry is in the running to become FIFA's World Player of the Year. I have expected it for a long time. Thierry is a complete athlete and complete football player. Now understanding of his class has spread slowly out of England and into Europe. To me he is the outstanding candidate for the award. He is a provider and a striker, a different player to Zidane. But the fact that both have been nominated tells you how good France are at the moment.

'I saw something special in Thierry when I brought him here, but I could never have predicted when he was 17 that he'd be the player he is today. You never know that. But certainly I was not surprised by his wonderful performance in Milan. He stays focused on his game and improves from year to year. There is more in the tank from him. "

ARSÈNE WENGER

" Once you reach a level in your career, people always expect you to deliver. So on that side it is not easy, but I understand it. I would rather be in that position than not. "

THIERRY HENRY

ARSENAL DIARY

Saturday 8 November
- The Gunners announce that David Bentley has signed a long-term contract with the club.
- On the day Spurs visit Highbury, Arsenal stage a series of activities to raise money for ChildLine, their charity of the season.

Saturday 22 November
- The Gunners' 3-0 victory over Birmingham at St Andrews, Arsène Wenger's 400th match in charge, wins the Scottish Life Performance of the Week Award from the League Managers Association.

Tuesday 25 November
- Thierry Henry, Zinedine Zidane and Brazil's Ronaldo are nominated for the World Player of the Year award.

Sunday 30 November
- Ex-Gunner Moritz Volz excels for Fulham against his old team-mates in the goalless draw at Highbury.

THE WIDER WORLD

Monday 10 November
- Peter Reid is sacked as manager of Leeds United.

Saturday 15 November
- Scotland beat Holland 1-0 in the first leg of their Euro 2004 qualifier. Wales earn a draw in Russia.

Wednesday 19 November
- Wales and Scotland are knocked out of Euro 2004, Wales falling 1-0 to the Russians, Scotland being hammered 6-0 by the Dutch.

Monday 24 November
- Bryan Robson takes over as manager of Bradford City.

Thursday 27 November
- Trevor Brooking is appointed FA director of football development.

Sunday 30 November
- England draw France, Croatia and Switzerland in Euro 2004.

FA CARLING PREMIERSHIP

30 November 2003

	P	HOME					AWAY					Pts
		W	D	L	F	A	W	D	L	F	A	
ARSENAL	13	5	1	0	12	6	5	2	0	16	4	33
Chelsea	13	5	1	0	15	5	5	1	1	12	4	32
Manchester United	13	5	1	1	14	4	5	0	1	11	4	31
Charlton Athletic	14	2	2	3	9	12	4	2	1	11	5	22
Fulham	13	3	2	2	12	9	3	1	2	12	9	21
Newcastle United	14	3	2	2	9	4	2	3	2	11	15	20
Birmingham City	13	2	3	2	6	7	3	2	1	5	4	20
Manchester City	13	2	2	2	12	9	3	1	3	10	9	18
Liverpool	13	2	1	3	8	8	3	2	2	10	6	18
Bolton Wanderers	14	2	4	1	7	4	2	2	3	6	15	18
Southampton	14	3	1	3	5	4	1	4	2	5	5	17
Leicester City	14	2	3	2	11	9	2	0	5	11	13	15
Portsmouth	14	4	0	3	15	8	0	3	4	2	12	15
Middlesbrough	13	2	1	4	6	10	2	2	2	5	5	15
Tottenham Hotspur	14	3	1	3	8	9	1	2	4	5	9	15
Blackburn Rovers	14	3	0	4	11	11	1	2	4	8	13	14
Aston Villa	14	3	3	1	7	5	0	2	5	4	12	14
Everton	14	3	2	2	11	7	0	2	5	4	12	13
Wolverhampton Wanderers	14	2	3	2	7	14	0	2	5	2	13	11
Leeds United	14	1	2	4	5	12	2	0	5	7	21	11

FORM GUIDE

W W W W W D [15 goals scored, 3 conceded]   W W L D L D [8 goals scored, 9 conceded]

ARSENAL 5

Aliadiere 24, 71, Kanu 68, Wiltord 79,
Fabregas 88

WOLVERHAMPTON WANDERERS 1

Rae 81

Substitutes					Substitutes
		Graham **STACK**	33	28	Andy **MARSHALL**	
Rami **SHAABAN**	24	Justin **HOYTE**	45	26	Joey **GUDJONSSON** ▪	1	Michael **OAKES**
▸ Olafur-Ingi **SKULASON**	55	▪ Frankie **SIMEK**	51	6	Paul **BUTLER**	14	Jorge **MANUEL SILAS**
◂ (Hoyte) 55		▪ Stathis **TAVLARIDIS**	27	12	Jody **CRADDOCK**	7	Shaun **NEWTON** ▸
▸ Ryan **SMITH**	56	Gael **CLICHY**	22	3	Lee **NAYLOR**		(Camara) 73 ◂
◂ (Bentley) 78		Francesc **FABREGAS**	57	24	Keith **ANDREWS**	11	Mark **KENNEDY** ▸
▸ Michal **PAPADOPULOS**	32	Patrick **VIEIRA**	4	8	Paul **INCE**		(Miller) 60 ◂
◂ (Aliadiere) 83		David **BENTLEY**	37	4	Alex **RAE**	29	Dean **STURRIDGE** ▸
Quincy **OWUSU-ABEYIE**	54	Sylvain **WILTORD**	11	17	Henri **CAMARA**		(Andrews) 68 ◂
		KANU	25	16	Kenny **MILLER**		
		Jeremie **ALIADIERE**	30	9	Nathan **BLAKE** ▪		

MATCH REPORT

Arsenal swept into the Quarter-Finals of the League Cup with a comprehensive victory which augured encouragingly for the club's future in both the long term and the short. Seven of the side that started against Wolves boasted a mere 13 first-team appearances between them, and when 16-year-old Francesc Fabregas completed the rout of the Premiership strugglers with the fifth goal near the end, he became the youngest scorer in the Club's history. Even more significantly for the Gunners' campaign, skipper Patrick Vieira made his comeback after two months' absence with a thigh injury, and dominated the midfield with all his customary majesty.

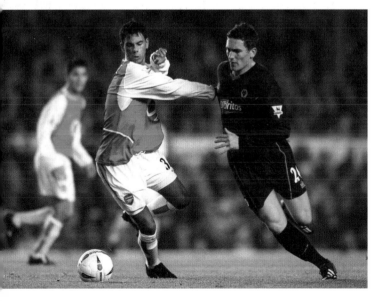

Jeremie Aliadiere capitalises on some loose defending by Wolves to open the scoring.

It was Wolves who launched the first attack of the night, but Stack dealt comfortably with Gudjonsson's free-kick after Miller had been fouled. But it was not long before Arsenal clicked into gear and started attacking Wolves. Twice Kanu might have capitalised, but first he miscued tamely from Hoyte's cross, then he shot against the outside of a post after leaving Gudjonsson, Ince and Craddock helpless with a mesmerising dribble. Yet for all the hosts' mounting supremacy, they were obliged to a defensive mistake for their breakthrough, Aliadiere seizing on a sloppy back-pass from Naylor before stroking neatly beyond the exposed Marshall.

Bentley, who looked particularly dangerous when he roamed to the left flank, might have doubled the advantage but his free-kick skimmed the crossbar. Wolves then almost grabbed an unexpected equaliser as Ince stretched Stack with a bouncing volley following a Rae corner.

However, the second half proved over-whelmingly one-sided as Arsène Wenger's young guns took charge. Kanu looked set to climax another typically dazzling run with a goal but was denied by the enterprising Marshall. Wiltord and Aliadiere then went close before the dam broke when substitute Skulason sent Wiltord clear on the right and the Frenchman's centre was converted by Kanu from five yards.

Now came the goal of the match from Aliadiere, who surged on to a Kanu delivery, then shimmied past Craddock and Butler before burying a powerful drive from the edge of the box. It was fitting that the masterful Vieira should be the next man to punish the demoralised Midlanders and he did so with a beautiful through-pass which sent in Wiltord for a clinical finish. At this point the likelihood of a retaliatory strike by

Wolves appeared remote in the extreme, but the spirited Rae refused to yield and shrugged off a challenge to net spectacularly with a rising shot from a narrow angle. Soon afterwards the four-goal margin was restored when Fabregas tapped in from close range to claim his place in the Highbury record books, as the youngest ever Arsenal scorer, and complete a hugely satisfying night's work for the Gunners.

There had been senior debuts for Simek, Skulason and Papadopulos; the slender experience of Stack, Clichy, Hoyte, Fabregas, Bentley and Smith had been extended, and Vieira had exceeded his manager's expectations by completing a full 90 minutes with no ill effects.

Fabregas makes history *as the Gunners' youngest ever scorer, netting the final goal to complete a resounding victory for Arsenal.*

DECEMBER

FA Barclaycard Premiership
Saturday 6 December 2003 at The Walkers Stadium, 3.00 p.m.
Attendance: 32,108 Referee: Rob Styles

FORM GUIDE

L L W W D W [1 goals scored, 6 conceded] W W W W D W [16 goals scored, 3 conceded]

LEICESTER CITY 1   ARSENAL 1
Hignett 90   Gilberto 60

Substitutes		Ian **WALKER**	1	1	Jens **LEHMANN** ▨		**SUBSTITUTES**
Danny **COYNE**	16	Callum **DAVIDSON**	14	28	Kolo **TOURE**	33	Graham **STACK**
Matt **ELLIOTT**	18	Steve **HOWEY**	24	23	Sol **CAMPBELL**	5	Martin **KEOWN** ▶
▶ Keith **GILLESPIE**	7	Riccardo **SCIMECA**	21	18	Pascal **CYGAN**		(Ljungberg) 88 ◀
◀ (Ferdinand) 76		Andrew **IMPEY**	2	3	Ashley **COLE** ■	22	Gael **CLICHY** ▶
▶ Craig **HIGNETT**	5	Ben **THATCHER**	33	8	Fredrik **LJUNGBERG**		(Bergkamp) 74 ◀
◀ (McKinlay) 59		Jordan **STEWART**	11	19	**GILBERTO**	11	Sylvain **WILTORD** ▶
▶ Paul **DICKOV**	22	Billy **MCKINLAY**	32	17	**EDU**		(Aliadiere) 67 ◀
◀ (Bent) 67		Jamie **SCOWCROFT**	10	7	Robert **PIRES**	25	**KANU**
		Marcus **BENT**	38	10	Dennis **BERGKAMP**		
	■	Les **FERDINAND**	9	30	Jeremie **ALIADIERE**		

MATCH REPORT

It was agonising for Arsenal as they were deprived of two points and the Premiership top spot with virtually the last kick of a hard-fought contest, after being reduced to ten men for the closing stages by the dismissal of Ashley Cole.

Without the services of Thierry Henry, who was nursing an injury, and Patrick Vieira, who was rested ahead of the crucial Champions League clash with Lokomotiv Moscow, the Gunners began steadily, though their characteristically fluent style was hindered both by a strongly gusting wind and by the fierce determination of Leicester City.

Thus the first half was a dogged affair in which Arsène Wenger's team mustered little in the way of attacking threat, while the improving Foxes, unbeaten in their last four outings, menaced only intermittently. Scowcroft rang the first alarm bell when his header from a Scimeca free-kick drifted narrowly wide of Lehmann's far post. Ferdinand then raced on to a cute through-ball from McKinlay

and swerved past the German keeper, only to slice wildly into the crowd from near the byline.

Pascal Cygan leaves Leicester's Marcus Bent
standing as he makes a clearing header.

However, Arsenal began to hit their high-quality stride immediately after the interval, when Pires found Gilberto with a clever pass and the Brazilian tested Walker from 22 yards. At the other end Bent tumbled under a challenge from Campbell but the referee waved away claims for a penalty. He then put an end to a clash between Lehmann and Ferdinand by brandishing yellow cards at both.

The Gunners were gaining the upper hand and their superiority paid off with a stunning counter-assault which Lehmann began by rolling the ball to Pires. The Frenchman dispatched an inch-perfect delivery down the left touchline to Bergkamp, who slipped past Thatcher and crossed for Gilberto to plunder his fourth goal of the campaign with a thunderous header from six yards.

Now, with Pires, Bergkamp and Aliadiere combining impressively, Arsenal began to purr. They nearly forged further ahead when Bergkamp's free-kick on the right was met by an acrobatic volley from Gilberto, which was pushed on to a post by the plunging Walker. Aliadiere attempted to pounce on the rebound but his effort was blocked, then hacked away by Scimeca.

With the Gunners' lead looking increasingly comfortable, Cole materialised on the right flank and launched himself into a two-footed challenge on Thatcher, with the inevitable upshot of a red card. Even thus depleted, the visitors looked the more likely side to score, until deep into stoppage time when Gillespie fed the ball back to Impey, who lofted a steepling cross into the Arsenal box. Scowcroft rose unchallenged to nod down to the charging Hignett, who nudged the equaliser past Lehmann from six yards.

There was barely time to restart the action before the referee blew the final whistle and a priceless opportunity to leapfrog League-leaders Chelsea, who had been held to a draw at Leeds, had been squandered at the death.

A thunderous header from a cross by Dennis Bergkamp brings Gilberto his fourth goal of the season on the hour mark.

DECEMBER

UEFA Champions League, Group Stage, Group B
Wednesday 10 December 2003 at Highbury, 7.45 p.m.
Attendance: 35,343 Referee: Lubos Michel, Slovakia

FORM GUIDE

W W W D W D [16 goals scored, 4 conceded]   W W D W D W [19 goals scored, 4 conceded]

ARSENAL 2
Pires 12, Ljungberg 67

LOKOMOTIV MOSCOW 0

Substitutes					Substitutes	
		Sergei **OVCHINNIKOV** 1	1	Jens **LEHMANN**		
Graham **STACK** 33	Kolo **TOURE** 28	16	Vadim **EVSEEV** ■	9	Ruslan **NIGMATULLIN**	
Martin **KEOWN** 5	Sol **CAMPBELL** 23	5	Sergei **IGNASHEVICH**	2	Gennadi **NIZHEGORODOV**	
Ray **PARLOUR** 15	Pascal **CYGAN** 18	14	Oleg **PASHININ**	30	Malkhaz **ASATIANI**	
EDU 17	Ashley **COLE** 3	17	Dmitri **SENNIKOV**	41	Sergei **GURENKO** ▸	
Sylvain **WILTORD** 11	Fredrik **LJUNGBERG** 8	28	Dmitri **KHOKHLOV**		(Buznikin) 46 ◂	
▸ **KANU** 25	**GILBERTO** 19	4	Jacob **LEKSETHO** ■■	99	Jorge **WAGNER**	
◂ (Bergkamp) 75	■ Patrick **VIEIRA** 4	10	Dmitri **LOSKOV**	77	Lessa **LEANDRO**	
Jeremie **ALIADIERE** 30	Robert **PIRES** 7	8	Vladimir **MAMINOV**	52	Winston **PARKS** ▸	
	Dennis **BERGKAMP** 10	15	Maxum **BUZNIKIN**		(Ashvetia) 46 ◂	
	Thierry **HENRY** 14	32	Mikhail **ASHVETIA**			

MATCH REPORT

Bottom of their Champions League qualifying group after three matches, top after six – that was the tale of Arsenal's stunning revival, completed by this comprehensive domination of Lokomotiv Moscow. It was the Gunners' third successive victory of their European campaign and the one which clinched their place in the knockout stage.

Needing a win to ensure progress, Thierry Henry and company began in imperious fashion and their early superiority was rewarded with a beautifully engineered goal in the 12th minute. The Frenchman outpaced his marker to seize possession on the right, then rolled the ball square to Pires, who burst between two defenders before netting with a powerful near-post drive.

Apart from one off-beam Khokhlov shot, the traffic continued to flow all one way as the hosts sought to build on their positive start. Bergkamp missed the target with a 30-yard curler, and then the Dutchman nudged a floated Ljungberg dispatch to Henry, who shaved an upright with a low clip. Next to threaten was Toure, whose searching cross was scooped out by

Thierry Henry fires narrowly wide after being put through by Dennis Bergkamp.

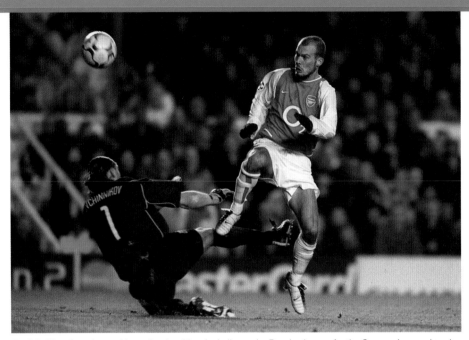

Freddie Ljungberg keeps his cool as he chips the ball over the Russian keeper for the Gunners' second goal.

Ovchinnikov to Ljungberg but the Swede's lob cleared the crossbar. Vieira was similarly inaccurate from close range after the keeper had parried a free-kick from Henry. In the final minute of the first half, an already unpromising situation for Lokomotiv deteriorated further when Leksetho was sent off for a second bookable offence.

The Gunners began the second period at high tempo. Twice Toure might have registered, first with a 20-yard howitzer which Ovchinnikov fingertipped to safety, then with a wild half-volley from a third of the distance. But Lokomotiv were not entirely without enterprise and Lehmann was required to block Parks from an acute angle following a slip by Cole. Arsenal returned to the attack with renewed momentum, but still the killer second goal proved frustratingly elusive. Pires pounced on a loose ball but swept marginally wide from 20 yards, Ljungberg's low shot demanded a full-length dive from Ovchinnikov and Bergkamp misdirected a free header from a cross by the overlapping Cole.

Finally, though, the pressure paid off with a typically stylish Arsenal incision. Vieira won the ball majestically in midfield and found Bergkamp, who flicked forward for Henry to hook into the path of Ljungberg, leaving the scampering Swede to dink the ball over the advancing keeper from eight yards.

Still a quarter of the contest remained and at last Lokomotiv mounted a series of concerted assaults. Khokhlov darted through the inside-left channel but Lehmann dealt smartly with his fizzing 20-yarder, Pires blocked Evseev in the box, Loskov fired wide from a free-kick and a Gurenko effort was smothered deftly by Lehmann.

Arsenal were always in control, however, and they concluded an eminently satisfying night's work with a keep-ball session which delighted the Highbury faithful. There was a happy ending for the Russians, too, as they qualified for the last 16 thanks to Dynamo Kiev's draw with Inter Milan.

DECEMBER

FORM GUIDE

W W D W D W [16 goals scored, 3 conceded]   L L W L W W [11 goals scored, 9 conceded]

ARSENAL 1
Bergkamp 11

BLACKBURN ROVERS 0

Substitutes						Substitutes
	Jens **LEHMANN**	1	1	Brad **FRIEDEL**		
Graham **STACK** 33	Kolo **TOURE**	28	11	Markus **BABBEL** ■	31	Peter **ENCKELMAN**
Martin **KEOWN** 5	Sol **CAMPBELL**	23	6	Craig **SHORT**	7	Garry **FLITCROFT**
▸ Ray **PARLOUR** 15	■ Pascal **CYGAN**	18	15	Andy **TODD** ■	21	Dino **BAGGIO** ▸
◂ (Bergkamp) 74	Ashley **COLE**	3	3	Vratislav **GRESKO** ■		(Babbel) 82 ◂
▸ **EDU** 17	Fredrik **LJUNGBERG**	8	23	Brett **EMERTON**	12	Steven **REID** ▸
◂ (Ljungberg) 84	■ **GILBERTO**	19	8	Kerimoglu **TUGAY**		(Gresko) 46 ◂
KANU 25	Patrick **VIEIRA**	4	24	Barry **FERGUSON** ■	9	Andy **COLE** ▸
	Robert **PIRES**	7	2	Lucas **NEILL**		(Gallagher) 57 ◂
	Dennis **BERGKAMP**	10	17	Paul **GALLAGHER**		
	Thierry **HENRY**	14	19	Dwight **YORKE**		

MATCH REPORT

Arsenal became the third club in 24 hours to top the Premiership as they edged a thrilling, high-quality encounter with Blackburn Rovers.

It's business as usual. Thierry Henry and Kolo Toure congratulate goalscorer Bergkamp.

Few visitors to Highbury attack the Gunners from the first whistle but Graeme Souness' men did just that and their boldness almost paid off after just 20 seconds, when Neill volleyed a cross into the path of Yorke, whose 15-yard toe-poke grazed the outside of Lehmann's post. Blackburn continued to flow forward smoothly and an Emerton dispatch demanded an athletic take from the German goalkeeper. Babbel might have done better with a far-post header from a Ferguson free-kick, but it was the hosts who seized the lead with only their first meaningful assault. The creator was the powerful Toure who surged down the right flank leaving Gresko in his wake before reaching the byline and pulling back for Bergkamp to slot home coolly from eight yards at the near post.

That was the signal for Arsenal to hit top gear, and now they threatened to overwhelm Rovers with a wave of fluent attacks. Although chance after chance was created, not one of them was converted into a goal: Ljungberg threaded a delightful pass to Henry, but Vieira slashed wide from his countryman's pull-back; Henry scuffed tamely from 30 yards; Pires bewitched several opponents with a sublime body-swerve only to curl his shot against an upright from the edge of the box.

The litany of near misses continued when a rebound from a Ljungberg effort was nodded weakly by Pires; Friedel saved bravely at the same Frenchman's feet, and then managed to block a side-foot from Henry after dazzling delivery work from Bergkamp.

The second period began in similar vein with Bergkamp sending Ljungberg clear in the inside-right channel, only for Friedel to repel the Swede's blast. Soon Blackburn reversed the flow and began to hold sway over an Arsenal side which showed signs of tiredness from their midweek European exertions. Cygan dealt decisively with a dangerous cross from Emerton, Tugay capped a buccaneering run with a powerful 25-yarder which cleared the crossbar and Babbel netted with a header from Ferguson's teasing centre, only for the 'goal' to be disallowed for a push on Toure.

Next Andy Cole sent in Ferguson but Lehmann brought off a splendid one-handed parry and, with the danger signals flashing, gradually the Gunners began to re-assert themselves as an attacking force.

Arsenal were denied a penalty after Todd had pushed Henry, a Ljungberg drive was blocked by Short and Henry's header from a Bergkamp free-kick was held by Friedel, who then dealt with two more shots from the Arsenal hitman.

Still the gallant visitors carried a potent threat, and they went close to equalising when Reid's corner was glanced on by Short, the plunging Lehmann pushed the ball out and Yorke scooped over the unguarded net from close range.

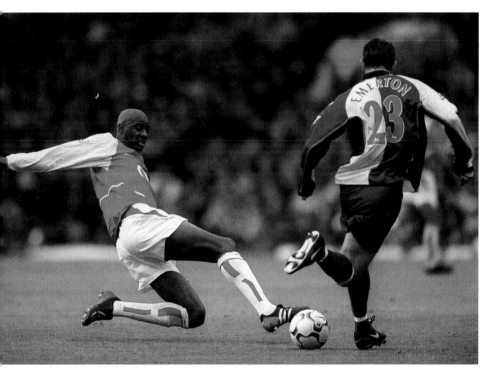

Skipper Patrick Vieira makes sure there's no way through for Blackburn's Emerton with a well-timed tackle.

DECEMBER

Carling Cup, Quarter-final
Tuesday 16 December 2003 at the Hawthorns, 8.00 p.m.
Attendance: 20,369 Referee: Matt Messias

WEST BROMWICH ALBION 0

ARSENAL 2
Kanu 25, Aliadiere 57

Substitutes						Substitutes	
Joe **MURPHY**	21	Russell **HOULT**	1	33	Graham **STACK**		
▶ Phil **GILCHRIST**	6	Sean **GREGAN**	14	12	**LAUREN**	Rami **SHAABAN**	24
◀ (Volmer) 66		Thomas **GAARDSOE**	24	5	Martin **KEOWN**	Frankie **SIMEK**	51
Adam **CHAMBERS**	22	Joost **VOLMER**	25	27	Stathis **TAVLARIDIS** ■	Jerome **THOMAS** ▶	53
▶ Artim **SAKIRI**	20	Bernt **HAAS**	2	22	Gael **CLICHY**	(Bentley) 82 ◀	
◀ (O'Connor) 71		James **O'CONNOR**	4	11	Sylvain **WILTORD**	Francesc **FABREGAS** ▶	57
▶ Lee **HUGHES**	19	Ronnie **WALLWORK**	7	15	Ray **PARLOUR**	(Aliadiere) 73 ◀	
◀ (Johnson) 39		Andy **JOHNSON**	10	17	**EDU**	Michal **PAPADOPULOS**	32
		Neil **CLEMENT**	3	37	David **BENTLEY**		
		Rob **HULSE**	15	25	**KANU**		
		Scott **DOBIE**	12	30	Jeremie **ALIADIERE**		

MATCH REPORT

Relying on a well-judged mixture of youth and experience, Arsenal eased into the Semi-finals of the Carling League Cup with a goal in each half, but if the scoreline implies a comfortable ride for the Premiership pacesetters then it is wholly misleading. West Bromwich Albion battled valiantly throughout, dominating large swathes of the action, but nothing went right for the First Division leaders. They struck the Gunners' woodwork twice and had a number of other good chances through-out the match.

The Baggies began in aggressive mode and Stack, Arsenal's impressive young goalkeeper, was forced to charge from his line in the first minute to thwart the onrushing Dobie. Albion, buoyed by their victories against Newcastle and Manchester United earlier in the competition, ratcheted up the pressure. Stack spilled a Clement free-kick but Kanu was on hand to clear the rebound. Albion thought they should have had a penalty when Keown impeded Johnson in the area, but the referee waved play on. Clement's surging raid down the left flank climaxed with a whipped cross which surprised Stack, rebounding to safety off the angle of upright

and crossbar. Gary Megson's men believed they had finally broken through when another Clement dispatch was nodded home from close-range by O'Connor, only for the strike to be ruled offside.

Gael Clichy demonstrates cool composure as he
clears the Arsenal lines under pressure.

Young marksman Jeremie Aliadiere salutes the travelling fans after putting the Gunners two goals ahead.

Then Arsenal turned the game on its head by taking the lead. Edu capitalised on a Wallwork error to work the ball out to Lauren on the right, Kanu's header from the resultant cross was parried by Hoult, and the Nigerian pounced to poke the loose ball into the corner of the net. Reacting gamely, Albion pushed forward, but Stack concluded their first-half frustration by saving a Hulse bicycle kick at full stretch.

Kanu menaced early in the second period but Hoult fielded his low shot. Then the Baggies returned to the offensive, with Stack denying Hulse with a brilliant block and Hughes blazing high from 12 yards with only the keeper to beat. Suddenly the prospect of a renewed siege was lifted by a howler from Hoult, whose miscued attempt to clear a backpass from Gaardsoe landed at the feet of the alert Aliadiere, the young Arsenal marksman swerving to his left before planting the ball into the unguarded goal.

Now two goals to the good the Gunners seized control and Aliadiere saw one fierce drive clutched by Hoult and another blocked by Gilchrist, an Edu scorcher was deflected away by Gaardsoe and Thomas set up Wiltord only for the Frenchman to fire too close to Hoult.

Even with only five minutes remaining Albion refused to bow to the pressure and Dobie almost set up a grandstand finish with a powerful volley from the edge of the box which clattered Stack's crossbar. Hughes then rose high to meet Sakiri's raking cross from the left, only for the ball to graze the outside of an upright.

Thus the Gunners were into the last four, and their young men had gained priceless experience. The significance for the likes of Stack, Clichy, Bentley and Aliadiere is incalculable.

DECEMBER

FA Barclaycard Premiership
Saturday 20 December 2003 at the Reebok Stadium, 3.00 p.m.
Attendance: 28,003 Referee: Graham Poll

FORM GUIDE

W W W L W W [11 goals scored, 5 conceded]   D W D W W W [11 goals scored, 2 conceded]

BOLTON WANDERERS 1

Pedersen 83

ARSENAL 1

Pires 57

Substitutes					Substitutes
	Jussi **JAASKELAINEN**	22	1	Jens **LEHMANN**	
Kevin **POOLE** 1	Ivan **CAMPO**	16	28	Kolo **TOURE**	33 Graham **STACK**
Anthony **BARNESS** 2	Simon **CHARLTON**	3	23	Sol **CAMPBELL**	5 Martin **KEOWN**
▸ Ibrahim **BA** 15	Nicky **HUNT**	18	18	Pascal **CYGAN**	15 Ray **PARLOUR** ▸
◂ (Campo) 78	Emerson **THOME**	26	22	Gael **CLICHY**	(Bergkamp) 69 ◂
Stelios **GIANNAKOPOULOS** 7	Ricardo **GARDNER**	11	8	Fredrik **LJUNGBERG**	17 **EDU**
▸ Henrik **PEDERSEN** 9	Per **FRANDSEN**	8	19	**GILBERTO**	25 **KANU**
◂ (Nolan) 75	Kevin **NOLAN**	4	4	Patrick **VIEIRA**	
	Youri **DJORKAEFF**	6	7	Robert **PIRES**	
	Jay-Jay **OKOCHA**	10	10	Dennis **BERGKAMP**	
	Kevin **DAVIES**	14	14	Thierry **HENRY**	

MATCH REPORT

Arsenal recorded their third draw in four Premiership outings as they were pegged back by a late Bolton equaliser at the climax of a pulsating encounter. In truth, the ever-improving Trotters deserved their point, earned in front of the Reebok Stadium's record attendance. The result left the Gunners sharing top spot with Chelsea, though Manchester United took over as Christmas leaders thanks to a Sunday victory at Tottenham.

Bolton began fluently and the lively Davies threatened with two early efforts, the first blocked by Toure, the second saved by Lehmann. It also took a timely intervention from Ljungberg to repel Thome's overhead kick. Arsenal retaliated quickly and twice Henry demonstrated his world-class pedigree, controlling the ball on his thigh before firing narrowly wide from 25 yards. He then shaved an upright with a cushioned volley from an acute angle.

Bolton were the next to threaten when an Okocha dispatch found Frandsen, whose pull-back to Djorkaeff was ballooned high from 12 yards. Now the action see-sawed to the other end where Toure capped a darting run with a cute pass to Bergkamp, whose finish was uncharacteristically wayward.

But the most inviting opening of the first period fell to Nolan, who resisted stiff challenges from a posse of defenders before unleashing a low cross-shot, which demanded a brilliant fingertip save from Lehmann. Still it was Arsenal who finished the half on the offensive when Vieira surged through the centre and slipped the ball to Henry, whose clipped cross reached Ljungberg, only for the Swede to miscue on the stretch from six yards.

After the break the Gunners enjoyed their most impressive spell, with Gilberto's 25-yarder warming the hands of Jaaskelainen and Henry carrying the ball half the length of the pitch before being denied by Charlton's superbly timed tackle. Soon they were rewarded with a goal when Bergkamp dispossessed Gardner and found Henry, who passed inside to Ljungberg; the Swede's shot was blocked by Jaaskelainen but only to Pires, who swept home from ten yards.

Bolton responded positively, with Campo and Okocha setting up Djorkaeff, who was foiled by Lehmann, then Okocha held his head in frustration after curling an exquisite free-kick against the outside of an Arsenal post.

Kolo Toure is a study in concentration as he beats Bolton's Djorkaeff to the ball.

Yet again the Trotters went close to levelling when Lehmann punched out a Djorkaeff cross to Frandsen, whose measured lob was net-bound until Pires popped up to head clear. But Sam Allardyce's men continued to probe and they plundered a spectacular equaliser. Thome delivered a long free-kick into the Gunners' box; the ball squirmed away from both Cygan and Davies and ran to Pedersen, who beat the flying Lehmann with an unstoppable half-volley from the edge of the box.

It was enough to secure a point and complete a memorable seven days for Bolton, who had already won at Chelsea and defeated Southampton to join Arsenal in the last four of the Carling League Cup.

Robert Pires seizes on a rebound to shoot Arsenal into the lead despite the presence of two Bolton defenders.

FORM GUIDE
W D W W W D [12 goals scored, 3 conceded]   D L D L L L [7 goals scored, 17 conceded]

ARSENAL 3
Craddock o.g. 13, Henry 20, 89

WOLVERHAMPTON WANDERERS 0

Substitutes					Substitutes
Graham **STACK**	33	Jens **LEHMANN**	1	1	Michael **OAKES**		Andy **MARSHALL**	28
Martin **KEOWN**	5	Kolo **TOURE**	28	22	Oleg **LUZHNY**	Mark **CLYDE**	23
▶ **EDU**	17	Sol **CAMPBELL**	23	6	Paul **BUTLER**	Shaun **NEWTON** ▶	7
◀ (Ljungberg) 71		Pascal **CYGAN**	18	12	Jody **CRADDOCK**	(Miller) 76 ◀
▶ Jeremie **ALIADIERE**	30	Gael **CLICHY**	22	3	Lee **NAYLOR**	Dean **STURRIDGE** ▶	29
◀ (Pires) 71		Fredrik **LJUNGBERG**	8	17	Henri **CAMARA**	(Camara) 85 ◀
KANU	25	Ray **PARLOUR**	15	4	Alex **RAE**	Steffen **IVERSEN**	19
		Patrick **VIEIRA**	4	8	Paul **INCE**		
		Robert **PIRES**	7	10	Colin **CAMERON**		
		Dennis **BERGKAMP**	10	11	Mark **KENNEDY**		
		Thierry **HENRY**	14	16	Kenny **MILLER**		

MATCH REPORT

Arsenal cruised to comprehensive victory over the Premiership's bottom side. The result was never in doubt after the predatory Gunners profited from two early errors by the unfortunate Jody Craddock. Arsène Wenger's men, who spent just four hours as League leaders before being overhauled by teatime winners Manchester United, dominated from the outset, with the Wolves' harassed rearguard failing to cope with their hosts' quickfire passing and fluid movement.

The assault began with a typically imaginative lofted dispatch from Pires to Henry, who tested Oakes with a sharp volley which demanded a reflex parry over the crossbar. The valiant goalkeeper, who would keep the scoreline within respectable limits with a string of acrobatic saves, was soon in action again, plunging to his right to repel a free-kick from Henry.

With Arsenal on song, it was ironic that when the breakthrough arrived it was rather scrappy. Henry's whipped corner was being miskicked past Oakes by Craddock as he was pressurised by Vieira. On that occasion the Wolves defender could claim he was unlucky, but there was no such excuse seven

minutes later when he dallied in possession and was robbed by Vieira, who set up Henry to net with a low placement from 12 yards.

Now the visitors were reeling and they might have fallen further behind when Henry's deflected 30-yard free-kick beat Oakes only to rebound from an upright before being hacked to safety. In the first 30 minutes of the match Wolves had offered little as an attacking force, although twice before the interval they managed to fashion clear scoring opportunities. First Camara eluded Toure and Bergkamp to find Cameron, whose delightful through-pass sent Miller clear on goal, only for the in-form Lehmann to pull off a superb block near the edge of his box. Then a Cygan clearance from Kennedy's corner fell to Camara and the Senegalese international's volley reached Craddock, who shot over the bar.

At the other end Parlour warmed Oakes' hands with a long-distance howitzer, and the Gunners continued in the ascendancy after the interval, with Bergkamp spearheading two incisive raids. The Dutchman found Henry with a raking delivery, and then sprinted to take the return pass, pirouetting

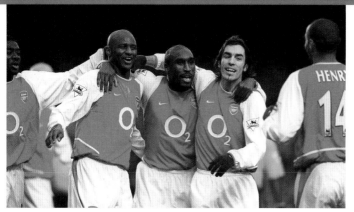

It's all smiles as Patrick Vieira takes the plaudits having set up Thierry Henry for his first goal.

past a desperate challenge but directing his shot marginally wide. Next he arrived at the climax of a slick interchange by Henry and Aliadiere, but his savage drive from ten yards was kept out by the legs of the increasingly beleaguered Oakes.

Former Gunner Oleg Luzhny was booked for a mistimed tackle on his old team-mate Edu, but there was no malice and the incident ended with grins all round. The last laugh went to the Brazilian, who pierced the Wolves defence with an exquisite pass to Henry, thus freeing the Frenchman for a final flourish. The runner-up in both the World and European Footballer of the Year polls jinked inside, swayed back towards the touchline and then rifled the third goal with an inch-perfect cross-shot. The gulf between the two sides could hardly have been illustrated more emphatically.

A sumptuous goal from the irrepressible Thierry Henry a minute from time wraps up a three-goal victory and another three points.

DECEMBER

FA Barclaycard Premiership
Monday 29 December 2003 at St Mary's Stadium, 8.00 p.m.
Attendance: 32,151 Referee: Steve Dunn

FORM GUIDE
W W W L W L [10 goals scored, 6 conceded]   D W W W D W [10 goals scored, 2 conceded]

SOUTHAMPTON 0   ## ARSENAL 1
Pires 35

Substitutes		Antti **NIEMI**	14	1	Jens **LEHMANN**		Substitutes
Paul **JONES**	1	Chris **BAIRD**	32	28	Kolo **TOURE**	33	Graham **STACK**
▸ Darren **KENTON**	22	Fitz **HALL**	15	23	Sol **CAMPBELL**	5	Martin **KEOWN** ▸
◂ (Baird) 59		Michael **SVENSSON**	11	18	Pascal **CYGAN**	12	**LAUREN** ▸
Chris **MARSDEN**	4	Danny **HIGGINBOTHAM**	19	22	Gael **CLICHY**		(Pires) 87 ◂
■ ▸ Neil **MCCANN**	10	Paul **TELFER**	33	8	Fredrik **LJUNGBERG**	17	**EDU** ▸
◂ (Telfer) 78		Rory **DELAP**	18	15	Ray **PARLOUR**		(Ljungberg) 73 ◂
▸ Brett **ORMEROD**	36	David **PRUTTON**	20	4	Patrick **VIEIRA**	25	**KANU** ▸
◂ (Griffit) 57		Leandre **GRIFFIT**	30	7	Robert **PIRES**		(Bergkamp) 74 ◂
		James **BEATTIE**	9	10	Dennis **BERGKAMP**		
		Kevin **PHILLIPS**	7	14	Thierry **HENRY**		

MATCH REPORT

A sumptuously executed goal by Robert Pires proved enough to beat Southampton and moved Arsenal to within a point of Manchester United at the top of the Premiership table. Thus the Gunners reached the turn of the year as the only undefeated team in English senior football.

Watched by the biggest home crowd in Southampton's history, the visitors began in imperious manner, threatening to overrun their more cautious hosts. At the core of this expansive approach was the majestic Vieira, who might have capped an early surge through the centre with the opening strike, but his enterprising one-two passing interchange with Bergkamp was smothered.

Soon Niemi, the Saints' busiest and most impressive performer on the night, was brought into action by the effervescent Toure who shot from 20 yards. Bergkamp then found Ljungberg inside the box only for the Swede to be crowded out by a posse of markers.

A shot by Phillips, which Lehmann gathered comfortably, offered brief

The ever-alert Freddie Ljungberg considers his options as he's closed down by Southampton's Rory Delap.

Poetry in motion.
Southampton defender
Fitz Hall keeps his eyes
on the ball as he tries
to tackle the flying
Thierry Henry.

cleared the crossbar with a wayward free-kick, and then Ljungberg brought a stunning reflex parry from Niemi at point-blank range after Higginbotham fluffed a clearance straight to the feet of the lurking Swede.

retaliation, but Arsenal returned immediately to the offensive with Niemi arching his back to tip over a deflected dipping drive from Henry. The Frenchman then bewildered several defenders before dispatching an inviting far-post cross which Bergkamp nodded into the side-netting, and Niemi was tested again by both Parlour and Pires, before finally Southampton began to move forward more purposefully.

But Southampton's attacks played straight into the counter-attacking Gunners' hands, as Bergkamp worked the ball to Henry, who split the Saints' rearguard with a rapier-like crossfield delivery which enabled Pires to stroke a low first-time shot beyond the keeper with consummate ease.

Towards the end of the first period a slip by Cygan almost let in Phillips but the former England marksman failed to capitalise, and thereafter Arsenal's ascendancy continued unabated. Henry

The Gunners continued to dictate matters throughout the third quarter of a lively contest, with Niemi nimbly denying both Henry and Ljungberg and Edu skying a hopeful effort, but Southampton mounted a late flurry of assaults in which Beattie and Phillips were prominent.

Through all this Arsenal – for whom the young French left-back Gael Clichy continued to perform creditably as deputy for the suspended Ashley Cole, and the central defensive partnership of Campbell and Cygan looked ever more sound – held firm without being unduly stretched.

The Gunners' victory was their 13th in the first half of a Premiership campaign in which their goals-against record of a mere dozen was second to none.

DECEMBER 2003

Arsenal.com PLAYER OF THE MONTH

Robert PIRES

" What is most important to me is that Arsenal win the League and that I play well. The idea of scoring 50 goals for the Club is a more personal question, but it is true that it would be a fantastic memory for me at the end of my career. I would be very proud if that were to happen. 'I have grown to love this Club, its culture and its supporters. Arsenal has become my oxygen. I feel at home among the English and I don't think I want to go anywhere else. "

ROBERT PIRES

" Robert's goal against Lokomotiv was a great finish and I know that he is feeling better and better about his game every time he plays, which is marvellous for us. "

PATRICK VIEIRA

" Robert is enjoying a fantastic season for Arsenal. With his control, his pace, the vision of his passing and, of course, his goals, he brings so much to the team. "

ARSÈNE WENGER

ARSENAL DIARY

Monday 15 December
- Thierry Henry finishes second to Zinedine Zidane in the World Footballer of the Year poll.
- Junior Gunners' Christmas party, sponsored by BT Yahoo and EA Sports and attended by the first team.

Monday 22 December
- Thierry Henry is pipped to the European Footballer of the Year award by Pavel Nedved of Juventus.

Tuesday 30 December
- Thierry Henry is voted French Player of the Year.

THE WIDER WORLD

Wednesday 3 December
- Liverpool and Manchester United, last season's finalists, are knocked out of the Carling Cup.

Friday 5 December
- England draw Wales, Northern Ireland, Poland, Austria and Azerbaijan in their qualifying group for World Cup 2006.

Tuesday 9 December
- Chelsea and Manchester United qualify for knockout phase of Champions League.

Wednesday 24 December
- Spurs announce that midfielder Michael Brown will join them from Sheffield United in the New Year.

FA CARLING PREMIERSHIP
28 December 2003

	P	HOME					AWAY					Pts
		W	D	L	F	A	W	D	L	F	A	
Manchester United	18	8	1	1	24	7	6	0	2	13	6	43
ARSENAL	18	7	2	0	16	6	5	4	0	18	6	42
Chelsea	18	6	1	1	17	7	6	2	2	16	9	39
Fulham	18	5	2	3	16	11	3	2	3	14	12	28
Charlton Athletic	18	3	3	3	13	14	4	3	2	13	8	27
Newcastle United	18	4	3	2	14	5	2	5	2	12	16	26
Southampton	18	5	1	3	11	6	2	4	3	7	8	26
Birmingham City	17	3	3	3	8	12	4	2	2	8	7	26
Liverpool	17	4	1	4	15	12	3	3	2	11	7	25
Bolton Wanderers	18	2	5	1	8	5	3	2	5	10	21	22
Middlesbrough	17	2	3	4	6	10	3	3	2	8	7	21
Aston Villa	18	4	3	1	10	7	1	3	6	6	16	21
Manchester City	18	2	3	3	13	11	3	2	5	12	14	20
Everton	18	4	3	2	14	9	1	2	6	8	16	20
Portsmouth	18	5	0	4	18	10	0	4	5	2	15	19
Blackburn Rovers	18	3	1	5	13	15	2	2	5	12	14	18
Tottenham Hotspur	18	4	1	4	14	13	1	2	6	5	15	18
Leicester City	18	2	5	3	13	13	2	0	6	13	16	17
Leeds United	18	2	4	4	9	15	2	1	5	8	22	17
Wolverhampton Wanderers	17	2	3	2	7	14	0	2	8	6	24	11

JANUARY

FA Cup, Third Round
Sunday 4 January 2004 at Elland Road, 4.05 p.m.
Attendance: 31,207 Referee: Rob Styles

FORM GUIDE

W D W D D L [7 goals scored, 7 conceded]   W W W D W W [10 goals scored, 1 conceded]

LEEDS UNITED 1   ARSENAL 4

Viduka 8   Henry 26, Edu 32, Pires 87, Toure 90

Substitutes					Substitutes
Scott **CARSON** 40	Paul **ROBINSON**	1	1	Jens **LEHMANN**	
Salomon **OLEMBE** 24	Frazer **RICHARDSON**	34	12	**LAUREN**	24 Rami **SHAABAN**
Seth **JOHNSON** 20	Michael **DUBERRY**	22	5	Martin **KEOWN**	28 Kolo **TOURE** ▶
▶ Lamine **SAKHO** 10	Matt **KILGALLON**	36	23	Sol **CAMPBELL**	(Ljungberg) 81 ◀
◀ (Bakke) 70	Ian **HARTE**	3	3	Ashley **COLE**	15 Ray **PARLOUR** ▶
▶ Aaron **LENNON** 25	Dominic **MATTEO**	21	8	Fredrik **LJUNGBERG**	(Edu) 81 ◀
◀ (Milner) 84	▨ Alan **SMITH**	17	19	**GILBERTO** ▨	7 Robert **PIRES** ▶
	Eirik **BAKKE**	19	4	Patrick **VIEIRA**	(Kanu) 81 ◀
	David **BATTY**	23	17	**EDU**	37 David **BENTLEY**
	James **MILNER**	38	25	**KANU**	
	Mark **VIDUKA**	9	14	Thierry **HENRY**	

MATCH REPORT

After conceding a freak goal during a faltering start, Arsenal recovered to turn on the style and record their third successive 4-1 victory at Elland Road. The Gunners' star performer was Thierry Henry, who scored a fabulous equaliser and set up the next two strikes. Manager Arsène Wenger had intended to rest the newly-crowned French Footballer of the Year, but was forced into a late change of plan when the replacement, Jeremie Aliadiere, had fallen ill.

Leeds began snappily, with Smith shooting high over the bar inside the first minute and Cole heading out a teasing cross from Milner shortly afterwards. Then the Yorkshiremen stunned the visitors by grabbing the lead in bizarre fashion.

Edu side-foots the Gunners into the lead from Henry's inch-perfect cross.

76

Substitute Robert Pires fires his tenth goal of the season three minutes from time.

There seemed to be no danger as Campbell completed a routine back-pass to Lehmann, but the goalkeeper took a heavy touch, then crashed his clearance into the onrushing Viduka and the ball rebounded into the empty net.

Thus jolted, Arsenal reacted with a fluent movement involving Cole and Edu which culminated in Henry volleying marginally high from 12 yards. But Leeds continued spiritedly, making a nonsense of their lowly league position. Milner tested Lehmann with a low shot at the climax of a jinking run, then Viduka was narrowly off-target with a 20-yard half-volley after Smith had nodded on Harte's steepling free-kick.

Gradually the Gunners' quality shone through and they levelled when Henry volleyed home from 12 yards, the cross being supplied by Ljungberg after fine work by Kanu. By now the visitors were in control and six minutes later they took the lead when Vieira found Henry on the left and the Frenchman's inch-perfect first-time cross was sidefooted home by Edu from eight yards.

More smiles for the boys from Brazil as Gilberto congratulates goalscorer Edu.

After the break Arsenal became ever more dominant as Kilgallon cleared off the line from Edu, Henry's free-kick was deflected wide by Viduka and Campbell shaved the crossbar with a header from Edu's corner.

Still Leeds struggled valiantly and Keown and Campbell had to make timely clearances, though most of the action was at the other end, where Henry went close and Robinson repelled a ferocious effort from Kanu. Ljungberg hit the side-netting after being set up by a marvellous flick from Henry, but there was no escape for tiring United when the Frenchman shrugged off a marker and squared for Pires, newly arrived from the substitutes' bench, to stroke home his tenth goal of the season three minutes from the end. Now the Gunners were rampant and rubbed in their superiority with a final strike which epitomised their endless flair and invention. Pires dinked the ball delicately into space for Toure to net with a precise side-footed volley at the far post.

The scoreline represented an uplifting first step for the Gunners in their attempt to reach a fourth successive FA Cup Final.

JANUARY

FA Barclaycard Premiership
Wednesday 7 January 2004 at Goodison Park, 8.00 p.m.
Attendance: 38,726 Referee: Alan Wiley

FORM GUIDE
D W W L W W [11 goals scored, 7 conceded]   W W D W W W [12 goals scored, 2 conceded]

EVERTON 1   ARSENAL 1
Radzinski 75   Kanu 29

Substitutes					Substitutes
Steve **SIMONSEN**	13	Nigel **MARTYN**	25	1	Jens **LEHMANN**	24	Rami **SHAABAN**
Joseph **YOBO**	20	Tony **HIBBERT**	28	28	Kolo **TOURE**	12	**LAUREN** ▶ ■
▶ Tobias **LINDEROTH**	22	Alan **STUBBS**	4	23	Sol **CAMPBELL**		(Toure) 20 ◀
◀ (Li Tie) 45		David **UNSWORTH**	6	18	Pascal **CYGAN**	19	**GILBERTO** ▶
▶ Francis **JEFFERS**	11	Gary **NAYSMITH**	15	3	Ashley **COLE**		(Ljungberg) 89 ◀
◀ (Kilbane) 70		Lee **CARSLEY**	26	8	Fredrik **LJUNGBERG** ■	17	**EDU** ▶
▶ Kevin **CAMPBELL**	9	Li **TIE**	12	15	Ray **PARLOUR** ■		(Kanu) 81 ◀
◀ (Radzinski) 87		Kevin **KILBANE**	14	4	Patrick **VIEIRA**	30	Jeremie **ALIADIERE**
		Wayne **ROONEY**	18	7	Robert **PIRES**		
		Tomasz **RADZINSKI**	8	25	**KANU**		
		Duncan **FERGUSON**	10	14	Thierry **HENRY**		

MATCH REPORT

The Gunners never hit top gear against a gutsy Everton playing at home. Arsenal conceded a late equaliser created by Francis Jeffers, the Arsenal striker on loan at Goodison Park.

The Merseysiders signalled their aggressive intent by starting with three front-runners – Ferguson, Radzinski and Rooney – yet Arsène Wenger's men were the first to threaten when Kanu

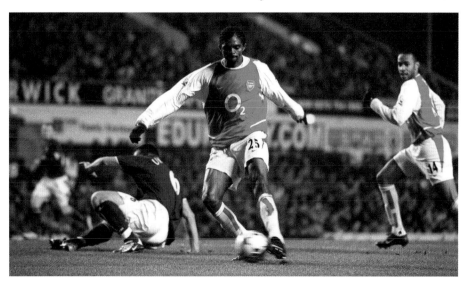

Kanu slots home his first Premiership goal in more than a year to give the Gunners a first-half lead.

struck a rising 25-yard drive which Martyn pulled from the air in the second minute. Thereafter Everton buzzed combatively, disrupting the visitors' more elegant style, and they almost took the lead after Rooney had hustled Cygan into overhitting a back-pass. From Carsley's resultant corner the ball rebounded towards the net from the shins of Cygan, demanding a full-stretch goal-line clearance by Cole.

Arsenal responded in devastating fashion. Henry found Ljungberg and the Swede clipped deftly into the path of Kanu, who strode past the lunging Unsworth before beating Martyn with a precisely angled shot to register his first Premiership strike for more than a year.

Eight minutes before the interval Everton spurned a gilded opportunity to draw level when Kilbane exchanged passes with Naysmith on the left flank and dispatched a cross to Rooney, who was untended only six yards from goal. Somehow the youthful prodigy, who had plundered a spectacular winner on the Gunners' previous visit to Goodison, nodded well wide and clutched his head in disbelief.

Arsenal started the second period on the front foot, with Henry shooting into Martyn's arms from 20 yards, but soon the hosts were menacing again with a twice-taken free-kick by Rooney. Ljungberg blocked the first effort and the second was punched away by Lehmann, who then dashed from his goal to repel a follow-up effort.

The German also diverted two headers from the towering Ferguson. Henry relieved the pressure after catching Unsworth in possession, but his attempt to set up Kanu for a second goal was foiled by a smart interception from Naysmith.

Meanwhile the Gunners' backline was looking admirably assured until it was undone with a

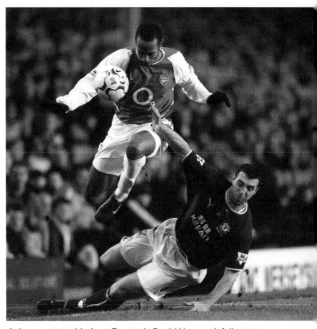

A desperate tackle from Everton's David Unsworth fails to stop an airborne Thierry Henry.

quarter of an hour remaining on the clock. Martyn launched a massive drop-kick, which was glanced on by Ferguson, and Cole miscued his attempt at a clearance, thereby allowing Jeffers to race towards goal with considerable pace and unleash a savage cross-shot. Lehmann pulled off a fabulous flying one-handed save but the loose ball landed at the left foot of Radzinski, who turned it home from the corner of the six-yard box.

After that both sides might have snatched all three points, but Pires was crowded out when about to shoot at one end, then the marauding Rooney suffered the same fate at the other.

In truth, a draw was a fair result and it enabled Arsenal to retain their unbeaten Premiership run, which now extended to 20 matches, a truly magnificent record.

FORM GUIDE
W D W W W D [12 goals scored, 3 conceded]   D D D L W W [7 goals scored, 5 conceded]

ARSENAL 4   MIDDLESBROUGH 1

Henry 38 pen, Queudrue o.g. 45,   Maccarone pen 86
Pires 57, Ljungberg 68

Substitutes		Arsenal			Middlesbrough		Substitutes	
Graham **STACK**	33	Jens **LEHMANN**	1	1	Mark **SCHWARZER**		Bradley **JONES**	35
Martin **KEOWN**	5	**LAUREN**	12	15	Danny **MILLS**	35	Stuart **PARNABY**	21
▸ Ray **PARLOUR**	15	Sol **CAMPBELL**	23	4	Ugo **EHIOGU**	21	Chris **RIGGOTT** ▸	5
◂ (Ljungberg) 72		Pascal **CYGAN**	18	6	Gareth **SOUTHGATE**	5	(Ehiogu) 46 ◂	
▸ **EDU**	17	Ashley **COLE**	3	3	Franck **QUEUDRUE**		(Ehiogu) 46 ◂	
◂ (Pires) 67		Fredrik **LJUNGBERG**	8	19	Stewart **DOWNING**	10	**JUNINHO** ▸	
▸ **KANU**	25	▪ **GILBERTO**	19	7	George **BOATENG**		(Job) 62 ◂	
◂ (Aliadiere) 46		Patrick **VIEIRA**	4	20	Guidoni **DORIVA** ▪	9	Massimo **MACCARONE** ▸	
		Robert **PIRES**	7	27	Boudewijn **ZENDEN**		(Doriva) 62 ◂	
		Jeremie **ALIADIERE**	30	16	Joseph-Desire **JOB**			
		Thierry **HENRY**	14	8	Szilard **NEMETH**			

MATCH REPORT

Before this comprehensive demolition of Middlesbrough by the free-scoring Gunners, the Teessiders' rock-like rearguard had been breached only five times in a dozen games. Truly it was a case of the irresistible force sweeping aside the apparently immovable object. Arsenal struck four

Thierry Henry scores from the spot in the 38th minute after Patrick Vieira had been fouled in the area by Middlesbrough defender Ugo Ehiogu.

times but might have doubled their tally as they submerged the visitors in wave after wave of superbly fluent attacks, leaving Boro to reflect on the size of their task as they prepared to face Arsène Wenger's team three more times in cup competitions before January was out.

The tone for this one-sided affair was set after a mere 40 seconds when Vieira sent Aliadiere sprinting clear of Southgate, only for the young Frenchman's low drive to be cleared by the trailing leg of the spread-eagled Schwarzer. Early on the Australian keeper was the busiest man on the field as he dealt with a curler by Henry and a low skimmer from Ljungberg, the product of a dashing left-flank run by the lively Aliadiere.

Boro did offer brief retaliation. Doriva hurrying Lehmann to repel a searing 30-yarder and Vieira

crowding out Boateng at the near post after Zenden had freed Job on the byline, but Arsenal's overall domination seemed certain to be rewarded, and so it proved. Pires took possession on the left and found Vieira inside the Boro box, where he was nudged to the ground by Ehiogu. Henry converted the spot-kick with gleeful aplomb, and then almost doubled the lead immediately after the restart with a wickedly bouncing free-kick which rebounded to safety off an upright.

No matter, a two-goal advantage was achieved shortly before the break when Pires was bundled over by Boateng and another Henry free-kick was sliced into his own net by the lunging Queudrue.

The second period began with a scintillating solo run by Henry, who left four opponents in his wake before releasing the ball to the offside Pires. That proved only a temporary reprieve for Middlesbrough as Southgate miscued a clearance to Pires, who wrong-footed Schwarzer with an ice-cool finish from 12 yards.

Now the Gunners needed only one more goal to unseat Manchester United as Premiership table-toppers. It arrived when the ball ran loose at the climax of a typically enchanting Kanu dribble, allowing Ljungberg to slot home with a low shot which entered the net via Schwarzer's fingertips and the far post. However, they were reduced to the status of joint leaders – equal with United on points, goal difference and goals scored – when Boro grabbed a late consolation. Lehmann had tripped Maccarone and the Italian sent the German the wrong way from the penalty spot.

Still Arsenal might have restored the four-goal margin, but an Edu screamer was blocked after Henry had created the opening by nutmegging the flabbergasted Mills near the corner flag, and then the French Footballer of the Year went even closer with a looping free-kick deep inside stoppage time.

An Arsenal huddle celebrates a job well done as Arsenal take a three-goal lead midway through the second half.

FORM GUIDE

W D W L W L [8 goals scored, 4 conceded]   D W W W D W [14 goals scored, 4 conceded]

ASTON VILLA 0   ARSENAL 2

Henry 29, 53 pen

Substitutes					Substitutes	
Stefan **POSTMA**	13	Thomas **SORENSEN**	1	1 Jens **LEHMANN**		
Dion **DUBLIN**	9	Mark **DELANEY**	2	12 **LAUREN**	Graham **STACK**	33
▸ Ulises **DE LA CRUZ**	15	Olof **MELLBERG**	4	23 Sol **CAMPBELL**	Martin **KEOWN**	5
◂ (Hendrie) 86		Ronny **JOHNSEN**	27	18 Pascal **CYGAN**	Ray **PARLOUR** ▸	15
▸ Liam **RIDGEWELL**	24	JLloyd **SAMUEL**	3	3 Ashley **COLE**	(Ljungberg) 76 ◂	
◂ (Barry) 86		Gareth **BARRY**	6	8 Fredrik **LJUNGBERG**	**EDU** ▸	17
▸ Peter **CROUCH**	16	Lee **HENDRIE**	7	19 **GILBERTO**	(Pires) 77 ◂	
◂ (Allback) 86		Thomas **HITZLSPERGER**	12	4 Patrick **VIEIRA**	Kolo **TOURE** ▸	28
		Marcus **ALLBACK**	14	7 Robert **PIRES**	(Kanu) 76 ◂	
		Peter **WHITTINGHAM**	17	25 **KANU**		
		Juan **PABLO ANGEL**	18	14 Thierry **HENRY**		

MATCH REPORT

Arsenal capitalised on Manchester United's shock defeat by bottom club Wolves to go two points clear in the race for the title.

Reflecting their recent improvement in form, Villa started brightly and threatened the Gunners with two early free-kicks, but Hendrie's effort was nodded out by Campbell and Angel failed to make contact with Hitzlsperger's teasing delivery. Gradually the visitors began to assert their quality and they went close to an opening goal when a Kanu thrust reached the byline and his low cross was sliced into the side-netting by Samuel.

The silky skills of Pires soon took centre stage as the Frenchman brought the best out of Sorensen with two fabulous strikes from distance. The first attempt followed Cole's high dispatch into Villa territory and a headed clearance by Samuel which fell to Pires on the right corner of the penalty area. Without pausing to control the dropping ball, he unleashed a dipping volley which demanded an acrobatic save from the Danish keeper. Sorensen barely had time to recover his balanced when Pires was shooting at his goal

Freddie Ljungberg twists his way past Aston Villa's Peter Whittingham in yet another Arsenal push on goal.

The quick-thinking Thierry Henry side-foots home a free-kick to give Arsenal the lead after half-an-hour.

again. This time the French midfielder surged past two opponents in midfield before hitting a low 25-yarder which would have curled inside a post but for Sorensen's desperate diving parry.

Arsenal continued to attack with increasing authority. When Vieira's charge towards the box was halted by a double foul, inflicted by Mellberg and Johnsen, referee Mark Halsey gave permission for an instant free-kick and Henry side-footed home from 20 yards with Villa still in the process of constructing their defensive wall. It was a bizarre goal – enterprising from the Gunners' point of view, outrageous from Villa's – but on the run of play Arsenal deserved the lead. At that point in the match the hosts had mounted only one genuinely menacing assault, when Allback spun on an Angel cross before shaving an upright with a low drive from 12 yards.

After the interval Lehmann scrambled along his line to repel a shot from Angel, who also sent a free-kick marginally high. But Arsène Wenger's men tightened their grip when Pires found Kanu, and the Nigerian was felled in the area by Mellberg; Henry clipped his penalty-kick to the left of Sorensen, who got a hand to the ball but could not keep it out.

Thereafter Pires and Henry, in particular, continued to lead Villa a merry dance, and Pires, Parlour and Toure all had chances to extend the lead.

Carling Cup, Semi-Final, first leg
Tuesday 20 January 2004 at Highbury, 7.45 p.m.
Attendance: 31,070 Referee: Steve Dunn

FORM GUIDE
W W W D W W [15 goals scored, 3 conceded]   D L W W L D [10 goals scored, 11 conceded]

ARSENAL 0   MIDDLESBROUGH 1
Juninho 53

Substitutes					Substitutes
	Graham **STACK**	33	1	Mark **SCHWARZER**	
Craig **HOLLOWAY** 44	Kolo **TOURE**	28	5	Danny **MILLS** ▪	Bradley **JONES** 35
Ashley **COLE** 3	Martin **KEOWN**	5	4	Ugo **EHIOGU**	Stuart **PARNABY** ▶ 21
Olafur-Ingi **SKULASON** 55	Pascal **CYGAN**	18	5	Chris **RIGGOTT**	(Mendieta) 81 ◀
▶ Jerome **THOMAS** 53	Gael **CLICHY**	22	3	Franck **QUEUDRUE** ▪	Stewart **DOWNING** 19
3(Owuso-Abeyie) 64	Ray **PARLOUR**	15	14	Gaizka **MENDIETA**	Michael **RICKETTS** 17
▶ Ryan **SMITH** 56	**GILBERTO**	19	7	George **BOATENG**	Joseph-Desire **JOB** ▶ 16
3(Bentley) 73	**EDU**	17	20	Guidoni **DORIVA**	(Maccarone) 78 ◀
	David **BENTLEY**	37	27	Boudewijn **ZENDEN**	
	KANU	25	10	**JUNINHO** ▪	
	Quincy **OWUSU-ABEYIE**	54	9	Massimo **MACCARONE**	

MATCH REPORT

Arsenal suffered the first defeat of their domestic campaign as Middlesbrough seized first-leg advantage in an enthralling semi-final encounter. Arsène Wenger was glad of the opportunity to give some young players the chance to play in such an important cup-tie, and though the Gunners mounted wave after wave of attacks, they failed to produce a breakthrough. As a result, the Teessiders claimed only their second victory at Highbury in 65 years.

Arsenal had started at a high tempo, their passes zipping sweetly across the wet surface, and Toure almost opened their account with a low cross-shot which fizzed past an upright after neat work by Parlour. But just as the Gunners seemed on the point of taking control, Boro reacted with a sudden flurry of

This is how it's done.
David Bentley is elegance itself as he sidesteps Middlesbrough's Gaizka Mendieta.

pressure which went perilously close to earning them the lead.

After Mendieta's stinging snap-volley had been blocked by Cygan, a slick passing interchange between Juninho and Boateng climaxed with the Brazilian rapping a 12-yard shot against a post, the ball rebounding into the arms of the grateful Stack. Next a Maccarone drive spun wide of the frame via Keown, before Arsenal retaliated with a succession of assaults in which the quicksilver Owusu-Abeyie and the skilful Bentley were prominent.

The action ebbed from end to end as the second half began, with Juninho's looping effort from the left corner of the box drawing a splendid flying save from Stack – an impressively reliable keeper between Arsenal's posts throughout the Carling Cup campaign – and Owusu-Abeyie almost setting up Kanu.

Then came the only goal of the night when Keown slipped under pressure from Queudrue and the ball was ferried from Mendieta to the unmarked Juninho, who gave Stack no chance with a firm shot inside the far post.

Two minutes later Maccarone almost sent in Juninho again, but the Gunners reacted positively, laying virtual siege to the Middlesbrough goal for lengthy periods. A powerful run from Toure led to a clever turn and brisk drive from Owusu-Abeyie but the ball skidded wide. A typical piece of Kanu magic took him to the byline only for Boateng to hack clear, and Bentley tried an ambitious overhead.

The one-way traffic was interrupted when Mills set up Maccarone, whose powerful curler demanded a diving save from Stack, but then the Gunners' frantic quest for an equaliser resumed unabated. Keown headed high from a Bentley supply and Edu sliced off-target from 25 yards. Bentley side-footed straight at Schwarzer after clever touches from Kanu and Thomas, Mills halted an enterprising dribble by the twinkle-toed Smith, and Toure fired wide from the edge of the box.

In the end, it could have been worse for the hosts. With time ebbing away, Middlesbrough took advantage of the space left by Arsenal's attacking enterprise. Job missed a golden opportunity to double their advantage when he prodded a Parnaby dispatch over a gaping net from six yards in the 87th minute, leaving the contest finely balanced for the second leg.

Quincy Owusu-Abeyie keeps his eyes on the ball as he seeks to set up another assault on the Middlesbrough goal.

FORM GUIDE
W W D W W L [12 goals scored, 4 conceded]   L W W L D W [9 goals scored, 9 conceded]

ARSENAL 4   MIDDLESBROUGH 1

Bergkamp 19, Ljungberg 28, 68,   Job 23
Bentley 90

Substitutes		Jens **LEHMANN**	1	1	Mark **SCHWARZER**		Substitutes
Graham **STACK**	33	**LAUREN**	12	15	Danny **MILLS**	35	Bradley **JONES**
Martin **KEOWN**	5	Kolo **TOURE**	28	5	Chris **RIGGOTT** ■	24	Andrew **DAVIES**
▸ Gael **CLICHY**	22	Sol **CAMPBELL**	23	3	Franck **QUEUDRUE**	10	**JUNINHO** ▸
◂ (VIEIRA) 55		Ashley **COLE**	3	21	Stuart **PARNABY** ■		(Job) 73 ◂
▸ David **BENTLEY**	37	Ray **PARLOUR**	15	14	Gaizka **MENDIETA**	8	Szilard **NEMETH** ▸
◂ (BERGKAMP) 84		Patrick **VIEIRA**	4	7	George **BOATENG** ■■		(Downing) 73 ◂
Quincy **OWUSU-ABEYIE**	54	**EDU**	17	19	Stewart **DOWNING**	9	Massimo **MACCARONE** ▸
		Robert **PIRES**	7	27	Boudewijn **ZENDEN** ■		(Ricketts) 73 ◂
		Fredrik **LJUNGBERG**	8	14	Joseph-Desire **JOB**		
		Dennis **BERGKAMP**	10	17	Michael **RICKETTS**		

MATCH REPORT

Arsenal brushed aside Middlesbrough in part three of the long-running saga between the two clubs, and maintained their bid to reach a fourth successive FA Cup Final. With Henry away, Kanu on international duty and Wiltord and Aliadiere injured, manager Arsène Wenger deployed Ljungberg and Bergkamp

The new striking partnership of Dennis Bergkamp and Freddie Ljungberg pays early dividends as the Dutchman slots the Gunners ahead after 20 minutes.

in a new strike partnership which yielded a decisive dividend, with the Swede plundering two goals and the Dutchman poaching another.

The Gunners settled quickly to their work and soon Pires netted with a glancing header from a looping Bergkamp dispatch, only to be denied by an offside flag. Boro's reprieve was short-lived, however, thanks largely to Parlour's refusal to give up what looked to be a lost cause. With the ball seemingly safe in the jurisdiction of Parnaby on the right byline, Parlour stole it and pulled back to Bergkamp, who netted via a deflection off Riggott.

Not that the combative visitors were rolling over meekly, and four minutes later they startled the Highbury faithful with an explosive equaliser. Downing launched a long free-kick from the left, Ricketts nodded down and Job held off a challenge from Toure to hit a rasping volley into the roof of Lehmann's net from the corner of the six-yard box.

Arsenal reacted positively and after Edu's penetrating delivery located Cole, the England left-back cut inside and tested Schwarzer with a curling drive from 16 yards. Campbell nodded into the arms of the big Australian from the ensuing corner. Still the Gunners poured forward and they were rewarded when Parlour's free-kick was headed by Campbell to Vieira; the Frenchman turned back to Ljungberg, who twisted first one way and then the other before forcing home a low shot from ten yards.

After the interval Arsenal began to dominate ever more comprehensively, with Pires running amok behind the front pair. The Frenchman almost set up Edu, then created a

shooting chance for Bergkamp, who fired through the legs of Mills but was foiled by the agile Schwarzer. Next it was Vieira's turn to be repelled by the keeper after shooting from 25 yards. The third goal finally arrived when a Pires cross from the left fell to Ljungberg, whose header from five yards was ruled to have crossed the line before Mendieta cleared, thus rendering Toure's follow-up effort redundant.

Middlesbrough manager Steve McLaren threw on three strikers – Maccarone, Nemeth and Juninho – in a desperate late bid to redress the balance, but that proved no more than a prelude to Arsenal's sweetest strike of the afternoon.

The ceaselessly creative Pires switched the ball to Bentley, a recent arrival from the substitutes' bench, and the extravagantly gifted young Englishman bewitched his markers with a shimmy before surprising Schwarzer with an inch-perfect chip from 20 yards with his unfavoured left foot.

It was a glorious flourish fit to cap an exhilarating team performance.

Substitute David Bentley caps a superb Arsenal performance with an inch-perfect, 20-yard chip just before the final whistle.

Arsenal.com PLAYER OF THE MONTH

Thierry **HENRY**

" Thierry is the best striker in the world. He is an intelligent, really clever player who creates chances and he scores goals. He is not selfish in front of goal, as you can see by the number of assists he gives.

One of his strengths is that he always believed in himself. He knows what he can do. He is a perfect example of how to work if you want to be successful. Now he looks like he can score in every game. "

PATRICK VIEIRA

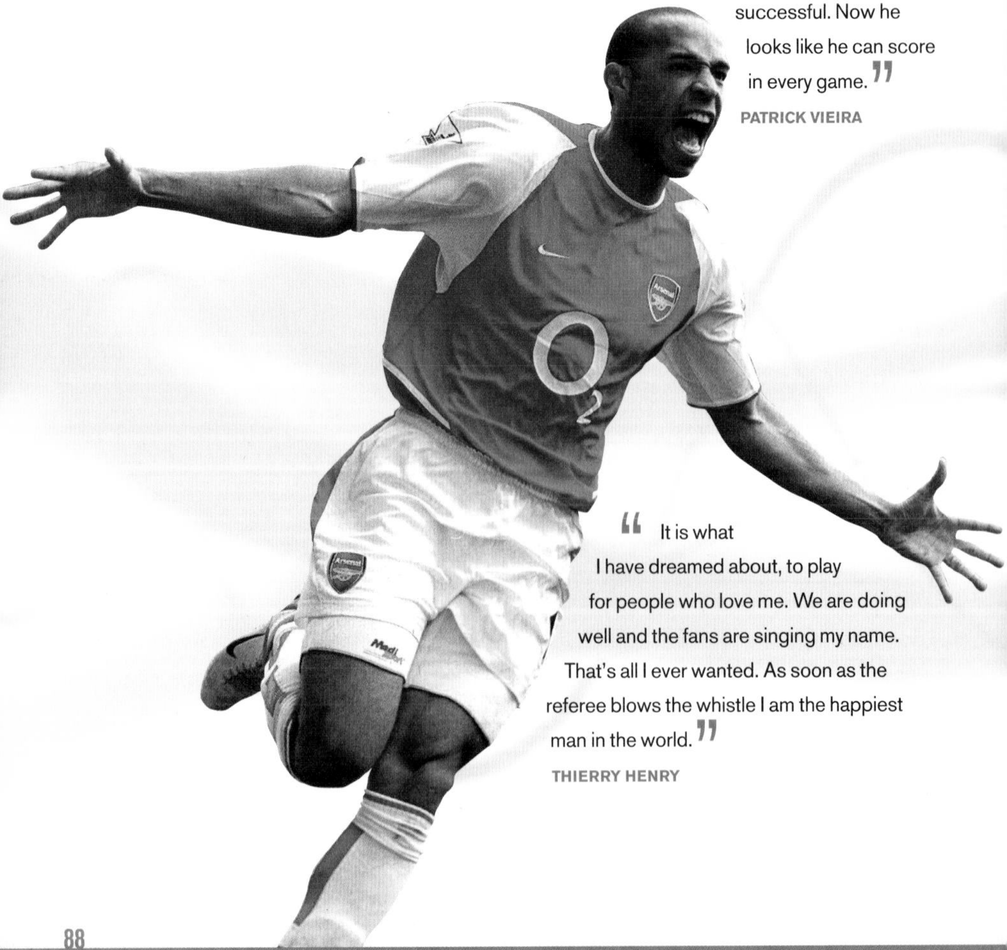

" It is what I have dreamed about, to play for people who love me. We are doing well and the fans are singing my name. That's all I ever wanted. As soon as the referee blows the whistle I am the happiest man in the world. "

THIERRY HENRY

ARSENAL DIARY

Saturday 3 January
- Arsène Wenger predicts there will be a winter break in 2004/2005.

Monday 12 January
- Thierry Henry is named in UEFA's team of the year for the third time.

Tuesday 13 January
- Forty-year-old former Highbury hero David Seaman retires due to injury.

Friday 16 January
- Moritz Volz completes a permanent move to Fulham for an undisclosed fee.
- West Ham sign Rami Shaaban on a month's loan.

Tuesday 27 January
- Arsenal announce the signing of José Antonio Reyes from Sevilla.

Wednesday 28 January
- The second leg of Arsenal's Carling Cup semi-final at Middlesbrough is postponed because of snow.

THE WIDER WORLD

Friday 9 January
- Southampton announce that Gordon Strachan is to step down as manager at season's end.

Tuesday 20 January
- Rio Ferdinand begins his eight-month ban, pending an appeal, for failing to take a drugs test.

Friday 23 January
- Manchester United pay Fulham £12.8 million for striker Louis Saha.

Wednesday 28 January
- Premiership chairmen vote in favour of a winter break for an experimental period of two seasons.
- Sir Alex Ferguson signs a new contract with Manchester United.

Friday 30 January
- Charlton's Scott Parker joins Chelsea for £10 million.

FA CARLING PREMIERSHIP

25 January 2004

	P	HOME					AWAY					Pts
		W	D	L	F	A	W	D	L	F	A	
ARSENAL	22	8	2	0	20	7	7	5	0	22	7	52
Manchester United	22	8	2	1	24	7	8	0	3	16	8	50
Chelsea	22	7	2	2	20	8	7	2	2	20	9	46
Charlton Athletic	22	4	3	3	15	14	6	4	2	16	9	37
Liverpool	22	5	1	4	16	12	4	5	3	16	12	33
Newcastle United	22	6	3	3	18	7	2	6	2	12	16	33
Fulham	22	6	2	3	18	12	3	2	6	16	20	31
Southampton	22	6	2	4	13	8	2	4	4	8	10	30
Birmingham City	21	4	3	3	10	13	4	3	4	9	12	30
Bolton Wanderers	22	3	6	2	12	9	4	2	5	14	24	29
Tottenham Hotspur	22	6	1	5	20	16	2	2	6	6	15	27
Aston Villa	22	6	3	2	15	10	1	3	7	6	17	27
Middlesbrough	21	3	4	5	11	15	3	3	3	9	11	25
Everton	22	5	4	3	16	11	1	2	7	9	18	24
Manchester City	22	2	6	3	17	15	3	2	6	14	18	23
Blackburn Rovers	22	3	1	6	16	19	3	4	5	16	17	23
Portsmouth	22	6	0	4	22	12	0	4	8	3	21	22
Leicester City	22	2	5	4	13	17	2	3	6	18	21	20
Wolverhampton Wanderers	22	4	5	2	14	18	0	2	9	6	26	19
Leeds United	22	2	4	5	9	16	2	1	8	10	28	17

W D W W L W [15 goals scored, 5 conceded]   D D L W D D [10 goals scored, 10 conceded]

ARSENAL 2
Tarnat o.g. 37, Henry 83

MANCHESTER CITY 1
Anelka 89

Substitutes						Substitutes	
		Jens **LEHMANN**	1	1	David **JAMES**		
Graham **STACK**	33	**LAUREN**	12	17	Sun **JIHAI**	25	Arni **GAUTUR ARASON**
▸ Pascal **CYGAN**	18	Kolo **TOURE**	28	22	Richard **DUNNE**	20	Steve **MCMANAMAN** ▸
◂ (Pires) 84		Sol **CAMPBELL**	23	5	Sylvain **DISTIN**		(Reyna) 76 ◂
▸ **EDU**	17	▪ Ashley **COLE**	3	18	Michael **TARNAT**	10	Antoine **SIBIERSKI**
◂ (Ljungberg) 59		Fredrik **LJUNGBERG**	8	29	Shaun **WRIGHT-PHILLIPS**	8	Robbie **FOWLER** ▸
David **BENTLEY**	37	▪ Ray **PARLOUR**	15	6	Claudio **REYNA**		(Bosvelt) 76 ◂
▸ José Antonio **REYES**	9	**GILBERTO**	19	26	Paul **BOSVELT**	11	Jonathan **MACKEN**
◂ (Bergkamp) 70		Robert **PIRES**	7	24	Joey **BARTON** ▪		
		Dennis **BERGKAMP**	10	28	Trevor **SINCLAIR** ▪		
		Thierry **HENRY**	14	31	Nicolas **ANELKA** ▪		

MATCH REPORT

It was a memorable afternoon. As the rain descended in torrents, José Antonio Reyes glittered through the gloom after rising from the bench for his debut. Henry scored from an explosive 25-yard drive which tore into the top corner of David James' net and Arsenal resumed their place as Premiership pacesetters by beating Manchester City in a manner both spectacular and controversial.

The game began with a series of brisk attacks by the hosts, who sliced through the City rearguard seemingly at will. Pires stole his way to the byline and his cross was half-cleared to skipper Ray Parlour, but his shot was blocked. Henry unleashed a fierce shot which was intercepted by Dunne and a minute later the Frenchman went even closer. Slick work by Ljungberg and Lauren had presented him with a six-yard tap-in, but somehow he turned the ball against an upright and it was scrambled to safety.

Jolted into activity by their let-off, City responded with a Barton shot which was blocked by Gilberto. Anelka then cut past two challenges before firing a sharp effort which was saved smartly by Lehmann. But just as Kevin Keegan's men appeared to be gaining a foothold, Arsenal took the lead. The referee waved play on

Freddie Ljungberg punches the air as Arsenal take the lead courtesy of an own-goal by City's Michael Tarnat.

Thierry Henry unleashes a superb 25-yard drive to put Arsenal two up ten minutes from time...

after Anelka went down, Parlour and Bergkamp ferried the ball to Henry, whose low cross was turned past his own keeper by Tarnat, with Ljungberg in close attendance.

With puddles forming on the pitch as the deluge intensified after the break, Arsenal continued to push forward. Bergkamp poked an effort into James' midriff and Cole almost capitalised on a loose throw by the England keeper. At the other end Sun Jihai drew an athletic stop from Lehmann, who then dealt comfortably with one header from Dunne and was tested more rigorously by another from Distin.

With 20 minutes remaining Reyes was brought on for his debut appearance and he immediately delighted the crowd with several deft touches before almost opening his Highbury goal account with a fierce drive which was charged down by James. But the Gunners finally made their mounting superiority pay in style when Pires found Henry on the left and, even as City claimed a free-kick for a supposed infringement, Thierry took one touch and then produced his masterpiece finish.

Still there was life in Manchester City, though, and they reduced the arrears when Wright-Phillips set up Anelka to sweep home in the last minute of normal time. That precipitated a spat between Anelka and Cole, which ended in the brandishing of red and yellow cards.

... and celebrates in time-honoured fashion.

FEBRUARY

Carling Cup, Semi-Final, second leg
Tuesday 3 February 2004 at The Riverside, 8.00 p.m.
Attendance: 28,781 Referee: Dermot Gallagher

FORM GUIDE
W L D W L W [11 goals scored, 12 conceded]   fD W W L W W [13 goals scored, 5 conceded]

MIDDLESBROUGH 2   ARSENAL 1
Zenden 69, Reyes o.g. 85   Edu 76

Substitutes					Substitutes
Bradley **JONES**	35	Mark **SCHWARZER**	1	33	Graham **STACK**		
▸ Stuart **PARNABY**	21	Danny **MILLS**	15	28	Kolo **TOURE**	13	Stuart **TAYLOR**
◂ (Greening) 64		Chris **RIGGOTT**	5	5	Martin **KEOWN** ■	45	Justin **HOYTE**
Stewart **DOWNING**	19	Gareth **SOUTHGATE**	6	18	Pascal **CYGAN**	55	Olafur-Ingi **SKULASON**
▸ Joseph-Desire **JOB**	16	■ Franck **QUEUDRUE**	3	3	Ashley **COLE**	54	Quincy **OWUSU-ABEYIE** ▸
◂ (Maccarone) 70		Gaizka **MENDIETA**	14	15	Ray **PARLOUR**		(Clichy) 82 ◂
Michael **RICKETTS**	17	Jonathan **GREENING**	12	4	Patrick **VIEIRA**	56	Ryan **SMITH**
		Guidoni **DORIVA**	20	17	**EDU**		
		Boudewijn **ZENDEN**	27	22	Gael **CLICHY**		
		JUNINHO	10	37	David **BENTLEY** ■		
		Massimo **MACCARONE**	9	9	José Antonio **REYES**		

MATCH REPORT

Arsène Wenger's policy of selecting a young side to play in this season's Carling Cup competition had already paid dividends as his players lined up for the second leg of this season's semi-final. Although they were 1-0 down from the first leg, the Gunners played more controlled football than Middlesbrough, and battled on valiantly with ten men for half the match following the dismissal of Martin Keown.

Boro, chasing the first major trophy in their 128-year history, began in cautious style and it was Arsenal who dominated the opening stages of the fourth meeting between the two clubs in 25 days. Clichy, Cole and the excellent Edu all threatened the home goal as the visitors attacked fluently. Yet it was the hosts who fashioned the best early chance when Juninho was challenged by Cole and the ball squirted into the path of Maccarone, who stroked wide from 12 yards.

The Gunners responded with a Cygan header into the side netting from Bentley's corner. Boro soon grew in confidence and after Queudrue turned Mendieta's free-kick back across goal, it took a stupendous block from Stack to prevent Maccarone

hooking home from close range. Thereafter Zenden, in particular, stretched Arsenal with his darting runs and flashing crosses. Shortly before the interval Keown was sent off for hauling back Maccarone.

Still, the Gunners started the second period positively and were aggrieved at not being awarded

David Bentley and Patrick Vieira combine to thwart *Middlesbrough's Boudewijn Zenden.*

Gael Clichy gets his head to the ball ahead of Boro's Joseph-Desire Job.

On his first start for the Gunners José Antonio Reyes ghosts past Guidoni Doriva but was unable to get his shot away.

a penalty when Reyes went down after sidestepping the plunging Schwarzer. Undaunted by their misfortune they continued to probe dangerously, with Vieira, Parlour and Edu working prodigiously hard in midfield, but Middlesbrough regrouped and midway through the half they doubled their advantage in the tie with a fine goal. Maccarone took possession on the left and found Mendieta, whose perfectly weighted pass sent in Zenden to flick the ball over the advancing Stack.

Arsenal refused to yield. Vieira earned a corner with a savage drive which demanded an agile parry from Schwarzer. Bentley delivered beautifully, the ball skewed off Vieira's back, then rebounded from an upright before Edu stooped bravely among the flailing feet to equalise on the night with a close-range header.

Now the outcome was back in the melting pot, but the Herculean labours of the below-strength Gunners were beginning to take their toll. Mendieta and Zenden both might have registered before the result was settled with an own goal. Juninho jinked in from the left and passed to Parnaby, who swerved past one tackle and was about to shoot when Reyes materialised with an attempted clearance which squeezed inside Stack's post with the goalkeeper helpless to intervene.

After that the Gunners pushed forward again, and Edu volleyed close, while Doriva, Job and Zenden all might have extended Boro's winning margin. The final whistle brought Arsenal's fine cup run to an end, but the youngsters who had put in so many fine performances during the competition will have benefited hugely from the experience. In the end, Arsenal were beaten but remained unbowed.

FA Barclaycard Premiership
Saturday 7 February 2004 at Molineux, 3.00 p.m.
Attendance: 29,392 Referee: Phil Dowd

FORM GUIDE
L W W D L D [5 goals scored, 6 conceded]   W W L W W L [13 goals scored, 6 conceded]

WOLVERHAMPTON WANDERERS 1

Ganea 26

ARSENAL 3

Bergkamp 9, Henry 58, Toure 63

Substitutes							Substitutes
Michael **OAKES**	1	Paul **JONES**	21	1	Jens **LEHMANN**		Graham **STACK** 33
Mark **CLYDE**	23	Denis **IRWIN**	2	12	**LAUREN**	12	Pascal **CYGAN** 18
Joey **GUDJONSSON**	26	Jody **CRADDOCK**	12	28	Kolo **TOURE**		Gael **CLICHY** 22
Jorge **MANUEL SILAS**	14	Paul **BUTLER**	6	23	Sol **CAMPBELL**		Ray **PARLOUR** 15
▸ Steffen **IVERSEN**	19	Lee **NAYLOR**	3	3	Ashley **COLE**		José Antonio **REYES** ▸ 9
◂ (Cort) 76		Kenny **MILLER**	16	19	**GILBERTO**		(Bergkamp) 55 ◂
		Colin **CAMERON**	10	4	Patrick **VIEIRA**		
		ALEX RAE	4	17	**EDU**		
		Mark **KENNEDY**	11	7	Robert **PIRES**		
		Viorel **GANEA**	20	10	Dennis **BERGKAMP**		
		Carl **CORT**	27	14	Thierry **HENRY**		

MATCH REPORT

The Gunners set a new club record of 24 games unbeaten at the start of a season and maintained their two-point advantage in the championship race with a hard-fought, but ultimately comfortable victory over struggling Wolves.

Faced by determined resistance from the recent conquerors of Manchester United, Arsenal made a smooth start against Wolves and took an early lead with a beautifully worked goal. Edu accelerated elegantly through midfield before slipping an incisive pass to his left, enabling Cole to turn the ball inside for Bergkamp to volley past Jones from 15 yards with the outside of his right foot.

The visiting Gunners continued to delight the eye and another smooth move flowed through Pires, Edu and Vieira

Dennis Bergkamp fires the Gunners ahead at the end of a superb move involving Edu and Ashley Cole.

who finally found Henry. His curling drive from wide on the left produced a full-length save from Jones, and Gilberto then dragged the rebound off-target from eight yards. But Dave Jones' relegation battlers showed admirably stern mettle, and after Irwin had fired narrowly wide from a free-kick, they responded with a high-quality equaliser. Cameron's corner was nodded back across goal by Craddock, setting up the untended Ganea to net with a clipped half-volley from 12 yards.

From an Arsenal perspective, it was a rare concession from a set-piece, and at this point lesser teams might have become rattled as Wolves, sensing their opportunity, tore forward with renewed vigour. Twice before the interval the hosts fashioned clear scoring opportunities, but the Gunners held firm. First Cameron freed Cort, only for the Molineux newcomer to mishit his shot, allowing Lehmann to scramble clear. Then Kennedy and Cameron played in Ganea, who was distracted in the act of shooting by Campbell's last-ditch intervention. Still Arsène Wenger's men remained potent on the break. Bergkamp tested Jones with a 20-yard volley which the veteran keeper palmed away at full stretch and a clipped shot which was repelled by a fist.

After the break Wolves probed again, and Irwin landed a free-kick on the roof of Lehmann's net. But then the League leaders assumed control with two goals in the space of five minutes. Vieira pushed a pass to the dangerously positioned Pires, who slipped a dispatch between two defenders and Henry raced on to register his 99th Premiership goal with a deftly measured cross-shot.

The same two creators were behind the Gunners' third strike, this time Pires delivering a steepling cross from the right to the far post, and Vieira turned it back for Toure to nod home unopposed from five yards. Soon afterwards the margin might have been extended still further when a high-speed break by Reyes and Henry left the Wolverhampton rearguard in tatters. The Spaniard's final pass was scooped from the Frenchman's toe by the courageous Jones.

Thereafter Arsenal were able to indulge in lengthy interludes of keep-ball, though they threatened intermittently to strike again, notably when Henry arrowed a through-ball to the scampering Cole, whose shot across Jones shaved the far post.

Lauren tussles for a bouncing ball with Wolves' Mark Kennedy.

FORM GUIDE
W L W W L W [12 goals scored, 6 conceded]   L D L W L D [5 goals scored, 9 conceded]

ARSENAL 2   SOUTHAMPTON 0
Henry 31, 90

Substitutes						Substitutes
Graham **STACK** 33	Jens **LEHMANN**	1	14	Antti **NIEMI** ▣		Paul **SMITH** 13
Pascal **CYGAN** 18	**LAUREN**	12	22	Darren **KENTON**		Chris **BAIRD** ▶ ▣ 32
▶ Gael **CLICHY** 22	Kolo **TOURE**	28	11	Michael **SVENSSON** ▣		(A. Svensson) 27 ◀
◀ (Reyes) 74	Sol **CAMPBELL**	23	19	Danny **HIGGINBOTHAM**		Fitz **HALL** 15
EDU 17	Ashley **COLE**	3	6	Stephen **CRAINEY**		Marian **PAHARS** ▶ 17
David **BENTLEY** 37	▣ Ray **PARLOUR**	15	33	Paul **TELFER**		(Le Saux) 82 ◀
	GILBERTO	19	18	Rory **DELAP**		James **BEATTIE** ▶ 9
	▣ Patrick **VIEIRA**	4	12	Anders **SVENSSON**		(Baird) 81 ◀
	Robert **PIRES**	7	3	Graeme **LE SAUX**		
	José Antonio **REYES**	9	36	Brett **ORMEROD**		
	Thierry **HENRY**	14	7	Kevin **PHILLIPS**		

MATCH REPORT

Thierry Henry plundered his 100th and 101st Premiership goals as the Gunners roared five points clear at the head of the pack. Though Arsenal performed well at times, Southampton gave a spirited display in their last game under the management of Gordon Strachan, and they might have easily slipped away from Highbury with a hard-earned point.

The early running was made by the hosts, who sliced through the visitors' rearguard twice in the opening minutes only for Niemi to deny Pires on both occasions. Strachan's men responded vigorously and soon Ormerod was claiming he had been baulked by Toure and Lehmann, but the referee ignored his claims

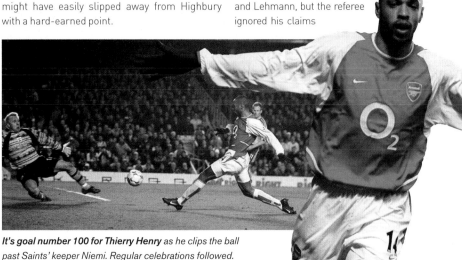

It's goal number 100 for Thierry Henry as he clips the ball past Saints' keeper Niemi. Regular celebrations followed.

for a penalty. There followed a succession of Southampton corners, two of which led to last-ditch clearances from Cole and Lauren. The action then switched to the other end where Henry was off-target with an ambitious half-volley from 20 yards.

Shortly afterwards he was celebrating his century of goals in the top division – the first of which was scored against Southampton in September 1999 – when Gilberto found Pires, who sent Thierry scampering clear on the left flank. Ignoring appeals for offside, he rode a despairing challenge from Kenton and clipped a neat shot past the diving Niemi, who managed to get a finger to the ball but could not keep it out.

As the first half was closing a lovely move involving Vieira and Pires created an opening for Reyes, but the Spaniard fired wide.

Southampton started the second period on the front foot, and soon Lehmann was twisting sharply to turn an awkward effort from the persistent Ormerod around an upright. Shortly afterwards the German keeper dealt with a spinning volley from Baird before the Gunners, as if recognising the danger signals from the determined Saints, began to mount pressure on Niemi's goal.

After Henry's centre skimmed the outstretched boot of the charging Reyes, Southampton launched a series of counter-attacks during which Ormerod went close with a cross-shot, Pires headed clear from the same opponent and Delap's deflected drive flashed wide of a post.

As time ticked away Strachan threw on Beattie and Pahars to join Ormerod and Phillips in a four-man forward line, but that left them vulnerable on the break and Henry almost settled the issue with a shot which went narrowly wide. It was not until the final minute that the Highbury faithful could breathe easily, when Henry kicked off his second century of Premiership goals. Parlour picked up the ball in midfield and spread it wide to Pires. His cross was missed by Gilberto, but Henry controlled the ball and cracked it past Niemi to ensure victory.

A thunderous free-kick just before time and Thierry Henry starts his second century of goals.

FORM GUIDE

L W W L W W [12 goals scored, 6 conceded]   W D W W W W [11 goals scored, 2 conceded]

ARSENAL 2   CHELSEA 1
Reyes 55, 61   **Mutu 40**

Substitutes						Substitutes
Graham **STACK**	33	Jens **LEHMANN**	1	23	Carlo **CUDICINI**	
Pascal **CYGAN**	18	**LAUREN**	12	15	Mario **MELCHIOT**	34 Neil **SULLIVAN** ▶
▶ Gael **CLICHY**	22	Kolo **TOURE**	28	13	William **GALLAS**	(Cudicini) 60 ◀
◀ (Reyes) 82		Sol **CAMPBELL**	23	26	John **TERRY**	29 Robert **HUTH**
▶ **EDU**	17	Ashley **COLE**	3	18	Wayne **BRIDGE**	10 Joe **COLE** ▶
◀ (Parlour) 51		Ray **PARLOUR**	15	19	Scott **PARKER**	(Gronkjaer) 69 ◀
David **BENTLEY**	37	**GILBERTO**	19	4	Claude **MAKELELE**	22 Eidur **GUDJOHNSEN** ▶
		Patrick **VIEIRA**	4	8	Frank **LAMPARD**	(Mutu) 64 ◀
		Robert **PIRES**	7	30	Jesper **GRONKJAER**	21 Hernan **CRESPO**
		Dennis **BERGKAMP**	10	7	Adrian **MUTU**	
		Jose Antonio **REYES**	9	9	Jimmy-Floyd	
					HASSELBAINK	

MATCH REPORT

Two brilliant goals in the space of six second-half minutes by José Antonio Reyes turned this tumultuously competitive London derby on its head as Arsenal knocked Chelsea out of the FA Cup for the fourth successive season. The Blues had been a goal to the good at the interval, courtesy of an explosive strike by Mutu, but they never recovered from the devastating double blow administered by the young Spanish star, and the holders finished in more comfortable control than the scoreline suggests.

The game began at a fierce tempo, with Chelsea forcing a rash of free-kicks which came to nothing. Arsenal's fluent passing almost paid off in the 11th minute when Bergkamp swivelled and passed to Gilberto, who executed a slick interchange with Pires, but was robbed by Terry in the act of shooting. Immediately the play moved to the opposite end of the pitch where Mutu crossed from the left for Gallas to test Lehmann at his near post.

Arsenal held sway for a prolonged spell during the first half. Cole set up Reyes for a cross-shot which didn't trouble Cudicini, Pires sidestepped a tackle before firing into the keeper's arms from 20 yards and Cudicini plunged courageously at the feet of several attackers. As the pressure increased, a sublime sequence of passing and movement culminated in Cole prodding goalwards from eight yards only for the keeper to block.

But gradually Chelsea reversed the flow. Lampard shot off target, Hasselbaink misdirected a free header from eight yards and Gronkjaer netted with a nod from Lampard's cross only to be frustrated by an offside flag. Finally the Blues' growing authority was rewarded when Lehmann's drop-kick was half-volleyed by Parker to Mutu, who swerved wide of Toure before hitting home a savage drive from 18 yards. In response, the Gunners fashioned two chances before the break. Bergkamp's fizzing 25-yarder was fielded cleanly by Cudicini, then Cole's effort from an acute angle was deflected for a corner.

Early in the second period Pires swept wide from 15 yards, and then Reyes strode on to centre stage. There seemed little imminent danger when Edu took possession on the right touchline and rolled the ball to the Arsenal newcomer, but he was not closed down and strode forward to rap an unstoppable

José Antonio Reyes strikes a magnificent 25-yarder to give the Gunners the lead and to show the Highbury faithful what he can do.

left-foot drive into the far top corner of Cudicini's net from 25 yards. Highbury exploded with joy.

Next Reyes saw two shots blocked in a chaotic interlude in the Chelsea goalmouth, but he was not to be denied. Vieira came out best in a challenge with Parker and passed on the blind side of Melchiot to the young Spaniard. He latched on to the penetrative despatch from his skipper to sidefoot what proved to be the winner. Substitute keeper Sullivan, called on for the injured Cudicini, managed a faint touch – but neither he, nor the lunging Terry on the line could repel this more subtle effort, and Highbury hailed its latest hero.

If that wasn't enough, Reyes scores a second six minutes later and can't contain his joy.

FEBRUARY

FORM GUIDE

D W W W W L [8 goals scored, 4 conceded]   W W L W W W [14 goals scored, 6 conceded]

CHELSEA 1   ARSENAL 2
Gudjohnsen 1   Vieira 14, Edu 21

Substitutes		Neil **SULLIVAN**	34	1	Jens **LEHMANN**		Substitutes
Marco **AMBROSIO**	31	Mario **MELCHIOT**	15	12	**LAUREN** ▪	33	Graham **STACK**
Marcel **DESAILLY**	6	William **GALLAS**	13	28	Kolo **TOURE**	18	Pascal **CYGAN**
▸ Joe **COLE**	10	▪ John **TERRY**	26	23	Sol **CAMPBELL**	8	Fredrik **LJUNGBERG** ▸
◂ (Gérémi) 73		Wayne **BRIDGE**	18	22	Gael **CLICHY**		(Bergkamp) 78 ◂
▸ Jesper **GRONKJAER**	30	Scott **PARKER**	19	19	**GILBERTO**	25	**KANU**
◂ (Parker) 62		Claude **MAKELELE**	4	4	Patrick **VIEIRA**	9	José Antonio **REYES**
▸ Jimmy-Floyd		▪ Frank **LAMPARD**	8	17	**EDU**		
HASSELBAINK	9	**GÉRÉMI**	14	7	Robert **PIRES**		
◂ (Mutu) 73		▪ Adrian **MUTU**	7	10	Dennis **BERGKAMP**		
		▪▪ Eidur **GUDJOHNSEN**	22	14	Thierry **HENRY** ▪		

MATCH REPORT

This was practically the perfect Saturday for Arsenal. After conceding a goal to title rivals Chelsea after only 27 seconds, the Gunners battled back to win, then walked off the pitch to learn that their Premiership lead over Manchester United had been stretched to seven points.

Player and fans unite in celebration as the Gunners go from one down to one up in the space of seven minutes.

The Blues made the best possible start to their bid for a first victory over Arsenal in 17 League games. Gérémi stole the ball from Vieira in midfield, then surged down the left flank before crossing for Mutu to flick on to Gudjohnsen, who side-footed coolly past Lehmann from a narrow angle at the far post.

The League-leaders were momentarily non-plussed and might have fallen further behind a minute later, but the untended Gallas skied wildly from a Mutu corner. But stung into retaliation, Arsenal began to pass with their customary fluency and soon a Pires corner caused havoc in the Chelsea rearguard, but Henry's volley was blocked and Campbell's follow-up from 20 yards was held safely by Sullivan.

The action began to see-saw as Gallas headed wide for the hosts and Henry was narrowly off-target at the other end with a volley from Bergkamp's divine crossfield delivery. When the equaliser materialised it was majestic in both conception and execution. Vieira won the ball and gave it to Bergkamp, then sprinted forward to receive the Dutchman's perfectly weighted return pass before slotting beautifully beyond the advancing Sullivan

from 12 yards. It was the ideal way for the skipper to atone for his earlier error.

Three minutes later Chelsea went close to regaining the lead when Parker sent in Gérémi on the left and the Cameroonian crossed to the far post, where Gudjohnsen's header was smothered by Clichy. Instead it was the Gunners who forged in front when Henry's corner was misjudged by Sullivan and the ball fell to Edu, who swivelled to net emphatically from six yards.

The frustrated Blues flowed forward for the remainder of the half, but Lehmann saved well when a Bridge centre was deflected by Toure, Terry shot limply after being chipped in by Makelele, and Gilberto pulled off a brilliant block from Bridge.

After the break Chelsea continued to make the running while the Gunners retained their composure and soaked up the mounting pressure. Mutu was freed in the box but stumbled and was robbed by Campbell, a Lampard snapshot crept wide, the excellent Clichy denied Mutu, and a wickedly arcing free-kick from Gérémi eluded three of his team-mates with the goal at their mercy.

Claudio Ranieri's team continued to push forward even after being reduced to ten men by the dismissal of Gudjohnsen on the hour for a second bookable offence, but Arsenal kept them at bay comfortably before creating two chances for Gilberto near the end. Both times the Brazilian was foiled by Sullivan, but it didn't matter. The points were safe, and the result from Old Trafford, where United drew with Leeds, was a sweet bonus.

An airborne Gilberto tests the Chelsea keeper Sullivan, but this time he failed to register.

101

UEFA Champions League, 1st Knockout Round, first leg
Tuesday 24 February 2004 at the Balaidos Stadium, 7.45 p.m.
Attendance: 21,000 Referee: Anders Frisk, Sweden

FORM GUIDE
L W L W W L [7 goals scored, 9 conceded]   W L W W W W [12 goals scored, 6 conceded]

CELTA VIGO 2   ARSENAL 3
Luis Edu 27, Ignacio 64   Edu 17, 58, Pires 80

Substitutes						Substitutes	
	Pablo **CAVALLERO**	1	1	Jens **LEHMANN**		Substitutes	
Jose **PINTO** 13	Juan **VELASCO**	2	12	**LAUREN**		Graham **STACK**	33
Fernando **CACERES** 4	Fernandez **SERGIO**	23	28	Kolo **TOURE**		Martin **KEOWN**	5
Pablo **CONTRERAS** 15	Eduardo **BERIZZO**	6	23	Sol **CAMPBELL**		Pascal **CYGAN** ▸	18
Sebastian **MENDEZ** 17	■ Silvio **SILVINHO**	3	22	Gael **CLICHY**		(Clichy) 90 ◂	
▸ Rogerio **VAGNER** 7	Peter **LUCCIN**	22	8	Fredrik **LJUNGBERG**		Justin **HOYTE**	45
◂ (Angel) 64	Jose **IGNACIO**	16	4	Patrick **VIEIRA**		David **BENTLEY** ▸	37
▸ Mauricio **PINILLA** 18	Lopez **ANGEL**	8	17	**EDU** ■		(Ljungberg) 90 ◂	
◂ (Edu) 75	Alexander **MOSTEVOI**	10	7	Robert **PIRES**		**KANU** ▸	25
Alejandro **JANDRO** 21	Luis **EDU**	19	9	José Antonio **REYES**		(Reyes) 78 ◂	
	Savo **MILOSEVIC**	9	14	Thierry **HENRY** ■		Francesc **FABREGAS**	57

MATCH REPORT

The Gunners took a mammoth stride towards the last eight of the Champions League, and recorded their first win on Spanish soil, thanks to a contrasting brace from man-of-the-match Edu and a masterful late strike from Robert Pires. The winning goal came as a relief after Arsenal had twice lost the lead to an enterprising Celta Vigo, who tasted European defeat at home for the first time in 25 matches. In truth, Arsène Wenger's men were not at their most expansive, but they turned on the style when it was needed to ensure an entertaining encounter.

Belying their lowly position in La Liga, Celta made most of the early running, but two menacing crosses from Angel came to nothing. Clichy was called into action and had to pull off a magnificent

A determined Kolo Toure convincingly out-muscles Celta Vigo's Rogerio Vagner.

Man-of-the-match Edu is congratulated after scoring his second to put Arsenal ahead for the second time.

Arsenal have the final word.

Robert Pires strikes the winner from just inside the penalty area despite the efforts of two Spanish defenders.

Celta almost made a sensational start to the second half when Mostevoi headed against the bar from a Luis Edu cross, then Ignacio fired into Lehmann's midriff. Henry responded with a mazy run and low drive which Cavallero parried, then the Frenchman clipped wide from close range

block on Milosevic after the former Aston Villa striker had been freed by Ignacio. Arsenal had signalled their own attacking intent when slick work from Ljungberg and Henry set up Reyes, only for his low shot to be gathered comfortably by Cavallero. The breakthough came when Pires swung in a free-kick, which was mis-headed by Edu, but the Brazilian's positive positioning and strong finish saw him scramble the ball home at the second attempt.

The game was held up for four minutes while Cavallero received treatment to a facial injury. But Celta were unbowed and they hit back when ex-Gunner Silvinho curled over a free-kick, which was glanced home emphatically from eight yards by the head of Luis Edu. Encouraged, the hosts continued to press and Silvinho was disappointed to see his penalty claim rejected following a collision with Toure. Luis Edu then seized on a misdirected clearance by Lehmann but the German recovered to save the resultant shot.

after a Reyes effort was blocked. Arsenal were looking increasingly dangerous and they reclaimed the lead in spectacular fashion when Edu jinked deftly on the edge of the box before dispatching a sublime curler with his right foot. It was a strike fit to win any contest.

Spurred on by the home crowd, Celta were keen to strike back quickly. When Mostevoi's corner was nodded down by Sergio to Ignacio, who converted from six yards, things were looking up for the home side. Celta scented a shock victory and Lehmann had to be at his best to clutch a swerving shot-cum-cross from Arsenal old-boy Silvinho.

But the final word was to rest with Arsenal. Vieira found Henry, who executed a dazzling interchange of passes with Pires which culminated in the midfielder netting with slide-rule accuracy from 16 yards. It was a wonderful goal to settle an exhilarating match.

FEBRUARY

FORM GUIDE

L W W W W [13 goals scored, 7 conceded] W W L L L W [9 goals scored, 9 conceded]

ARSENAL 2
Pires 2, Henry 4

CHARLTON ATHLETIC 1
Jensen 59

Substitutes					Substitutes
	Jens **LEHMANN**	1	1	Dean **KIELY**	
Stuart **TAYLOR** 13	**LAUREN**	12	12	Herman **HREIDARSSON**	25 Simon **ROYCE**
▸ Pascal **CYGAN** 18	Kolo **TOURE**	28	24	Jonathan **FORTUNE**	18 Paul **KONCHESKY**
◂ (Pires) 88	Sol **CAMPBELL**	23	6	Mark **FISH**	23 Michael **TURNER**
▸ **GILBERTO** 19	Ashley **COLE**	3	19	Luke **YOUNG**	17 Shaun **BARTLETT**
◂ (Ljungberg) 74	Fredrik **LJUNGBERG**	8	4	Graham **STUART**	21 Jonatan **JOHANSSON** ▸
KANU 25	Patrick **VIEIRA**	4	2	Radostin **KISHISHEV**	(Kishishev) 78 ◂
▸ José Antonio **REYES** 9	**EDU**	17	10	Claus **JENSEN**	
◂ (Bergkamp) 74	Robert **PIRES**	7	8	Matt **HOLLAND**	
	Dennis **BERGKAMP**	10	11	Paolo **DI CANIO**	
	Thierry **HENRY**	14	35	Carlton **COLE**	

MATCH REPORT

Arsenal got off to a whirlwind start with two goals in the opening four minutes, but fourth-placed Charlton fought back and came within an inch of forcing a draw when they rapped an upright deep inside stoppage time. Despite that close call, the Gunners tightened their grip on the Premiership title race, ending the day nine points ahead of both their nearest rivals, Chelsea and Manchester United.

The Gunners, unbeaten in the League for 300 days, took just 90 seconds to seize the lead when Henry exchanged passes with Ljungberg and the Swede's low cross was poked home from four yards by Pires. It was the Frenchman's 50th goal for the club. Charlton were still reeling when the margin was doubled. Bergkamp sent Vieira surging down the left and the captain's searching delivery was controlled by Henry, who wrong-footed Fortune and Hreidarsson before shooting past Kiely.

Now the Arsenal machine purred sweetly, with the ball being switched fluently from man to man, and as the first half wore on they created a succession of scoring opportunities. An Edu daisycutter

Arsenal are one up after 90 seconds as Robert Pires registers his 50th goal for the club.

bobbled narrowly wide from 30 yards, Ljungberg accepted a pass from Henry before cutting inside to draw a sharp tip-over from Kiely, Pires' delicate touch fed Henry but the Frenchman volleyed straight at the goalkeeper, and Edu curled a 25-yard free-kick the wrong side of an upright.

All Charlton could muster in reply before the interval was an off-target volley from Di Canio and a chip from Jensen which cleared the crossbar, but they came out fighting in the second half. Soon it required a saving tackle from Ashley Cole to deny his namesake, Carlton, then both Stuart and Di Canio unleashed powerful shots which were blocked.

Though frustrated, the Addicks continued to show defiance and they were rewarded when Jensen bent an exquisite free-kick around the Gunners' defensive wall and into Lehmann's net via a post. That served as a wake-up call and now the League leaders returned to the offensive with a vengeance. First Pires sent Henry clear on goal, but the top scorer's stinging drive was repelled by the legs of Kiely, then Bergkamp's hanging free-kick was nodded wide by Vieira from six yards with the net gaping. Henry's 30-yard free-kick demanded a full-length dive from Kiely and, as Highbury was engulfed in a sudden snow flurry, the same marksman clipped the crossbar with a dipping effort from a narrow angle.

Still the visitors remained dangerous, and Stuart might have done better than misdirect his header back across goal after a cross from Carlton Cole had eluded Lehmann. Reyes fired a low 25-yarder just off target, but the Highbury faithful were whistling for the end as Di Canio and company

gathered themselves for a final assault, and the nervous fans suffered when an 18-yard overhead kick from Johansson defeated Lehmann's dive before slapping a post on its way to safety.

Thus Charlton had perished valiantly, but the three points were no more than Arsenal deserved.

Having scored a second after four minutes Thierry Henry *continued to test the Charlton defence.*

Patrick Vieira rises to head at goal but was unable to add to Arsenal's tally for the afternoon.

FEBRUARY 2004

Arsenal.com PLAYER OF THE MONTH
EDU

" My confidence is very good because I've been playing in more games. I'm happy with my form and it might be the best I've ever played for Arsenal, but I've only been here for two or three years and I'm sure there's a lot more to show the supporters. I am 25 years old and have plenty of seasons in me.

When you are with a good team like Arsenal you have to keep improving all the time to stay in the squad. I'm trying hard to do that and I think I have made progress. I'm thinking a lot quicker now because the game is faster over here. Everything is going so well for me and the team is doing fantastic as well. I just hope it will continue. "

EDU

" It seems that people keep discovering Edu now that he has scored important goals against Chelsea and Celta Vigo, but I have always considered him as a regular player and he has done well in many big games. He had injuries when he first came over, and after coming through those difficulties you can only be stronger. "

ARSÈNE WENGER

ARSENAL DIARY

Sunday 1 February
- Before the Highbury clash with Manchester City, David Seaman is presented with a commemorative award to mark his 13 great years as a Gunner.

Saturday 21 February
- Dennis Bergkamp makes his 253rd League appearance for Arsenal, thus breaking the Premiership record by a foreign player at one club previously held by Peter Schmeichel of Manchester United.

Monday 23 February
- Arsenal announce they have secured the required £357 million funding to build a new stadium at Ashburton Grove.
- Arsène Wenger pledges his future to the Gunners until at least 2007.

Saturday 28 February
- Robert Pires completes his first half-century of goals for the Gunners in the 2-1 victory over the Addicks.

THE WIDER WORLD

Tuesday 3 February
- Wales fail in their appeal against Russia's qualification for Euro 2004 on the grounds of a player's failed drug test.

Wednesday 4 February
- Spurs are the victims of incredible FA Cup fight-back by ten-man Manchester City, who recover from 3-0 down to win at White Hart Lane.

Saturday 14 February
- Ten-man Manchester United oust Manchester City from the FA Cup.

Wednesday 18 February
- England draw 1-1 in friendly with Portugal; Republic of Ireland draw 0-0 with Brazil; Wales beat Scotland 4-0; Northern Ireland lose 4-1 to Norway but score their first goal in 14 matches.

Saturday 21 February
- Welsh legend John Charles dies at the age of 72.

FA CARLING PREMIERSHIP
29 February 2004

	P	HOME					AWAY					Pts
		W	D	L	F	A	W	D	L	F	A	
ARSENAL	27	11	2	0	26	9	9	5	0	27	9	67
Chelsea	27	8	2	3	22	10	10	2	2	26	11	58
Manchester United	27	9	3	2	30	13	9	1	3	21	12	58
Newcastle United	26	8	3	3	23	9	8	2	1	14	18	41
Charlton Athletic	27	5	3	5	21	22	6	4	4	17	12	40
Liverpool	25	6	2	4	18	13	4	6	3	18	14	38
Aston Villa	27	7	4	2	19	12	3	3	8	13	20	37
Fulham	27	7	3	4	22	16	3	3	7	17	22	36
Birmingham City	25	5	4	3	14	14	4	5	4	11	14	36
Tottenham Hotspur	26	7	2	5	28	23	3	2	7	11	19	34
Bolton Wanderers	26	3	7	3	15	14	5	3	5	17	26	34
Southampton	27	6	4	4	16	11	2	5	6	11	16	33
Middlesbrough	25	3	4	6	11	16	5	3	4	16	15	31
Everton	27	6	4	4	21	15	1	4	8	12	24	29
Blackburn Rovers	27	3	3	7	20	24	4	4	6	19	20	28
Manchester City	27	2	7	4	17	16	4	2	8	19	23	27
Wolverhampton Wanderers	27	5	5	3	17	22	0	4	10	7	30	24
Portsmouth	25	6	1	5	22	14	0	4	9	6	25	23
Leicester City	27	2	7	5	14	23	2	4	7	23	28	23
Leeds United	26	3	4	6	13	20	2	2	9	11	31	21

FORM GUIDE

D L L D W D [6 goals scored, 8 conceded] W W W W W W [14 goals scored, 6 conceded]

PORTSMOUTH 1   ARSENAL 5

Sheringham 90   Henry 25, 50, Ljungberg 43, 57,
Toure 45

Substitutes					Substitutes
Harald **WAPENAAR** 25	Shaka **HISLOP**	1	1	Jens **LEHMANN**	Stuart **TAYLOR** 13
Kevin **HARPER** 7	Linvoy **PRIMUS**	2	12	**LAUREN**	Pascal **CYGAN** 18
▶ Steve **STONE** 19	Petri **PASANEN**	34	28	Kolo **TOURE**	Gael **CLICHY** ▶ 22
◀ (Berkovic) 46	Arjan **DE ZEEUW**	6	23	Sol **CAMPBELL**	(Vieira) 72 ◀
▶ Richard **HUGHES** 22	Alexei **SMERTIN**	30	3	Ashley **COLE**	David **BENTLEY** ▶ 37
◀ (Quashie) 70	Nigel **QUASHIE**	11	8	Fredrik **LJUNGBERG**	(Ljungberg) 72 ◀
▶ Teddy **SHERINGHAM** 10	AMDY **FAYE**	15	4	Patrick **VIEIRA**	**KANU** ▶ 25
◀ (Mornar) 77	Eyal **BERKOVIC**	39	17	**EDU**	(Henry) 72 ◀
	Matthew **TAYLOR**	14	19	**GILBERTO**	
	Ayegbeni **YAKUBU**	20	14	Thierry **HENRY**	
	Ivica **MORNAR**	37	9	José Antonio **REYES**	

MATCH REPORT

Arsenal swept imperiously into the semi-finals of the FA Cup, overwhelming Portsmouth with five goals in one destructive 32-minute spell. So irresistible was the Gunners' free-flowing attacking flair that even the Pompey fans gave Arsène Wenger's men two standing ovations, at half-time and at the final whistle.

The visitors served notice of their intentions as early as the second minute when Cole and Henry combined to set up Reyes for a thunderous 20-yard half-volley which rattled the hosts' crossbar before arcing to safety. Mornar, Smertin and Taylor threatened briefly at the other end, before Henry demonstrated Arsenal's colossal self-confidence by launching a shot from 40 yards!

The Portsmouth keeper was soon pressed into more urgent action. This time he could not prevent the Gunners taking the lead. A clever run from Reyes caused chaos in the Portsmouth defence, Vieira found Ljungberg, and an interception ran to Henry, who swerved past a challenge before hammering unstoppably past Hislop from 10 yards.

Now, Arsenal seized control. Vieira headed powerfully past an upright from a Reyes corner, Edu

saw two efforts flash wide and another saved by Hislop, and Henry's twisting scamper ended with De Zeeuw blocking his shot. Something had to give and it did when Edu played a smart one-two interchange with Vieira before freeing the darting Ljungberg to beat Hislop with a firm cross-shot.

Desperate for the break to regroup, Pompey found themselves three behind before the half-time

One: *an unstoppable left-foot shot from Thierry Henry gives Arsenal the lead.*

whistle had blown. The home defence failed to clear a corner and allowed Toure to swivel on a loose ball and net with a low drive.

Yakubu might have reduced the arrears early in the second period, but the Nigerian shot wildly from a De Zeeuw knockdown. That rather forlorn foray proved no more than a forerunner of further grief for Harry Redknapp's side. First, Reyes passed to Ljungberg, the Swede touched back to Henry and the Frenchman delivered a perfectly placed 25-yard side-foot which bounced over Hislop's despairing clutch on its way inside the far post. Then Toure ran powerfully through midfield and slipped the ball to Ljungberg, who jinked wide of a would-be tackler before hitting an 18-yard shot which deflected past Hislop.

Two: *Freddie Ljungberg celebrates after putting Arsenal two goals to the good.*

Now the Gunners were five to the good, and with the outcome emphatically decided, they resorted to lengthy periods of keep-ball, punctuated by occasional attempts to increase the scoreline, with Reyes, Henry and Ljungberg all going close.

But Portsmouth refused to lie down and, to their immense credit, they finally began to make inroads into the Arsenal defence. Primus nodded narrowly off-target, then Yakubu deserved better fortune when his fierce header from a Stone cross cannoned off the crossbar and down on to the line before being cleared. The assault intensified, with Taylor shooting against a post and the rebound bouncing over the bar via Campbell.

A consolation goal was the least they merited, and it materialised in the last minute when Hughes knocked down a Stone delivery and Sheringham evaded Campbell to steer past Lehmann from close range.

Three: *Kolo Toure nets with a low drive and Arsenal lead 3-0 before the half-time whistle.*

MARCH

UEFA Champions League, 1st Knockout Round, second leg
Wednesday 10 March 2004 at Highbury, 7.45 p.m.
Attendance: 35,402 Referee: Pierluigi Collina, Italy

FORM GUIDE

W W W W W W [16 goals scored, 6 conceded]   W W L L L L [9 goals scored, 15 conceded]

ARSENAL 2   CELTA VIGO 0

Henry 14, 34

Substitutes						Substitutes
	Jens **LEHMANN**	1	1	Pablo **CAVALLERO**		
Graham **STACK** 33	**LAUREN**	12	2	Juan **VELASCO**	13	Jose **PINTO**
Martin **KEOWN** 5	Kolo **TOURE**	28	23	Fernandez **SERGIO**	15	Pablo **CONTRERAS** ▸
Pascal **CYGAN** 18	Sol **CAMPBELL**	23	4	Fernando **CACERES** ▮▮		(Silvinho) 21 ◂
Gael **CLICHY** 22	Ashley **COLE**	3	3	Silvio **SILVINHO**	17	Sebastian **MENDEZ**
▸ **GILBERTO** 15	Fredrik **LJUNGBERG**	8	16	Jose **IGNACIO**	20	Mora **JESULI** ▸
◂ (Edu) 70	Patrick **VIEIRA**	4	22	Peter **LUCCIN**		(Luccin) 29 ◂
▸ **KANU** 25	**EDU**	17	28	OUBINA **BORJA**	7	Rogerio **VAGNER** ▸
◂ (Bergkamp) 77	Robert **PIRES**	7	11	Gustavo **LOPEZ**		(Lopez) 70 ◂
▸ Jose Antonio **REYES** 9	Dennis **BERGKAMP**	10	10	Alexander **MOSTOVOI**	19	Luis **EDU**
◂ (Pires) 70	Thierry **HENRY**	14	18	Mauricio **PINILLA**	9	Savo **MILOSEVIC**

MATCH REPORT

The Gunners turned in an efficient performance to see off their Spanish opponents and move smoothly into the quarter-finals. Thierry Henry contributed a first-half brace to end his 10-match Highbury scoring drought in Europe's premier competition as the overwhelmingly superior Gunners strolled past Celta Vigo with ease.

Perversely in view of what was to follow, it was the visitors who made the sprightlier start, with Campbell deflecting one Luccin drive into the hands of Lehmann and blocking another. Next a driving run from Pinilla might have proved productive had he heard the scream of the unmarked Mostovoi to his left, but then the tide turned irrevocably as Arsenal took the lead on the night – and a 4–2 advantage overall – with their first meaningful attack. Bergkamp latched on to a loose ball, pirouetted away from a challenge and split the Celta defence with an exquisite outside-of-the-foot dispatch to Henry, who beat Cavallero at his near post with a fierce cross-shot.

The Gunners assumed command, stroking passes around at will, though

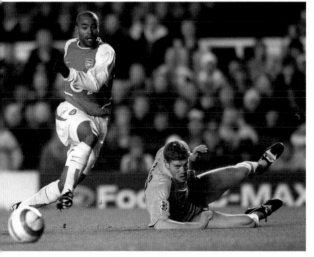

Ashley Cole stands firm, as Celta Vigo's Sergio is frustrated that his team could not built on their sprightly start.

Thierry Henry fires a cross-shot past the Spanish keeper Cavallero to give Arsenal a one-goal lead on the night and a two-goal lead overall.

Luccin sounded a faint warning note with a dipping 30-yarder which Lehmann turned over his crossbar and Ignacio sliced wide from the resulting corner. A neat link between Cole and Bergkamp sent the Arsenal left-back scurrying into the Spanish box only to steer his shot wide, but it was merely a reprieve for Celta. Pires located Ljungberg on the right, the Swede exchanged passes with Bergkamp and Henry was on hand to force home a deflected cross from close range.

Late in the first half Pinilla squandered an inviting chance to reply, and Lehmann turned away a curling free-kick from Lopez. The action then switched ends as Pires and Ljungberg fashioned a chance for Henry to complete a hat-trick, only for Cavallero to bring off a terrific block.

With the outcome settled barring a minor miracle, the second period began gently, with Arsenal in exhibition mode and Celta intent on damage limitation. Both sides played attractively, though, and Pires might have stretched the lead but for a courageous parry from Cavallero. Lehmann

turned a header from Caceres around an upright and a Lopez free-kick was charged down.

Bergkamp was lucky to escape serious injury and unfortunate not to be awarded a penalty when Cavallero planted a foot in his chest. But Celta then went down to ten men when Contreras was given a second yellow after fouling substitute Reyes. Cavallero then made a more legitimate intervention, charging from his area to foil Henry, who was in pursuit of a superb through-ball from Gilberto. The Brazilian, who was in lively form after rising from the bench to replace his countryman, Edu, then delivered a flighted cross to the head of the unmarked Ljungberg, who nodded the ball wide from six yards.

Shortly before the end Pinilla was similarly wasteful when set up by Velasco, but even had the young centre-forward hit the target it would not have threatened Arsenal's fifth successive Champions League victory.

FORM GUIDE
D L W D L D [8 goals scored, 9 conceded]   W W W W W W [16 goals scored, 6 conceded]

BLACKBURN ROVERS 0

ARSENAL 2
Henry 57, Pires 87

Substitutes				Substitutes
Peter **ENCKELMAN** 31	Brad **FRIEDEL** 1	1 Jens **LEHMANN**	33 Graham **STACK**	
▸ Markus **BABBEL** 11	Lucas **NEILL** 2	12 **LAUREN**	18 Pascal **CYGAN** ▸	
◂ (Todd) 84	Andy **TODD** 15	28 Kolo **TOURE**	(Pires) 89 ◂	
▸ Vratislav **GRESKO** 3	Craig **SHORT** 6	23 Sol **CAMPBELL**	22 Gael **CLICHY** ▸	
◂ (Douglas) 77	Michael **GRAY** 33	3 Ashley **COLE**	(Reyes) 77 ◂	
Nils-Eric **JOHANSSON** 14	Brett **EMERTON** 23	19 **GILBERTO**	37 David **BENTLEY**	
▸ Dwight **YORKE** 19	Kerimoglu **TUGAY** 8	4 Patrick **VIEIRA**	25 **KANU**	
◂ (Jansen) 73	▥ Martin **ANDRESEN** 25	17 **EDU** ▥		
	Jonathon **DOUGLAS** 26	7 Robert **PIRES**		
	Matt **JANSEN** 10	9 José Antonio **REYES**		
	Andy **COLE** 9	14 Thierry **HENRY**		

MATCH REPORT

Thierry Henry's 30th goal of the season and a 14th strike by Robert Pires were enough to ensure that Arsène Wenger's men cleared a potentially awkward hurdle in the chase for the title.

Blackburn started enterprisingly, belying their lowly league position, and putting early pressure on Sol Campbell and company. Tugay's skill set up an opening for Jansen but Sol Campbell brought off a timely block, then Ashley Cole cleared off the line following Short's looping header from an Emerton corner.

As if stung by his side's initial lethargy, Vieira began to dominate midfield, commencing with a characteristic surge to the edge of the Blackburn box which ended with

a delicate dispatch to Pires, whose attempted cross to Henry was cut out by Todd. The visitors began to flow more smoothly and Pires, Reyes and Gilberto worked a glimpse at goal for Henry,

Ashley Cole is the first to congratulate
Thierry Henry after the Frenchman
notched his 30th goal of the season.

who swivelled to hit a stinging 15-yarder which demanded a sharp parry from Friedel.

Henry then took a quick free-kick that swerved inches wide of a post. He was then the central figure in the game's most contentious moment. As Friedel threw up the ball to punt it downfield, Henry nipped in to rob him, then strode on to find the net. To the consternation of the Arsenal faithful, who saw the striker's actions as a moment of skilful opportunism, the referee signalled a Blackburn free kick for infringement.

Disappointed but not discouraged, the Gunners continued to threaten, with Pires cutting in from the left to curl a shot on to the roof of the net and Reyes thundering down the same flank before firing a rasping drive narrowly wide of the far upright. The nearest Blackburn came to breaking through was when Andy Cole juggled the ball past Toure and hit a fierce volley from an acute angle which Lehmann did well to smother cleanly.

After the interval, Rovers continued to battle gamely to improve the Premiership's worst home record, but then Short conceded a free-kick against Henry some 25 yards from goal and the Frenchman bent an exquisite free-kick past the plunging Friedel at his near post. Soon afterwards Pires went close to doubling the lead but his effort was deflected into the goalkeeper's custody, then Blackburn threw extra men forward in search of an equaliser and began to stretch the Arsenal rearguard.

Vieira, who was outstanding even by his dynamic standards, headed out one menacing attempt from the busy Emerton, then Yorke's trickery created time and space for Andy Cole to deliver a telling cross, which just eluded the outstretched boot of Douglas at the far post.

The Gunners needed a clincher and it arrived at the climax of a fluent move initiated on the left by Clichy and moving on through Pires and Vieira to Gilberto. The Brazilian slightly mishit a cross-shot which Friedel managed to palm against an upright, only for the alert Pires to hammer home the rebound from eight yards.

Not to be outdone, *Robert Pires fires his 14th three minutes from time to wrap up the points for the Gunners.*

FORM GUIDE
W W W W W W [16 goals scored, 5 conceded]   D D L L L L [5 goals scored, 12 conceded]

ARSENAL 2
Pires 16, Bergkamp 24

BOLTON WANDERERS 1
Campo 41

Substitutes		Jens **LEHMANN**	1	22	Jussi **JAASKELAINEN**		Substitutes
Graham **STACK**	33	**LAUREN**	12	18	Nicky **HUNT**	1	Kevin **POOLE**
▸ Pascal **CYGAN**	18	Kolo **TOURE**	28	5	Bruno **N'GOTTY**	2	Anthony **BARNESS**
◂ (Pires) 88		Sol **CAMPBELL**	23	26	Emerson **THOME**	8	Per **FRANDSEN** ▸
▸ Fredrik **LJUNGBERG**	8	▪ Ashley **COLE**	3	3	Simon **CHARLTON**		(Nolan) 76 ◂
◂ (Gilberto) 69		**GILBERTO**	19	7	Stelios **GIANNAKOPOULOS**	37	Dwight **PEZZAROSSI**
KANU	25	Patrick **VIEIRA**	4	16	Ivan **CAMPO**	32	Ricardo **VAZ TE**
José Antonio **REYES**	9	**EDU**	17	4	Kevin **NOLAN** ▪		
		Robert **PIRES**	7	10	Jay-Jay **OKOCHA**		
		Dennis **BERGKAMP**	10	9	Henrik **PEDERSEN** ▪		
		Thierry **HENRY**	14	14	Kevin **DAVIES**		

MATCH REPORT

Against plucky Bolton, Arsenal equalled the record of 29 unbeaten games at the start of an English top-flight season – set by Leeds United in 1973/1974 and Liverpool in 1987/1988. First the runaway Premiership leaders charmed Highbury with a superlative show of passing,

Another cracker from Robert Pires as his 20-yarder flies on its way into the Bolton net.

movement and finishing on their way to an apparently unassailable two-goal lead. But when the Trotters bounced back unexpectedly into contention with a goal shortly before the interval, the Gunners began to twitch, and as the final whistle sounded they were hanging on nervously.

Gale-force winds had delayed the start for 15 minutes while loose scaffolding outside the stadium was made safe. Bolton then made an early attacking sortie which ended with Nolan slicing a volley wide, but then Arsenal settled into their customary imperious rhythm. Henry led the way, and almost notched a spectacular opener when he swivelled on to a Vieira dispatch before rocking Jaaskelainen's crossbar with a sudden 30-yarder.

Arsène Wenger's side seemed irresistible and so it proved as they fashioned an exquisite goal. The ball was ferried with precision from Edu to Vieira to Pires and back out to the Brazilian on the left. Edu lofted forward to Bergkamp, who cushioned deftly into the path of Pires, enabling the Frenchman to take one elegant stride before curling an unerring 20-yarder into the far corner of Jaaskelainen's net.

The assault continued with Gilberto feeding Henry for a cross-cum-shot which was headed away by Charlton. A Pires corner was almost turned home by Gilberto, and Jaaskelainen smothered a Cole effort at his near post after slick work by Bergkamp and Pires.

All that was merely the prelude to the second breakthrough, masterminded by Pires, whose through-ball enabled Henry to spring the visitors' offside trap and cross for Bergkamp to net emphatically from eight yards.

Not unreasonably, the home fans expected the floodgates to open, but they were stunned into momentary silence when Giannakopoulos delivered from the left, N'Gotty's drive was only half-cleared and Campo pounced to fire high into Arsenal's net from eight yards. Bolton might have levelled before the break when Giannakopoulos' glancing header from Pedersen's cross clipped the bar and the fightback continued in the second half with Edu being forced to rescue Lehmann after the German had misjudged a centre from Hunt. Davies then missed with a free header from another dispatch from the increasingly dangerous Giannakopoulos.

The situation evoked uncomfortable echoes of the Reebok during the previous spring when a Bolton revival had cost the Gunners two points and the initiative in the title race, and now they strove determined to stifle any hint of a repeat. Henry brought a flying save from Jaaskelainen following a Campo miskick, Pires skied from a Gilberto knock-back and it took desperate saving tackles by Charlton and N'Gotty to frustrate Ljungberg and Henry. Despite a late save from a Davies header, Arsenal contained Bolton and controlled play for three more points.

Kolo Toure bursts down the right flank leaving Bolton's Jay-Jay Okocha in his wake.

MARCH

UEFA Champions League, Quarter-Final, first leg
Wednesday 24 March 2004 at Stamford Bridge, 7.45 p.m.
Attendance: 40,778 Referee: Manuel Gonzalez, Spain

FORM GUIDE
L W W D W W [7 goals scored, 3 conceded]   W W W W W W [16 goals scored, 5 conceded]

CHELSEA 1   ARSENAL 1
Gudjohnsen 53   Pires 59

Substitutes						Substitutes	
		Marco **AMBROSIO**	31	1	Jens **LEHMANN**	Substitutes	
Neil **SULLIVAN**	34	William **GALLAS**	13	12	**LAUREN**	Graham **STACK**	33
▸ Mario **MELCHIOT**	15	Marcel **DESAILLY**	6	28	Kolo **TOURE**	Martin **KEOWN**	5
◂ (Gudjohnsen) 86		John **TERRY**	26	23	Sol **CAMPBELL**	Pascal **CYGAN**	18
Robert **HUTH**	29	Wayne **BRIDGE**	18	3	Ashley **COLE**	Gael **CLICHY**	22
GÉRÉMI	14	Scott **PARKER**	19	8	Fredrik **LJUNGBERG**	**GILBERTO** ▸	19
Jesper **GRONKJAER**	30	Claude **MAKELELE**	4	4	Patrick **VIEIRA**	(Bergkamp) 72 ◂	
▸ Joe **COLE**	10	Frank **LAMPARD**	8	17	**EDU**	**KANU**	25
◂ (Parker) 72		Damien **DUFF**	11	7	Robert **PIRES**	José Antonio **REYES** ▸	9
▸ Hernan **CRESPO**	21	Eidur **GUDJOHNSEN**	22	10	Dennis **BERGKAMP**	(Ljungberg) 78 ◂	
◂ (Mutu) 72		Adrian **MUTU**	7	14	Thierry **HENRY**		

MATCH REPORT

Arsenal stretched their unbeaten sequence against Chelsea to an astonishing 17 games and seized the advantage of an away goal as the enthralling first act of this Champions League quarter-final drama finished all square. At one point, after Chelsea had taken the lead, the Gunners were on the rack. But they came from behind to frustrate their London neighbours for the third time this season, the equaliser coming from the in-form Robert Pires, his fifth strike in six games.

Arsenal were the more coherent side during the initial exchanges, dominating possession with their precise and patient approach play. Lauren fashioned an early opening for Bergkamp, playing his first away match in European competition for more than a year, but Ambrosio dived to save, then the Dutchman delivered a raking cross from the left only for the unmarked Campbell to nudge wide with a free header from six yards.

Although Chelsea had begun cautiously, they gradually emerged from their shell. Toure halted a dangerous Duff run with a crisp tackle, Makelele and Gudjohnsen set up Parker but the midfielder mishit his drive, then Parker reached the byline only for the long arm of Lehmann to clutch his attempted cross.

At the other end Ambrosio spilled a fizzing drive from Bergkamp, but the Blues continued to buzz menacingly either side of the interval and they went

The French connection. Thierry Henry gets the better of his compatriot William Gallas.

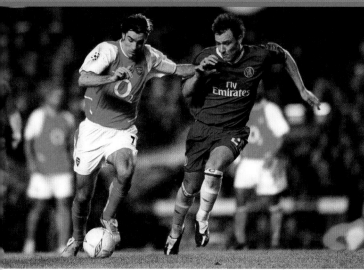

It's head to head as Robert Pires goes up against Chelsea defender John Terry.

Now the contest became more even, with Henry threatening to unhinge the hosts' rearguard, while Duff and Gudjohnsen posed a lively threat to the visitors. But just as Chelsea were gathering themselves for a late assault, they were reduced to ten men by the dismissal of Desailly for a second bookable offence, and thereafter opted mainly for safety.

perilously close to snatching the lead when a Lampard 25-yarder was deflected inches wide by Campbell. For Arsenal it proved to be the briefest of reprieves. Lampard launched a long ball forward, Lehmann rushed from his line to clear but his kick hit the charging Gudjohnsen, who calmly turned the rebound into the net from the left edge of the area.

Now the Gunners were rocking and Chelsea had a succession of opportunities to press home their advantage. Campbell cleared a Duff cross, Parker sent Gudjohnsen into the box but the Icelander's short centre found Toure rather than one of three waiting attackers, then Lehmann parried both a Lampard drive and the close-range follow-up from Duff.

Lesser teams might have wilted, but the Gunners produced the perfect response in the form of an equaliser which was magnificent in both construction and execution. Edu found Vieira, who ferried the ball left to the advancing Cole; Lampard and Terry were slow to react to the full-back's floated cross and Pires rose majestically to head past Ambrosio from 12 yards.

Even so, either Henry or Crespo could have plundered late glory for their respective sides, but neither camp was dismayed by the final whistle.

Freddie Ljungberg tussles with Chelsea captain Marcel Desailly.

FORM GUIDE
W W W W W D [14 goals scored, 4 conceded]

L D W D L W [9 goals scored, 9 conceded]

ARSENAL 1
Henry 49

MANCHESTER UNITED 1
Saha 86

Substitutes		Jens **LEHMANN**	1	13	Roy **CARROLL**		Substitutes
Graham **STACK**	33	**LAUREN**	12	2	Gary **NEVILLE**	14	Tim **HOWARD**
▶ Pascal **CYGAN**	18	Kolo **TOURE**	28	6	Wesley **BROWN**	3	Phil **NEVILLE**
◀ (Ljungberg) 82		Sol **CAMPBELL**	23	27	Mikael **SILVESTRE**	8	Nicky **BUTT**
▶ **GILBERTO**	19	▦ Gael **CLICHY**	22	22	John **O'SHEA**	20	Ole **GUNNAR**
◀ (Reyes) 77		Fredrik **LJUNGBERG**	8	24	Darren **FLETCHER**		**SOLSKJAER** ▶
▶ Dennis **BERGKAMP**	10	Patrick **VIEIRA**	4	10	Eric **DJEMBA-DJEMBA**		(Fletcher) 72 ◀
◀ (Pires) 85		**EDU**	17	16	Roy **KEANE**	9	Louis **SAHA** ▶
KANU	25	Robert **PIRES**	7	11	Ryan **GIGGS**		(Djemba-Djemba) 59 ◀
		José Antonio **REYES**	9	18	Paul **SCHOLES** ▦		
		Thierry **HENRY**	14	10	Ruud **VAN NISTELROOY**		

MATCH REPORT

Arsenal set a new 30-game record for an unbeaten start to an English season and ensured that the champions remained 12 points adrift of Arsène Wenger's side after a compelling, high-octane contest. A special goal, even by the high standards of Thierry Henry, appeared likely to have secured victory, but Manchester United snatched a late equaliser to preserve their pride.

In view of the high stakes, the game got off to a fabulously open start, with Neville almost setting up Scholes in the opening minute, then two Keane scorchers were blocked. The Gunners responded in kind and twice Ljungberg was thwarted at the last, by a Brown tackle and Carroll's parry at his near post. The Irish goalkeeper also made a brave stop at the feet of Reyes. The action see-sawed to the other end, where Djemba-Djemba dinked over Campbell before

testing Lehmann with a 20-yard volley, after which Arsenal enjoyed a period of marked superiority.

Vieira delivered a cute pass to Reyes, but Carroll saved with his legs; a hammer-blow from Henry was deflected wide by Djemba-Djemba, and Carroll

Thierry Henry, Robert Pires and Lauren celebrate after the number 14 had given the Gunners the lead with a superb strike.

The exciting José Antonio Reyes forces his way between United defenders Silvestre and Gary Neville.

clutched a curling free-kick from Henry to his midriff. The tempo quickened as Giggs set up a clear shooting chance for Scholes, who miskicked from 12 yards, then Pires twice went close for Arsenal and Henry raced on to a Ljungberg delivery only to lose control of the ball as he sidestepped Carroll.

All that a tremendous first half lacked was a goal. When it materialized, shortly after half-time, it was memorable. When Henry exchanged passes with Reyes some 30 yards out there appeared no immediate danger to United's goal, but the Frenchman unleashed a sudden, swerving drive which ripped into the net above Carroll's unavailing plunge.

It was a strike fit to decide any contest and most teams might have been flattened by it. But the visitors responded defiantly and when Campbell appeared to clip Giggs in the box, Arsenal hearts were in mouths until the referee waved away United's concerted appeals for a penalty.

Seeing their slim championship hopes receding even further, Sir Alex Ferguson's side began to mount pressure and Lehmann held a Keane flick from a Fletcher cross. The Gunners remained potent on the break, though, and Carroll made a brilliant close-range block from Reyes and Ljungberg scuffed his shot after being sent in by Pires.

Still United refused to yield and their persistence paid off when Scholes found Solskjaer on the right and his low cross eluded both van Nistelrooy and Toure but was converted by Saha at the far post.

Even then, either side might have won, with the unmarked van Nistelrooy heading straight at Lehmann from a Giggs delivery, and Henry nodding wide of an empty net after Carroll had beaten out a point-blank effort from Lauren.

MARCH 2004

Arsenal.com PLAYER OF THE MONTH

Thierry HENRY

"People have been trying to say that we are a one-man or two-man team, but I think the others are doing their jobs, too. We are all fighting for each other. For example, when we drew at Chelsea in the Champions League, I felt I was closely marked, but that didn't stop Robert Pires from heading a terrific goal. Someone is always there at the right time. That day it was Robert, who is always in the box; two weeks ago it was Dennis Bergkamp and Edu; before that it was me, before that José Reyes, before that someone else. We are a team."

THIERRY HENRY

"Both of our goals against Southampton came from Thierry, who is so exceptional. His first took him to 100 in the Premiership, which is a superb achievement, especially as he has scored them in such a short space of time. When he came to us it took him a few games before the goals started going in – and since then they just haven't stopped. He was always going to be a success because he works so hard and has so much love for football."

ARSÈNE WENGER

ARSENAL DIARY

Friday 5 March
- Arsenal directors attend a symbolic signing of the final documents regarding the Club's new stadium at Ashburton Grove.

Wednesday 10 March
- Arsenal announce that Martin Keown has been granted a testimonial at season's end.

Friday 12 March
- Arsenal draw London neighbours Chelsea in the quarter-finals of the Champions League.

Saturday 20 March
- Dennis Bergkamp and Edu are the joint recipients of the latest Barclaycard Premiership Player of the Month award.

THE WIDER WORLD

Thursday 4 March
- Southampton appoint Paul Sturrock as their manager.

Tuesday 9 March
- Manchester United crash out of the Champions League, thanks to a late goal by Porto; Chelsea see off Stuttgart to reach the quarter-finals.

Friday 19 March
- Leeds United announce their £22m takeover by a local consortium.

Sunday 29 March
- The FA announce that Sven-Goran Eriksson has contracted to be England manager until 2008.

FA CARLING PREMIERSHIP

28 March 2004

		HOME					AWAY					
	P	W	D	L	F	A	W	D	L	F	A	Pts
ARSENAL	29	12	2	0	28	10	10	5	0	29	9	73
Chelsea	30	10	2	3	29	13	11	2	2	28	11	67
Manchester United	29	10	3	2	33	13	9	1	4	22	16	61
Liverpool	29	8	2	4	22	13	4	7	4	20	18	45
Newcastle United	29	9	3	3	26	10	2	9	3	15	20	45
Birmingham City	30	8	4	4	23	17	4	5	5	14	19	45
Aston Villa	30	7	4	3	19	14	5	3	8	19	21	43
Charlton Athletic	30	6	3	6	23	24	6	4	5	18	15	43
Fulham	30	8	3	4	24	16	3	4	8	18	24	40
Southampton	30	8	4	4	19	11	2	5	7	11	17	39
Middlesbrough	30	5	4	6	17	19	5	4	6	18	20	38
Tottenham Hotspur	30	8	2	5	29	23	3	2	10	11	24	37
Everton	30	7	5	4	23	16	1	5	8	13	25	34
Bolton Wanderers	29	3	7	4	15	16	5	3	7	18	30	34
Manchester City	30	3	8	4	21	17	4	2	9	20	25	31
Blackburn Rovers	30	3	3	9	21	28	5	4	6	21	20	31
Portsmouth	30	7	2	5	24	15	1	4	11	8	30	30
Leicester City	29	2	8	5	15	24	3	4	7	24	28	27
Leeds United	30	4	5	6	17	23	2	2	11	12	37	25
Wolverhampton Wanderers	30	5	5	4	17	26	0	4	12	9	36	24

APRIL

FA Cup Semi-Final
Saturday 3 April 2004 at Villa Park, 12 noon
Attendance: 39,939 Referee: Graham Barber

FORM GUIDE
W W W W D D [13 goals scored, 4 conceded]   D W D L W D [9 goals scored, 8 conceded]

ARSENAL 0   MANCHESTER UNITED 1

Scholes 32

Substitutes						Substitutes	
		Jens **LEHMANN**	1	13	Roy **CARROLL**	Substitutes	
Graham **STACK**	33	▪ **LAUREN**	12	2	Gary **NEVILLE**		Tim **HOWARD**	14
Martin **KEOWN**	5	▪ Kolo **TOURE**	28	6	Wesley **BROWN**	3	Phil **NEVILLE** ▸
▸ **KANU**	25	Sol **CAMPBELL**	23	27	Mikael **SILVESTRE**		(Solskjaer) 75 ◂
◂ (Edu) 76		Gael **CLICHY**	22	22	John **O'SHEA**	19	Eric **DJEMBA-DJEMBA**
▸ José Antonio **REYES**	9	Fredrik **LJUNGBERG**	8	7	Cristiano **RONALDO**	8	Nicky **BUTT**
◂ (Aliadiere) 57		Patrick **VIEIRA**	4	16	Roy **KEANE**	12	David **BELLION** ▸
▸ Thierry **HENRY**	14	**EDU**	17	24	Darren **FLETCHER**		(Ronaldo) 84 ◂
◂ (Pires) 58		▪ Robert **PIRES**	7	18	Paul **SCHOLES** ▪		
		Dennis **BERGKAMP**	10	11	Ryan **GIGGS**		
		Jeremie **ALIADIERE**	30	20	Ole Gunnar **SOLSKJAER**		

MATCH REPORT

In a typically tight and dramatic FA Cup semi-final encounter the Gunners twice struck Manchester United's woodwork, dominated possession for lengthy periods, but ultimately paid the price for not converting their scoring chances and fell to a solitary goal by Paul Scholes.

Though Arsène Wenger opted to leave Thierry Henry on the bench ahead of a punishing schedule of games, Arsenal made a blistering start and United were lucky to survive their opening salvoes. In the third minute Edu nodded forward to Bergkamp, whose first shot was blocked by Carroll and his follow-up was headed off the line by the diving Brown. When the resultant corner was cleared to Edu, the Brazilian chipped against the crossbar from 20 yards and it seemed certain that Toure would nod the rebound into the empty net, but Carroll materialised to palm the header away.

Having been reprieved three times in the space of a minute, United responded by mounting a wave of retaliatory attacks, mostly through the mercurial Ronaldo. Lehmann blocked Solskjaer on the byline, Giggs weaved past several challenges before the German caught his shot, and a free-kick from

In complete control: Sol Campbell keeps the ball away from the lunging Ole Gunnar Solskjaer.

Scholes was scrambled clear. Arsenal relieved the pressure through a storming run by Campbell, who set up Bergkamp to flight a delivery from the right, which was headed over from six yards by the untended Pires.

That was to prove the Gunners' best chance of the contest and, after being denied a penalty following a Silvestre handball, soon they were rueing the miss as United snatched the lead. Gary Neville dispatched an astute through-pass to Giggs, who rolled the ball across the box for Scholes to rifle past Lehmann from 15 yards.

Arsenal attempted to hit back quickly but the Manchester United held firm and it wasn't until first-half stoppage time that a breakthrough looked likely. Pires floated a free-kick into the area and Keane, under heavy pressure from Vieira, clipped his own upright with a miscued clearance.

Having escaped once more, it was United who fashioned the first chance of the second period, but after Fletcher's volley was smothered, the Gunners pinned their opponents back, with the arrival of substitutes Reyes and Henry stretching Sir Alex Ferguson's team to the limit. Reyes surged menacingly through the middle only to be crowded out, then the Spaniard found Edu with a clever flick only for the Brazilian to scoop wide.

Arsenal continued to probe the United defence, in which Brown was outstanding, but another volley from Henry flashed beyond a post and a scorching Reyes drive didn't trouble Carroll.

Inevitably, the Gunners left themselves increasingly vulnerable to the counter and United might have doubled their lead in the 90th minute when Giggs' cross snaked narrowly beyond Bellion, but still the cup holders refused to give in. In added time a Ljungberg cross caused mayhem, then Henry fired high before Arsenal finally submitted to their first FA Cup defeat since May 2001.

United keeper Roy Carroll palms Toure's header off the line to prevent the Gunners taking an early lead.

APRIL

UEFA Champions League, Quarter-Final, second leg
Tuesday 6 April 2004 at Highbury, 7.45 p.m.
Attendance: 35,486 Referee: Markus Merk, Germany

FORM GUIDE
W W W D D L [8 goals scored, 4 conceded]   D W W D W W [11 goals scored, 4 conceded]

ARSENAL 1   CHELSEA 2
Reyes 45   Lampard 51, Bridge 87

Substitutes						Substitutes	
Graham STACK	33	Jens LEHMANN	1	31	Marco AMBROSIO		
Martin KEOWN	5	■ LAUREN	12	15	Mario MELCHIOT	Neil SULLIVAN	34
Gael CLICHY	22	Kolo TOURE	28	13	William GALLAS ■	Robert HUTH	29
GILBERTO	19	Sol CAMPBELL	23	26	John TERRY	GÉRÉMI	14
KANU	25	Ashley COLE	3	18	Wayne BRIDGE	Joe COLE ▶ ■	10
Sylvain WILTORD	11	Fredrik LJUNGBERG	8	19	Scott PARKER	(Duff) 82 ◀	
▶ Dennis BERGKAMP	10	Patrick VIEIRA	4	4	Claude MAKELELE	Jesper GRONKJAER ▶	30
◀ (Henry) 81		EDU	17	8	Frank LAMPARD	(Parker) 46 ◀	
		Robert PIRES	7	11	Damien DUFF	Adrian MUTU	7
		José Antonio REYES	9	22	Eidur GUDJOHNSEN	Hernan CRESPO ▶	21
		Thierry HENRY	14	9	Jimmy-Floyd	(Hasselbaink) 82 ◀	
					HASSELBAINK ■		

MATCH REPORT

Arsenal failed to reach the semi-finals of the Champions League as Chelsea came from behind to snatch victory in the dying minutes and smash their 17-match hoodoo against the Gunners. Only three days after elimination from the FA Cup, it was a savage blow for Arsène Wenger's men to take, especially as they had been the better team in the first half of a ceaselessly frenetic contest. After Reyes had put the hosts in front on the stroke of half-time, Frank Lampard equalised early in the

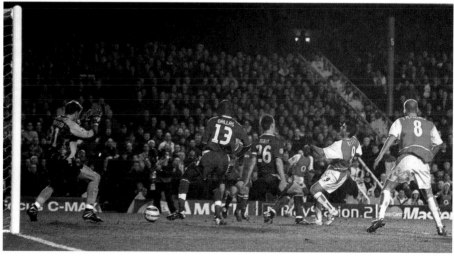

José Antonio Reyes latches onto a deflection to lash Arsenal into the lead just on half-time.

second period and Bridge claimed the spoils as extra-time beckoned.

Initial indications had been positive for the Gunners, with the excellent Edu fizzing a low drive narrowly wide, then sending in Henry to swerve past Terry before firing over Ambrosio's crossbar. Soon Ljungberg and Reyes combined sweetly to set up an even more inviting chance for Henry, but the Frenchman side-footed the wrong side of an upright.

Little had been seen of Chelsea as an attacking force to that point, but a Gudjohnsen step-over allowed Duff to race past Campbell before shaving Lehmann's near post with a bobbling shot. In the main, though, the Blues were reduced to speculative efforts as Arsenal created a succession of openings, mostly from the left flank; Henry saw several efforts blocked, then Pires bulged the side-netting with a flashing header from a Cole cross.

Finally the Gunners achieved their deserved breakthrough when Lauren's delivery from the right was nodded across goal by Henry, the ball deflected off Ljungberg and Reyes netted from six yards.

After the interval Chelsea, who had replaced midfielder Parker with right-winger Gronkjaer, looked far more potent and quickly plundered an equaliser. A Duff cross was cleared by Edu to Makelele, whose swirling 30-yarder was pushed out by Lehmann, allowing Lampard to sweep home from eight yards.

Arsenal might have regained the advantage almost immediately but a pinball sequence in the visitors' box ended with Henry firing off-target. The Blues then almost nosed ahead when a Lampard snapshot whistled fractionally off-target. The Gunners hit back spiritedly with Reyes forcing Ambrosio to parry and Toure demanding a tip-over from the Italian with an explosive effort from nearly 40 yards.

But now Chelsea began to grow ominously in authority, with Lampard and Gudjohnsen going close, then Ashley Cole clearing off his line from the Icelandic international. Finally the pressure paid off when Gronkjaer played a crossfield ball to Bridge, who strode forward to execute a neat one-two interchange with Gudjohnsen before slotting neatly past the exposed Lehmann from 12 yards.

Thanks to the away-goals ruling, that left Arsenal needing two strikes in three minutes, and they almost managed one when Toure was presented with a free header from a Pires dispatch, only to nod tamely into the arms of Ambrosio. It was a disappointing night for the Gunners and signalled the end of another exciting European adventure.

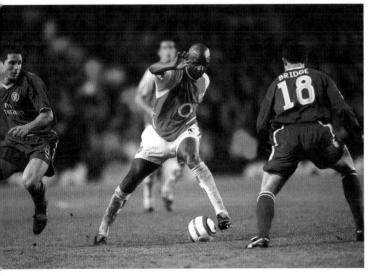

Patrick Vieira uses clever footwork to keep the ball from Chelsea's Frank Lampard and Wayne Bridge.

FORM GUIDE

W W D D L L [7 goals scored, 6 conceded]　　　　L W W L D W [9 goals scored, 4 conceded]

ARSENAL 4　　LIVERPOOL 2

Henry 31, 50, 78, Pires 49　　Hyypia 5, Owen 42

Substitutes				Substitutes	
Rami SHAABAN	24	Jens LEHMANN	1	1 Jerzy DUDEK	
▸ Martin KEOWN	5	LAUREN	12	23 Jamie CARRAGHER	29 Patrice LUZI
◂ (Keown) 90		Kolo TOURE	28	4 Sami HYYPIA	2 Stephane HENCHOZ
Gael CLICHY	22	Sol CAMPBELL	23	25 Igor BISCAN	13 Danny MURPHY ▸
▸ EDU	17	Ashley COLE	3	18 John-Arne RIISE	(Diouf) 85 ◂
◂ (Pires) 72		Fredrik LJUNGBERG	8	9 El-Hadji DIOUF	28 Bruno CHEYROU
José Antonio REYES	9	GILBERTO	19	16 Dietmar HAMANN	5 Milan BAROS ▸
		Patrick VIEIRA	4	17 Steven GERRARD	(Heskey) 66 ◂
		Robert PIRES	7	7 Harry KEWELL	
		Dennis BERGKAMP	10	8 Emile HESKEY	
		Thierry HENRY	14	10 Michael OWEN	

MATCH REPORT

Digging deep into apparently bottomless reserves of character, Arsenal twice bounced back from behind to overwhelm Liverpool and stretch their Premiership lead over Chelsea to seven points. The highlight was one of the goals of the season by hat-trick man Thierry Henry, who shrugged off a back injury to spearhead the Gunners' attack.

Yet it was fourth-placed Liverpool, themselves desperate for points to cement their Champions League place, who started more confidently and seized an early lead. The Gunners rearguard remained rooted as Kewell delivered a deep corner to Gerrard, who directed the ball back across goal for the diving Hyypia to glance neatly beyond Lehmann.

With the visitors prodigiously industrious in midfield, Arsène Wenger's side looked vulnerable, and when Owen raced on to a raking dispatch from Riise, it took a perfectly timed last-ditch challenge by Campbell to stop him. Next Kewell went close to doubling the Merseysiders' advantage but his snap-volley was deflected narrowly wide, then the unmarked Hyypia nodded marginally high from the resultant corner.

However, it wasn't all one-way traffic, and Dudek pulled off a sharp save to thwart Ljungberg from an acute angle, but then it was Liverpool pressing forward again, with Owen shooting over Lehmann's goal. The Gunners needed to reverse the flow and they did so with style when Pires freed Henry to advance on Dudek and fire under the keeper's body for the equaliser.

A classic Arsenal one-two as first Pires strokes the ball past Dudek for the equaliser…

... and 70 seconds later Thierry Henry scores one of the goals of the season to give the Gunners the lead.

Still Gérard Houllier's men remained defiant and they regained the ascendancy shortly before the break when Gerrard stepped away from Vieira and found Owen, who gave Campbell the slip before converting the chance with icy composure.

At this point, lesser teams might have melted away, but Arsenal responded to adversity as they had done throughout the season and within five minutes of the re-start they had turned a pulsating contest on its head. First Henry split the Liverpool defence with a clever delivery to Ljungberg, whose deft lay-off sent in Pires to stroke past Dudek from close range. Then, just 70 seconds later, Henry took possession near the centre circle, slalomed past the bewildered Hamann and Carragher, and slotted the ball wide of the hopelessly exposed keeper. It was an individual effort of stunning quality, fit

to win any game. The Highbury faithful, who had been subjected to an afternoon of unabated tension, exploded in a thunderous mixture of glee and relief. Even the normally cool Arsène Wenger cut loose to celebrate with joyous abandon.

Still, though, with 40 minutes remaining there was work to be done, and several thrusts by Kewell and Owen had the home fans on tenterhooks. Henry spurned a gilded opportunity to make the game safe when he missed the target with a free header, but he finally settled matters when he rounded off a Bergkamp-inspired move, albeit with a fortunate rebound off Dudek.

That bit of luck was the least the French master deserved for yet another inspirational performance.

Sol Campbell congratulates the scorers on their contribution to Arsenal's victory.

127

APRIL

FA Barclaycard Premiership
Sunday 11 April 2004 at St James' Park, 4.05 p.m.
Attendance: 52,141 Referee: Paul Durkin

FORM GUIDE

L W W L W D [11 goals scored, 6 conceded] W D D L L W [9 goals scored, 8 conceded]

NEWCASTLE UNITED 0   ARSENAL 0

Substitutes					Substitutes
Steve **HARPER** 12	Shay **GIVEN**	1	1	Jens **LEHMANN**	
Titus **BRAMBLE** 19	Aaron **HUGHES**	18	12	**LAUREN**	24 Rami **SHAABAN**
▸ Lee **BOWYER** 29	Andy **O'BRIEN**	5	28	Kolo **TOURE**	5 Martin **KEOWN**
◂ (Ambrose) 79	Jonathan **WOODGATE**	27	23	Sol **CAMPBELL**	22 Gael **CLICHY** ▸
▸ Hugo **VIANA** 45	Olivier **BERNARD**	35	3	Ashley **COLE**	(Cole) 90 ◂
◂ (Robert) 79	Darren **AMBROSE**	17	11	Sylvain **WILTORD**	7 Robert **PIRES** ▸
Shola **AMEOBI** 23	Jermaine **JENAS**	9	19	**GILBERTO**	(Wiltord) 79 ◂
	Gary **SPEED**	11	4	Patrick **VIEIRA** ▪	10 Dennis **BERGKAMP** ▸
	Lauren **ROBERT**	32	17	**EDU**	(Reyes) 79 ◂
	Craig **BELLAMY**	10	9	José Antonio **REYES**	
	Alan **SHEARER**	9	14	Thierry **HENRY**	

MATCH REPORT

Arsenal extended their unbeaten sequence in this season's Premiership campaign to 32 games and ended Newcastle's run of eight straight home wins. Arsène Wenger's men were happy enough as they returned south, having finished a hectic spell of four matches in nine days against top-quality opposition, and boasting a seven-point lead in the championship race with six games remaining.

It was the hard-working Magpies who had made the more impressive start, with Speed freeing Bellamy to charge into Arsenal's box, only for the Welshman's tame shot to be gathered easily by Lehmann. Soon, the big German was pressed into more meaningful action as Shearer crossed from the right and Bellamy delivered a clever flick from eight

yards which took a slight deflection off Toure and appeared to be creeping inside a post. Lehmann was equal to the challenge, however, changing direction to sprawl full-length and pull off a magnificent save.

Thereafter the contest became scrappy, with both sides struggling to come to terms with an uneven surface, but gradually the Gunners began

Sol Campbell was at his commanding best at St James' Park to deal with Newcastle's twin striking threat of Craig Bellamy and Alan Shearer.

On his first start since December Sylvain Wiltord shows his trickery on the ball to get past Aaron Hughes.

to exert steady pressure. Henry was off-target with a long-range speculator, and then Reyes juggled brilliantly before crossing for Edu, who was foiled in front of the net only by a superb challenge by Bernard. A minute later the Brazilian returned the compliment to Reyes, only for the Spaniard to fire wide, and a surge by Henry ended with a disappointing shot.

But the most inviting opportunity of the first-half fell to Wiltord when he intercepted a back-pass by Jenas, then scuffed his shot a foot wide of an upright with Given helpless. It was a frustrating moment for the ring-rusty Frenchman, who was making his first start since December.

Newcastle opened the second period with intent, but several free-kicks came to nothing. Bellamy couldn't control a deft flick by Shearer, and Bernard drove wastefully into the side-netting.

Once again, though, it was the visitors who emerged as the more convincing unit as the half wore on, and Given had to plunge courageously at the feet of Reyes following an exhilarating left-flank charge by Vieira. A breakthrough appeared inevitable when Henry sprung United's offside trap, but after swerving wide of Given, he side-footed against the outside of the near post from an acute angle.

Henry continued to threaten and after almost setting up Vieira, then having a shot blocked, he curled a delightful cross to Reyes, who had only Given to beat from five yards but nodded against the keeper's legs. Still, despite his recent back injury and his serial exertions, Henry was not exhausted. He climaxed one spellbinding dash with a searing shot which just cleared the crossbar.

In the end, both teams were reasonably happy with a point from the game, with Arsenal closing in on the title and Newcastle seeking Champions League qualification.

ARSENAL 5   LEEDS UNITED 0
Pires 6, Henry 27, 32 pen, 49, 67

Substitutes					Substitutes
Graham **STACK**	33	Jens **LEHMANN**	1	1 Paul **ROBINSON**	Scott **CARSON** 40
Martin **KEOWN**	5	**LAUREN**	12	2 Gary **KELLY**	Matthew **KILGALLON** 36
▸ **EDU**	17	Kolo **TOURE**	28	15 Stephen **CALDWELL**	Nick **BARMBY** ▸ 7
◂ (Gilberto) 69		Sol **CAMPBELL**	23	22 Michael **DUBERRY**	(Radebe) 72 ◂
▸ Ray **PARLOUR**	15	Gael **CLICHY**	22	3 Ian **HARTE**	Aaron **LENNON** 25
◂ (Pires) 73		Sylvain **WILTORD**	11	11 Jermaine **PENNANT**	Simon **JOHNSON** ▸ 39
▸ José Antonio **REYES**	9	**GILBERTO**	19	5 Lucas **RADEBE**	(Viduka) 84 ◂
◂ (Bergkamp) 73		Patrick **VIEIRA**	4	21 Dominic **MATTEO**	
		Robert **PIRES**	7	38 James **MILNER**	
		Dennis **BERGKAMP**	10	17 Alan **SMITH**	
		Thierry **HENRY**	14	9 Mark **VIDUKA**	

MATCH REPORT

An awesome four-goal salvo from the incomparable Thierry Henry swept Arsenal to the brink of the Championship and left Leeds teetering precariously close to relegation. The Yorkshiremen were the last team to beat the Gunners in the Premiership way back in May 2003, but this time they were demolished comprehensively as the French maestro extended his phenomenal tally for the club to 150 strikes in 251 games.

Thierry Henry latches on to Gilberto's pass to put Arsenal two up.

The danger signals for Eddie Gray's men began flashing in the fourth minute when Pires wriggled to the byline and pulled back a low cross to Wiltord who lashed wide from six yards. But there was no lack of precision two minutes later when Wiltord laid off neatly to Bergkamp, whose instant through-ball into the path of Pires was converted with a superlative trademark curler from 18 yards. It was Pires' 18th senior goal of the campaign, a fabulous achievement for a midfielder.

A lesser side than Leeds might have lay down and died, but instead they fought back spiritedly, with the combative Smith prominent in a succession of attacks. He was wildly off target with one volley from 20 yards, but then he charged past two challenges and was deep inside the Arsenal box when he was halted by Campbell. Thus encouraged, Viduka brought a save from Lehmann, then delivered a teasing cross which Clichy sliced over his own crossbar.

But the visitors' resurgence was halted in emphatic fashion when Gilberto's astute pass enabled Henry to unhinge United's offside trap before racing on to slide the ball past Robinson.

An exquisite sidefoot shot gives Henry the fifth hat-trick of his Arsenal career.

Next Bergkamp raced on to a Wiltord flick and attempted to slip past Duberry, who hand balled in the box; Henry netted from the spot with an impudent chip into the middle of goal and suddenly the contest was effectively over.

As Leeds had enjoyed more possession and managed more shots than the rampant Gunners at this point, the score-line seemed a trifle harsh, but still United battled gamely, though Harte's attempt to signal defiance with a long-distance free-kick ended in a sorry mishit.

After the interval, Arsenal's dominance became total and they moved even further ahead with an example of counter-attacking at its most devastating.

Gilberto, who performed magnificently throughout, took possession on the edge of his own area, then surged forward before releasing Henry who slotted the ball unerringly past the exposed Robinson, thus completing the fifth hat-trick of his Arsenal career.

Now Highbury was rocking, the ecstatic supporters roaring for more, and Pires almost provided it when he sent Wiltord scampering goalwards, only for a 15-yard curler to finish fractionally the wrong side of a post. The Gunners remained irresistible though and Henry almost brought the house down when he took a Pires lay-off in his stride, burst past four Leeds defenders and, even as he was fouled from behind, side-footed immaculately beyond Robinson for his fourth, and Arsenal's fifth, goal of an unforgettable night.

There might have been even more as Reyes and Henry went close, but Arsenal were content with victory and a ten-point lead at the Premiership summit.

Henry's smile says it all – four goals, the match ball and the man of the match trophy.

APRIL

FA Barclaycard Premiership
Sunday 25 April at White Hart Lane, 4.05 p.m.
Attendance: 36,097 Referee: Mark Halsey

FORM GUIDE
L L L L D L [2 goals scored, 11 conceded]   D L L W D W [11 goals scored, 6 conceded]

TOTTENHAM HOTSPUR 2

Redknapp 62, Keane pen 90

ARSENAL 2

Vieira 3, Pires 35

Substitutes					Substitutes
	Kasey **KELLER**	13	1	Jens **LEHMANN** ▨	
Lars **HIRSCHFIELD** 33	Stephen **KELLY**	34	12	**LAUREN**	33 Graham **STACK**
▸ Goran **BUNJEVCEVIC** 5	Anthony **GARDNER**	30	28	Kolo **TOURE**	5 Martin **KEOWN**
◂ (Taricco) 90	Ledley **KING**	26	23	Sol **CAMPBELL**	22 Gael **CLICHY**
▸ Gustavo **POYET** 14	Mauricio **TARICCO**	3	3	Ashley **COLE**	17 **EDU** ▸
◂ (Kelly) 79	Simon **DAVIES**	29	15	Ray **PARLOUR**	(Parlour) 67 ◂
Rohan **RICKETTS** 27	Michael **BROWN**	6	19	**GILBERTO**	9 José Antonio **REYES** ▸
▸ Jermain **DEFOE** 18	▨ Jamie **REDKNAPP**	15	4	Patrick **VIEIRA**	(Bergkamp) 80 ◂
◂ (Jackson) 46	Johnnie **JACKSON**	32	7	Robert **PIRES**	
	▨ Robbie **KEANE**	10	10	Dennis **BERGKAMP**	
	Frederic **KANOUTE**	9	14	Thierry **HENRY**	

| MATCH REPORT

The Gunners won the Premiership title in the White Hart Lane sunshine, clinching their crown without losing a match and enshrining Arsène Wenger as the first Arsenal manager to win three Championships. Tottenham, the old enemy, made a gallant fight of it in the end, and denied their ebullient visitors victory with a dramatic late recovery from two goals down.

The Gunners dominated the first-half with a typically masterful exhibition of attacking fluency that yielded two sumptuous goals. The opening strike encapsulated the characteristic counter-attacking brilliance of a side which led the table since early January. Spurs won a corner which was taken by Jackson, and misheaded by Gardner to the feet of Henry. The Frenchman seized on the gift, and carried the ball for 50 yards before dispatching a clever pass to release Bergkamp on the left flank. Without breaking his stride, the Dutchman curled a perfect low cross behind the Spurs defence and Vieira climaxed a lung-bursting 100-yard sprint to prod home with an outstretched boot from six yards.

Arsenal sought to build on their early advantage, with Bergkamp looking particularly dangerous, but

gradually Spurs established a foothold in the contest and Taricco almost produced a shock equaliser when he exchanged passes with Keane before catching Lehmann off his line with a 30-yard curler which landed on the top of the net.

Patrick Vieira celebrates after his lung-bursting run *and shot gave the Gunners a third-minute lead.*

Kanoute threatened on a couple of occasions, but then the Gunners re-established authority with a move which flowed from Pires to Bergkamp to Vieira and back to Pires, who sidefooted his 19th goal of the season from the corner of the six-yard box.

Tottenham, still needing points to be mathematically safe from relegation, responded with a Kanoute effort which was gathered by Lehmann and Davies volleyed fractionally high, but it was the Gunners who finished the half in clear control, with both Bergkamp and Henry going close.

Now it's two as Ashley Cole prepares to celebrate with goalscorer Robert Pires, Patrick Vieira and Thierry Henry.

Understandably the champions-elect eased off a little in the second period, but still Henry carried the most potent threat of any man on the field and he drew a sharp diving save from Keller with a wickedly bouncing drive. However, Spurs hit back out of the blue when Defoe broke down the left, Brown ferried the ball to Redknapp and the Spurs captain rifled home unstoppably from 25 yards.

Henry might have restored the two-goal cushion when sent in by Pires, but he poked wide from 12 yards, then Pires hit the bar following a blunder by Gardner.

Meanwhile both Redknapp and Defoe prompted deft tip-overs from Lehmann with rasping free-kicks, but just when it seemed the points were secure, Keane and Lehmann became entangled as they vied to reach a Brown corner. The upshot was a booking for both men and a penalty for Spurs, which was dispatched unerringly by Keane. But not even that could take the gloss off Arsenal's glorious day. With the title finally in the bag, the Gunners partied joyfully on the pitch, led by skipper Patrick Vieira, fittingly as prominent in the celebration as he had been throughout the whole momentous campaign.

Arsène Wenger smiles with relief and pride as the Gunners celebrate winning the Premiership title.

APRIL 2004

Arsenal.com PLAYER OF THE MONTH

Thierry HENRY

❝ It was important for our fans to win the title at White Hart Lane. That made it special for them. So many times this season people have talked about the way we play for each other. They have forgotten about the way we fight for each other, too, and we did that against Tottenham. You can't win a title just because you play fancy football. ❞

THIERRY HENRY

❝ No one could deserve the PFA Player of the Year award more than Thierry Henry. I'm probably a bit biased, but I think he's been unbelievable for us this season. He has scored so many great goals. Our success has been a team effort but we owe this title to Thierry as well. ❞

ASHLEY COLE

ARSENAL DIARY

Tuesday 13 April
- Uncapped Edu is called into the Brazil squad for their forthcoming friendly with Hungary.

Thursday 15 April
- Thierry Henry and Patrick Vieira are among six nominees to become PFA Footballer of the Year; Kolo Toure is nominated in the 'Young Player' category.

Friday 16 April
- Ray Parlour returns to first-team contention after nearly two months out with injury.
- Former Gunner Paul Merson takes temporary charge of Walsall following the sacking of manager Colin Lee.

Sunday 25 April
- Thierry Henry is voted PFA Footballer of the Year on the day Arsenal regain the Premiership crown.

Wednesday 28 April
- Arsenal sign the Dutch forward Robin van Persie from Feyenoord.

THE WIDER WORLD

Tuesday 6 April
- Monaco fight back from 5-2 down to knock Real Madrid out of the Champions League.

Wednesday 7 April
- Deportivo La Coruña recover from 4-1 first-leg deficit to defeat European champions AC Milan 5-4 on aggregate. Porto beat Lyon in the other quarter-final.

Tuesday 13 April
- Roy Keane declares his availability for an international comeback with the Republic of Ireland.

Thursday 15 April
- Referees reveal there will be a clampdown on diving in 2004/2005.

Sunday 18 April
- Diego Maradona is rushed to hospital in Buenos Aires with breathing difficulties.

Wednesday 21 April
- Ron Atkinson resigns as an ITV commentator after an unguarded remark about Chelsea's Marcel Desailly.

FA CARLING PREMIERSHIP

26 April 2004

		HOME					AWAY					
	P	W	D	L	F	A	W	D	L	F	A	Pts
ARSENAL	34	14	3	0	38	13	10	7	0	31	11	82
Chelsea	35	10	4	3	29	13	12	2	4	32	16	72
Manchester United	35	12	3	3	36	14	10	2	5	25	19	71
Liverpool	35	9	3	5	26	14	5	8	5	23	22	53
Newcastle United	34	11	4	3	32	13	2	10	4	15	21	53
Aston Villa	35	8	6	3	23	17	6	4	8	23	24	52
Fulham	35	9	4	5	29	20	4	5	8	20	24	48
Charlton Athletic	35	6	5	6	25	26	7	4	7	19	19	48
Birmingham City	35	8	5	5	26	21	4	7	6	16	23	48
Bolton Wanderers	35	5	8	4	20	18	7	3	8	22	34	47
Southampton	34	8	4	5	20	13	4	5	8	19	22	45
Middlesbrough	35	7	4	7	23	22	5	5	7	18	22	45
Blackburn Rovers	35	4	3	10	23	30	7	4	7	26	27	40
Portsmouth	34	9	2	5	28	16	2	5	11	11	32	40
Everton	35	8	5	5	26	18	1	7	9	16	30	39
Tottenham Hotspur	35	8	4	6	32	27	3	2	12	12	29	39
Manchester City	35	3	9	5	25	23	4	5	9	23	28	35
Leeds United	35	5	6	7	22	28	3	2	12	14	43	32
Leicester City	35	2	10	6	16	27	3	4	10	26	33	29
Wolverhampton Wanderers	35	6	5	6	21	32	0	6	12	14	41	29

FORM GUIDE
L L W D W D [12 goals scored, 8 conceded]   W D L L D D [9 goals scored, 9 conceded]

ARSENAL 0   BIRMINGHAM CITY 0

Substitutes						Substitutes
		Jens **LEHMANN**	1	1	Ian **BENNETT**	
Rami **SHAABAN**	24	**LAUREN**	12	26	Oliver **TEBILY**	13	Colin **DOYLE**
▸ Martin **KEOWN**	5	Kolo **TOURE**	28	4	Kenny **CUNNINGHAM**	15	Martin **TAYLOR**
◂ (Bergkamp) 90		Sol **CAMPBELL**	23	25	Matthew **UPSON**	6	Aliou **CISSE**
Ray **PARLOUR**	15	Ashley **COLE**	3	23	Jamie **CLAPHAM**	10	Bryan **HUGHES** ▸
▸ Robert **PIRES**	7	Fredrik **LJUNGBERG**	8	22	Damien **JOHNSON** ▪		(Dunn) 76 ◂
◂ (Ljungberg) 69		**GILBERTO**	19	8	Robbie **SAVAGE** ▪	14	Stern **JOHN** ▸
▸ Jeremie **ALIADIERE**	30	Patrick **VIEIRA**	4	32	Stephen **CLEMENCE**		(Morrison) 72 ◂
◂ (Reyes) 79		José Antonio **REYES**	9	11	Stan **LAZARIDIS**		
		Dennis **BERGKAMP**	10	16	David **DUNN**		
		Thierry **HENRY**	14	19	Clinton **MORRISON**		

MATCH REPORT

With the title safely in the bag, the Gunners never reached full throttle against a well-organised Birmingham side, and the result was an unmemorable stalemate. Though the visitors

Dennis Bergkamp in command: *the imperious Dutchman was in fine form against Birmingham, but the Gunners were unable to break the deadlock against the well-organised Midlanders.*

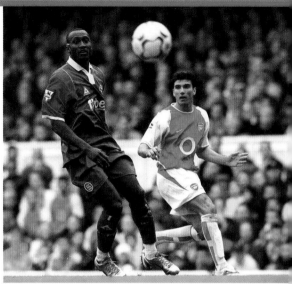

José Antonio Reyes, making his tenth appearance of the season, came closest to scoring on an afternoon when chances were rare.

needed points to press for a UEFA Cup place, they were wary of pushing men forward, having been mercilessly exposed by Arsenal's devastating counter-attacking style at St Andrews earlier in the season, so they crowded the midfield. Thus the two sides cancelled each other out to such an extent that neither managed a shot on target until midway through the second half.

Yet the new Champions had started in sprightly enough fashion, indulging in several extravagant flourishes which had the fans, who were in the mood to celebrate, roaring for more. Henry embarked on a typically penetrative run through the inside-right channel, then found Bergkamp with a slick backheel which unhinged the City rearguard, only for the Dutchman's shot to be deflected into the arms of the grateful Bennett. There were lovely touches, too, from Gilberto and Vieira, but the only threat on goal during the first-half came from Reyes – making his tenth League appearance of the campaign, thus qualifying for a title medal – who met an enticing cross from Bergkamp only to volley wide from 15 yards.

After the break it was the same old story of Arsenal dominating possession but, for the most part, being held comfortably by the determined Blues. Henry might have broken the deadlock but he curled wide from a quickly-taken free-kick, then he hit a cross-shot which was saved by Bennett.

By then, Birmingham were beginning to venture forth with a little more boldness, and the industrious Dunn set up Clemence, whose low 20-yarder was gathered comfortably by the under-employed Lehmann. Soon after that, City created the most inviting scoring opportunity of the match when Lazaridis robbed Lauren and crossed from the left to Morrison, who miskicked embarrassingly when eight yards from goal.

That escape appeared to remind the Gunners that their unbeaten Premiership record might, after all, be under threat, and they responded with a series of late sorties. The surging Gilberto set up Reyes to cross but the Spaniard's curving delivery ran clear, a low Bergkamp drive was blocked, then Pires sent Henry scampering to the byline, only for a combination of Cunningham and Bennett to deal with the Frenchman's near-post dink. Finally Bergkamp wriggled free in Birmingham's box and stumbled under an untidy challenge from Hughes, but the referee waved away the aggrieved Dutchman's appeal for a penalty.

Perhaps the most compelling drama of the afternoon was reserved until the dying seconds when Keown, eager to compile enough appearances to secure his third title gong, was sent on to replace Bergkamp in the front line. There was just time for Pires to arc a free-kick into the Birmingham goal area, but there was to be no fairytale winner for the veteran defender, and City held on to become the fourth side to avoid League defeat at Highbury all season.

FORM GUIDE
W D W W W D [10 goals scored, 5 conceded]   L W D W D D [12 goals scored, 6 conceded]

PORTSMOUTH 1   ARSENAL 1
Yakubu 30   Reyes 50

Substitutes					Substitutes
Harald **WAPENAAR**	25	Shaka **HISLOP**	1	1	Jens **LEHMANN**	
Richard **DUFFY**	31	John **CURTIS**	33	12	**LAUREN**	24	Rami **SHAABAN**
Kevin **HARPER**	7	Arjan **DE ZEEUW**	6	28	Kolo **TOURE**	5	Martin **KEOWN** ▶
▶ Ivica **NORDAR**	37	Dejan **STEFANOVIC**	3	23	Sol **CAMPBELL** ▢		(Reyes) 90 ◀
◀ (Yakubu) 80		Matthew **TAYLOR**	14	3	Ashley **COLE**	22	Gael **CLICHY**
Teddy **SHERINGHAM**	10	Steve **STONE**	19	37	David **BENTLEY**	25	**KANU** ▶
		Amdy **FAYE**	15	15	Ray **PARLOUR** ▢		(Bentley) 61 ◀
		Nigel **QUASHIE**	11	4	Patrick **VIEIRA**	30	Jeremie **ALIADIERE** ▶
		Richard **HUGHES**	22	8	Fredrik **LJUNGBERG**		(Ljungberg) 90 ◀
		Lomana Tresor **LUA LUA**	32	9	José Antonio **REYES**		
		Aiyegbeni **YAKUBU**	20	14	Thierry **HENRY**		

MATCH REPORT

A first League strike by José Antonio Reyes kept the Gunners on course for the first undefeated top-flight campaign since Preston North End proved to be invincible in 1888–89. But the record attempt came under serious threat from a spirited and enterprising Portsmouth side, who led at the interval and exerted late pressure on the visitors' goal.

Arsenal made an assured opening, oozing style and panache, and they almost seized an early lead when Ljungberg's effort was blocked and a swerving follow-up from Parlour demanded a full-length save from Hislop. Pompey, unbeaten in seven games and showing vast improvement since the Gunners had knocked them out of the FA Cup in March, hit back venomously. Yakubu started by surging through the centre to force

Lehmann into a dive, then Lua Lua charged past Campbell before firing wide.

The game developed into an attractively open contest and soon the lively Reyes fashioned three scoring chances in quick succession. He volleyed high from a cushioned dispatch from Ljungberg,

David Bentley works hard to keep
control of the midfield.

José Antonio Reyes fashioned three scoring chances in quick succession in the first half and finally got his reward with the equaliser five minutes after half-time.

saw a close-range effort deflected for a corner and hit a rasping drive which clipped Hislop's crossbar after flicking off the shoulder of Campbell.

But even as the Champions threatened to take control, Portsmouth edged in front when Toure misjudged a long ball from Taylor, allowing the sprinting Yakubu to squeeze a shot past Lehmann from an acute angle with the outside of his right foot. Almost immediately Henry twice went close to equalising, only to be foiled by a sharp parry from Hislop and a well-timed tackle by the stretching Stone. At the other end Yakubu nodded off-target from Stone's cross and Lehmann blocked Lua Lua's path to goal, but after the interval it was Portsmouth who lived dangerously as a shot from Henry was turned against the angle of post and bar by Hislop and Taylor completed the clearance.

However, parity was achieved from the resultant corner when a loose header fell to the predatory young Spaniard, Reyes, who netted with a low volley from the edge of the box.

For a spell, Arsenal looked the likelier winners, but Reyes scooped high after completing a delightful passing interchange with Henry. Portsmouth refused to fold, roaring forward in a late offensive which was repelled mainly due to the heroics of Lehmann. The big German stood up brilliantly to block Yakubu after the powerful Nigerian had raced clear of the Gunners defence, then he flung himself towards the top left corner of his goal to repel a powerful free-kick from Stefanovic.

Still ten minutes remained, and it seemed possible that Arsenal might stumble at the 36th Premiership hurdle, but they remained steadfast to the end and were honoured by a resounding ovation from the generous home fans. It was the eighth time during the League season that Arsène Wenger's resilient team had come from behind to avoid defeat, as much a testimony to their remarkable sang-froid and self-belief as to their glorious ability.

MAY

FA Barclaycard Premiership
Sunday 9 May 2004 at Loftus Road, 4.05 p.m.
Attendance: 18,102 Referee: Mike Dean

FORM GUIDE

D W L D W D [8 goals scored, 5 conceded]　　　　W D W D D D [12 goals scored, 5 conceded]

FULHAM 0　　ARSENAL 1

Reyes 9

Substitutes				Substitutes	
	Edwin **VAN DER SAR**	1	1	Jens **LEHMANN**	
Mark **CROSSLEY** 12	Moritz **VOLZ**	2	12	**LAUREN**	33 Graham **STACK**
Mark **HUDSON** 20	Ian **PEARCE**	35	28	Kolo **TOURE**	5 Martin **KEOWN** ▶
Bobby **PETTA** 26	▨ Alain **GOMA**	24	23	Sol **CAMPBELL**	(Ljungberg) 87 ◀
▶ Brian **MCBRIDE** 8	Carlos **BOCANEGRA**	34	3	Ashley **COLE**	22 Gael **CLICHY** ▶
◀ (Inamoto) 58	Martin **DJETOU**	17	8	Fredrik **LJUNGBERG**	(Pires) 78 ◀
▶ Collins **JOHN** 36	Junichi **INAMOTO**	6	15	Ray **PARLOUR** ▨	10 Dennis **BERGKAMP**
◀ (Djetou) 58	▨ Sean **DAVIS**	23	4	Patrick **VIEIRA** ▨	30 Jeremie **ALIADIERE** ▶
	Sylvain **LEGWINSKI**	5	7	Robert **PIRES**	(Reyes) 71 ◀
	Steed **MALBRANQUE**	14	9	José Antonio **REYES**	
	Luis **BOA MORTE**	11	14	Thierry **HENRY** ▨	

MATCH REPORT

Arsenal returned to winning ways after three successive draws and moved to within one game of rewriting modern football history by remaining unbeaten throughout a whole Premiership campaign. Victory at Fulham came courtesy of an uncharacteristic clanger by one of the world's

It's that man again: *José Antonio Reyes seizes on van der Sar's mistake to tap in the simplest of goals.*

most reliable goalkeepers, Edwin van der Sar, but after plundering so many wonderful goals on the title trail, the Gunners were more than entitled to a rare scrappy one.

The Champions began majestically, as though intent on sweeping aside their London rivals without delay, and van der Sar was forced to dive at the feet of Ljungberg following a fantastic through-ball by Parlour in the second minute. As Arsenal continued to flow forward, Davis blocked a shot from Reyes and Cole's dangerous cutback from the byline was hacked away, then the early pressure paid off in unexpected fashion. Djetou delivered a routine back-pass which van der Sar miscontrolled, then he attempted to dribble round the advancing Reyes, who won the ball before slipping it joyously into the empty net.

Gael Clichy shows maturity beyond his years to keep possession from Fulham's Steed Malbranque and Silvain Legwinski.

Fulham, who were bidding for their highest ever League finish, reacted positively, gradually forcing the visitors back and creating a succession of scoring opportunities. The most inviting was set up and missed by two former Gunners, Inamoto sending in Boa Morte, whose point-blank effort was repelled superbly by Lehmann. Next Inamoto found Malbranque, whose scooped drive from the edge of the box brushed the side netting. Inamoto then fired into Lehmann's midriff from 15 yards.

At the other end an adroit header from Cole did not extend van der Sar, and the second half commenced with Fulham continuing to hold territorial sway. Malbranque went close with a spectacular overhead from a Davis cross then Campbell smothered a Legwinski effort, but the Gunners remained menacing on the break and Reyes shot into van der Sar's side-netting from 20 yards.

Fulham boss Chris Coleman threw on extra attackers and, midway through the second-half, McBride ignored unmarked colleagues to volley wastefully wide, Cole foiled Legwinski, then Volz,

yet another ex-Gunner, surged into the box to fire narrowly wide of the far post.

As the hosts became increasingly desperate, so Arsène Wenger's men looked to counter intelligently. Henry reached the left byline but his cross was intercepted, Ljungberg and Clichy combined neatly but were halted at the edge of Fulham's area, and the French teenager embarked on a 50-yard run, culminating in a low shot which was fielded by van der Sar.

With five minutes remaining, Fulham won a free-kick on the edge of Arsenal's area, but Malbranque's first effort failed to pierce the wall and his second was skied into the crowd. Two minutes later the French midfielder almost reached a flick-on from McBride and that proved to be his team's last meaningful chance.

Fittingly on a day when Arsenal moved to the threshold of a unique Premiership achievement, the final word was left to Henry, whose last-minute free-kick from 27 yards demanded an alert tip-over from van der Sar.

FORM GUIDE
D W D D D W [9 goals scored, 3 conceded]   L L L D D W [6 goals scored, 8 conceded]

ARSENAL 2   LEICESTER CITY 1

Henry pen 46, Vieira 66   Dickov 26

Substitutes						Substitutes
Graham **STACK**	33	Jens **LEHMANN**	11	1	Ian **WALKER**	Danny **COYNE** ▸	16
▸ Martin **KEOWN**	5	**LAUREN**	12	3	Frank **SINCLAIR** ◾	(Walker) 78 ◂	
◂ (Ljungberg) 87		Kolo **TOURE**	28	44	Nikos **DABIZAS**	Paul **BROOKER** ▸	12
Ray **PARLOUR**	15	Sol **CAMPBELL**	23	25	Matt **HEATH**	(Freund) 76 ◂	
▸ **EDU**	17	Ashley **COLE**	3	11	Jordan **STEWART**	Keith **GILLESPIE**	7
◂ (Pires) 70		Fredrik **LJUNGBERG**	8	38	Marcus **BENT**	Steve **GUPPY**	27
▸ José Antonio **REYES**	9	**GILBERTO**	19	13	Steffen **FREUND**	Trevor **BENJAMIN** ▸	20
◂ (Bergkamp) 82		Patrick **VIEIRA**	4	32	Billy **MCKINLAY**	(Dickov) 85 ◂	
		Robert **PIRES**	7	8	Lilian **NALIS**		
		Dennis **BERGKAMP**	10	10	James **SCOWCROFT**		
		Thierry **HENRY**	14	22	Paul **DICKOV**		

MATCH REPORT

Arsenal's unbeatable team capped their sensational season with the perfect finale, coming from behind to defeat Leicester as a sun-kissed Highbury rocked with ecstatic jubilation. The relegated visitors threatened to be party-poopers by plundering a first-half lead through former Gunner Paul Dickov, but the incomparable Henry and the colossus Vieira turned the tables after the interval.

The Champions poured forward in waves from the first minute, but an extremely disciplined and well organised City side were not going to roll over lightly, frustrating Arsène Wenger's men with a packed midfield behind lone frontman Dickov. During the opening exchanges Gilberto and Henry were off target with long-range snap-shots, Ljungberg shaved an upright with a low drive across goal and Pires was crowded out at the end of a typically mesmerising run. Henry was as irrepressible as usual, but his dart to the byline was thwarted by a Dabizas interception and a 35-yard free-kick was tipped over the crossbar by Walker.

Captain Fantastic: *Patrick Vieira settles the worries of the Arsenal fans with a simple but classic goal midway through the second half…*

But suddenly the crowd was stunned into silence as Leicester scored a high-quality goal with their first telling attack. Sinclair burst down the right and cut inside past Vieira before floating a cross to the far post, where the diminutive Dickov nodded beyond Lehmann.

The Gunners didn't panic, and laid siege to the City goal for the remainder of the half. Bergkamp miscued with two efforts, Pires was marginally wide with a glorious bender from the left flank, Henry shot high, and Walker saved at the feet of two marauders after repelling another swerving attempt from Pires.

For all Arsenal's clear superiority, an air of apprehension circulated the ground during the break, but it was dispelled in the first minute of the second half when a Bergkamp dispatch freed Cole, who was bundled to the ground in the box for a clear penalty. Henry sent Walker the wrong way from the spot – thus becoming the first Gunner since Ronnie Rooke 56 years earlier to notch 30 League goals in a season – and now the hosts tightened their grip on the momentous occasion.

As the pressure on the Leicester goal intensified, Henry almost sent in Ljungberg, Walker pipped Gilberto to a free-kick by the Frenchman and Toure headed high.

During a brief flurry at the other end, City alleged a handball by Gilberto but their penalty appeal was denied. Then the Gunners put the game beyond doubt with a goal of pure quality. Confronted by a packed defence, Bergkamp released a masterful through-pass to the charging Vieira, who rounded Walker and tapped into the empty net as Highbury erupted with glee.

Now it was time for festival football, and Arsenal obliged in characteristic style. Henry almost increased the lead with an audacious long-distance placement, a Ljungberg scorcher was turned over by substitute keeper Coyne, and Reyes nearly forced home from close range.

All that remained was for Keown to be called from the bench to qualify for a title medal in his final senior game for the club, a fitting end to an unforgettable afternoon.

The team celebrate an incredible achievement as Arsenal are crowned champions after the first unbeaten League season for 115 years.

MAY 2004

Arsenal.com PLAYER OF THE MONTH

Patrick VIEIRA

" The year has gone fantastically for the whole team and I've enjoyed every second of captaining these players. I'm quite happy with my own form and I would say that it's been the best I've played in the last three years. All injuries are behind me now and I've been getting stronger and stronger all the way to the end of the season.

It's the third time we've won the title during my time at Arsenal and we've really enjoyed ourselves. We've been at the top of our game longer this time than for the previous two titles. It looks as though the team spirit is getting better every year. This was a real team effort. I was happy to be voted third in the Footballer of the Year poll, but really that's an award for the strikers and Thierry deserves it. I'm just delighted to be in the top three as a midfielder. "

PATRICK VIEIRA

ARSENAL DIARY

Sunday 9 May
- Thierry Henry becomes the first player to be voted Footballer of the Year by the Football Writers Associations in successive seasons.

Friday 14 May
- Martin Keown will leave at the end of the season.

Sunday 16 May
- More than a quarter of a million supporters turned out for Arsenal's victory parade from Highbury to Islington Town Hall.

Monday 17 May
- Arsene Wenger is named Manager of the Year for the third time.

Tuesday 18 May
- Premiership commission one-off trophy for Arsenal to mark their unbeaten League season.

THE WIDER WORLD

Saturday 1 May
- Leicester are relegated from the Premiership, Wolves are effectively demoted.

Sunday 2 May
- Leeds lose their Premiership foothold.

Wednesday 5 May
- Chelsea lose their Champions League semi-final to Monaco.

Saturday 22 May
- Manchester United win the FA Cup, beating Millwall 3-0 in the final.

Wednesday 26 May
- Alan Smith joins Manchester United from Leeds for £7 million.
- Porto beat Monaco 3-0 in the European Cup Final.

FA CARLING PREMIERSHIP

15 May 2004

		HOME					AWAY					
	P	W	D	L	F	A	W	D	L	F	A	Pts
ARSENAL	38	15	4	0	40	14	11	8	0	33	12	90
Chelsea	38	12	4	3	34	13	12	3	4	33	17	79
Manchester United	38	12	4	3	37	15	11	2	6	27	20	75
Liverpool	38	10	4	5	29	15	6	8	5	26	22	60
Newcastle United	38	11	5	3	33	14	2	12	5	19	26	56
Aston Villa	38	9	6	4	24	19	6	5	8	24	25	56
Charlton Athletic	38	7	6	6	29	29	7	5	7	22	22	53
Bolton Wanderers	38	6	8	5	24	21	8	3	8	24	35	53
Fulham	38	9	4	6	29	21	5	6	8	23	25	52
Birmingham City	38	8	5	6	26	24	4	9	6	17	24	50
Middlesbrough	38	8	4	7	25	23	5	5	9	19	29	48
Southampton	38	8	6	5	24	17	4	5	10	20	28	47
Portsmouth	38	10	4	5	35	19	2	5	12	12	35	45
Tottenham Hotspur	38	9	4	6	33	27	4	2	13	14	30	45
Blackburn Rovers	38	5	4	10	25	31	7	4	8	26	28	44
Manchester City	38	5	9	5	31	24	4	5	10	24	30	41
Everton	38	8	5	6	27	20	1	7	11	18	37	39
Leicester City	38	3	10	6	19	28	3	5	11	29	37	33
Leeds United	38	5	7	7	25	31	3	2	14	15	48	33
Wolverhampton Wanderers	38	7	5	7	23	35	0	7	12	15	42	33

Unbeaten in the League, the Premiership champions celebrate with ecstatic fans at Highbury

CELEBRATION

Salute the Untouchables of 2003/2004. Not only did they win the Championship without losing a game, rewriting modern sporting history in the process, but they also did it in style, serving up some of the most brilliant attacking play in living memory. When the ball was flowing smoothly, often as if by magic, between Henry, Pires, Vieira, Bergkamp and company, it was an exhilarating sight to behold for all who prize what is extraordinary in sport. For Arsène Wenger, celebrating his second Premiership crown in two years and his third in eight attempts since arriving at Highbury in the autumn of 1996, it was a handsome vindication of his beliefs and methods. As he put it so eloquently, it was an achievement which people will still be talking about in 50 years time, thus conferring on the team a footballing immortality which has been granted to very few.

There was a point in the season, during the spring, when it seemed possible that even greater triumph was at hand. The elusive Treble, encompassing the FA Cup and the Champions League as well as the domestic title, did not appear beyond the glorious Gunners. That particular dream evaporated within the space of four days, through defeats by Manchester United and Chelsea respectively, but those disappointments were offset by mounting excitement over the undefeated League sequence which was moving inexorably towards its remarkable climax.

Captain Patrick Vieira, a truly inspirational leader and a massive force on the pitch

Thierry Henry ends the season as the Premiership's top scorer and possibly the world's best striker

Every member of the squad deserves enormous credit, but pride of place must go to the majestic Thierry Henry, who topped the Premiership scoring charts with 30 strikes. He was selected as Footballer of the Year by both his fellow footballers and the sporting press, and was second only to his countryman Zinedine Zidane in FIFA's World Player of the Year poll. It wasn't only the goals that he scored, and those he created for his colleagues, that made Thierry's contribution so special. It was the sheer unadulterated brilliance of so much of his general play, memories of which will be preserved forever in the mind's eye of those privileged enough to witness it on a regular basis.

Then there was Patrick Vieira, confirming his stature as an inspirational leader in the tradition of Tony Adams. He was a monumentally influential figure in midfield, a potent amalgam of colossal talent and overwhelming desire to succeed. Robert Pires touched new heights, his classy midfield promptings garnished by 19 goals; Dennis Bergkamp returned to his majestic best in the twilight of a career which will continue for at least one more term; Kolo Toure was the find of the season alongside the magnificent Sol Campbell in central defence; Edu emerged as a top-quality all-rounder in midfield, the list could go on almost indefinitely.

High points included three 2-1 victories over Chelsea, the late header by Ashley Cole against Dynamo Kiev which rejuvenated the Champions League bid in the autumn, sumptuous 5-1 victories in Milan against Internazionale and at Portsmouth in the FA Cup. The rousing fightback to beat Liverpool at Highbury underlined the Gunners' status as the top team in the land at a time when lesser sides might have been undermined by cup reverses.

As for the future, it could hardly be brighter. The manager and leading players have affirmed their loyalty to the Arsenal cause, gifted youngsters such as José Antonio Reyes, Gael Clichy, David Bentley and new signing Robin van Persie offer mouth-watering prospects. The imminent move to a new ground opens up fresh horizons and even higher hopes for the future.

It is hard to imagine there has ever been a more exciting time to follow the Gunners!

Kolo Toure proves to be a worthy addition to the squad in his second season at the Club

ENGLAND 2003/2004

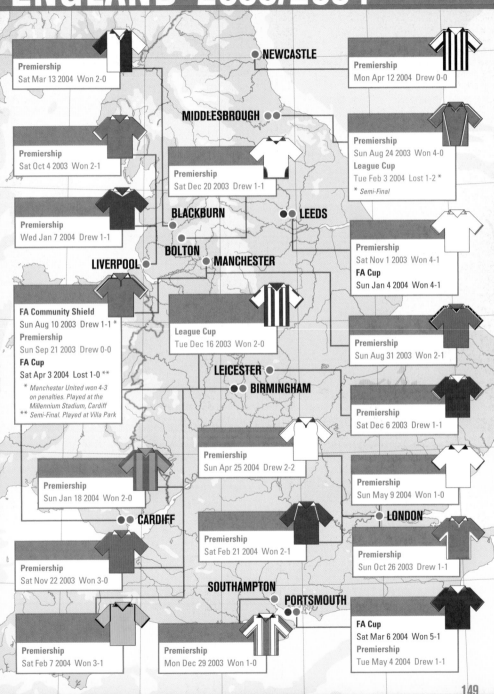

NEWCASTLE

Premiership
Sat Mar 13 2004 Won 2-0

Premiership
Mon Apr 12 2004 Drew 0-0

MIDDLESBROUGH

Premiership
Sat Oct 4 2003 Won 2-1

Premiership
Sat Dec 20 2003 Drew 1-1

Premiership
Sun Aug 24 2003 Won 4-0
League Cup
Tue Feb 3 2004 Lost 1-2 *
Semi-Final

Premiership
Wed Jan 7 2004 Drew 1-1

BLACKBURN

LEEDS

BOLTON

LIVERPOOL

MANCHESTER

Premiership
Sat Nov 1 2003 Won 4-1
FA Cup
Sun Jan 4 2004 Won 4-1

FA Community Shield
Sun Aug 10 2003 Drew 1-1 *
Premiership
Sun Sep 21 2003 Drew 0-0
FA Cup
Sat Apr 3 2004 Lost 1-0 **

  * Manchester United won 4-3
    on penalties. Played at the
    Millennium Stadium, Cardiff
** Semi-Final. Played at Villa Park

League Cup
Tue Dec 16 2003 Won 2-0

Premiership
Sun Aug 31 2003 Won 2-1

LEICESTER

BIRMINGHAM

Premiership
Sat Dec 6 2003 Drew 1-1

Premiership
Sun Apr 25 2004 Drew 2-2

Premiership
Sun May 9 2004 Won 1-0

Premiership
Sun Jan 18 2004 Won 2-0

CARDIFF

Premiership
Sat Feb 21 2004 Won 2-1

LONDON

Premiership
Sat Nov 22 2003 Won 3-0

Premiership
Sun Oct 26 2003 Drew 1-1

SOUTHAMPTON

PORTSMOUTH

Premiership
Sat Feb 7 2004 Won 3-1

Premiership
Mon Dec 29 2003 Won 1-0

FA Cup
Sat Mar 6 2004 Won 5-1
Premiership
Tue May 4 2004 Drew 1-1

149

ARSENAL ON THE ROAD

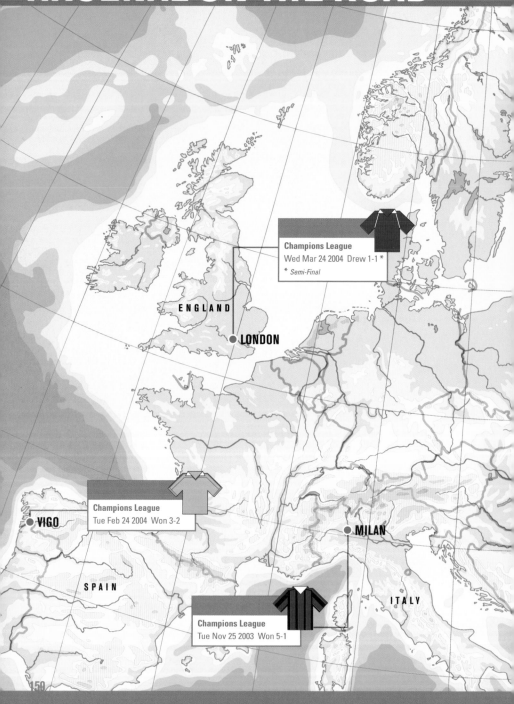

Champions League
Wed Mar 24 2004 Drew 1-1 *
* *Semi-Final*

ENGLAND

● LONDON

Champions League
Tue Feb 24 2004 Won 3-2

● VIGO

● MILAN

SPAIN

Champions League
Tue Nov 25 2003 Won 5-1

ITALY

EUROPE 2003/2004

RUSSIA

Champions League
Tue Sep 30 2003 Drew 0-0

● MOSCOW

● KIEV

UKRAINE

Champions League
Tue Oct 21 2003 Lost 1-2

FA BARCLAYCARD PREMIERSHIP

Date	Opponents (Venue)	Score	League Position
Sat Aug 16	Everton (H)	2-1	4
Sun Aug 24	Middlesbrough (A)	4-0	1
Wed Aug 27	Aston Villa (H)	2-0	1
Sun Aug 31	Manchester City (A)	2-1	1
Sat Sep 13	Portsmouth (H)	1-1	1
Sun Sep 21	Manchester United (A)	0-0	1
Fri Sep 26	Newcastle United (H)	3-2	1
Sat Oct 4	Liverpool (A)	2-1	1
Sat Oct 18	Chelsea (H)	2-1	1
Sat Oct 26	Charlton Athletic (A)	1-1	1
Sat Nov 1	Leeds United (A)	4-1	1
Sat Nov 8	Tottenham Hotspur (H)	2-1	1
Sat Nov 22	Birminghm City (A)	3-0	1
Sun Nov 30	Fulham (H)	0-0	1
Sat Dec 6	Leicester City (A)	1-1	2
Sun Dec 14	Blackburn Rovers (H)	1-0	1
Sat Dec 20	Bolton Wanderers (A)	1-1	1
Fri Dec 26	Wolverhampton W (H)	3-0	1
Mon Dec 29	Southampton (A)	1-0	2
Wed Jan 7	Everton (A)	1-1	2
Sun Jan 10	Middlesbrough (H)	4-1	1
Sat Jan 18	Aston Villa (A)	2-0	1
Sun Feb 1	Manchester City (H)	2-1	1
Sat Feb 7	Wolverhampton W (A)	3-1	1
Tue Feb 10	Southampton (H)	2-0	1
Sat Feb 21	Chelsea (A)	2-1	1
Sat Feb 28	Charlton Athletic (H)	2-1	1
Sat Mar 13	Blackburn Rovers (A)	2-0	1
Sat Mar 20	Bolton Wanderers (H)	2-1	1
Sun Mar 28	Manchester United (H)	1-1	1
Fri Apr 9	Liverpool (H)	4-2	1
Mon Apr 12	Newcastle United (A)	0-0	1
Fri Apr 16	Leeds United (H)	5-0	1
Sun Apr 25	Tottenham Hotspur (A)	2-2	1
Sat May 1	Birmingham City (H)	0-0	1
Tues May 4	Portsmouth (A)	1-1	1
Sun May 9	Fulham (A)	1-0	1
Sat May 15	Leicester City (H)	2-1	1

UEFA CHAMPIONS LEAGUE

Date	Opponents (Venue)	Score
Wed Sep 17	Inter Milan (H)	0-3
Tue Sep 30	Lokomotiv Moscow (A)	0-0
Tue Oct 21	Dynamo Kiev (A)	1-2
Wed Nov 5	Dynamo Kiev (H)	1-0
Tue Nov 25	Inter Milan (A)	5-1
Wed Dec 10	Lokomotiv Moscow (H)	2-0
Tue Feb 24	Celta Vigo (A)	3-2
Wed Mar 10	Celta Vigo (H)	2-0
Wed Mar 24	Chelsea (A)	1-1
Tue Apr 6	Chelsea (H)	1-2

FA CUP

Date	Opponents (Venue)	Score
Sun Jan 4	Leeds United (A)	4-1
Sun Jan 24	Middlesbrough (H)	4-1
Sun Feb 15	Chelsea (H)	2-1
Sat Mar 6	Portsmouth (A)	5-1
Sat Apr 3	Manchester United (*)	0-1

*played at Villa Park

CARLING CUP

Date	Opponents (Venue)	Score
Tue Oct 28	Rotherham United (H)	1-1
(Arsenal won 9-8 on pens)		
Tue Dec 2	Wolverhampton W (H)	5-1
Tue Dec 16	West Bromwich A (A)	2-0
Tue Jan 20	Middlesbrough (H)	0-1
Tue Feb 3	Middlesbrough (A)	1-2

FA COMMUNITY SHIELD

Date	Opponents (Venue)	Score
Sun Aug 10	Manchester United (*)	1-1
(Manchester United won 4-3 on penalties)		
* played at Millennium Stadium, Cardiff		

APPEARANCES (SUBS IN BRACKETS) AND GOALS

Player	Premiership App	Gls	FA Cup App	Gls	Carling Cup App	Gls	Champions League App	Gls	Community Shield App	Gls	Totals App	Gls
J ALIADIERE	3 (7)	0	1	0	3	4	0 (1)	0	0	0	7 (8)	4
D BENTLEY	1	0	0 (2)	1	4	0	0 (1)	0	0	0	5 (3)	1
D BERGKAMP	21 (7)	4	3	1	0	0	4 (2)	0	1	0	29 (9)	5
S CAMPBELL	35	1	5	0	0	0	9	0	1	0	50	1
G CLICHY	7 (5)	0	1 (3)	0	5	0	1	0	0	0	14 (8)	0
A COLE	32	0	4	0	1	0	9	1	1	0	47	1
P CYGAN	10 (8)	0	0	0	3	0	2 (1)	0	0	0	15 (9)	0
EDU	13 (17)	2	4 (1)	1	4	1	7 (1)	3	0 (1)	0	28 (20)	7
C FABREGAS	0	0	0	0	2 (1)	1	0	0	0	0	2 (1)	1
GILBERTO	29 (3)	4	3	0	1	0	5 (3)	0	1	0	39 (6)	4
T HENRY	37	30	2 (1)	3	0	0	10	5	1	1	50	39
J HOYTE	0 (1)	0	0	0	2	0	0	0	0	0	2 (1)	0
F JEFFERS	0	0	0	0	0	0	0	0	0 (1)	0	0 (1)	0
KANU	3 (7)	1	1 (2)	0	4	2	1 (6)	0	0	0	9 (15)	3
M KEOWN	3 (7)	0	1	0	3	0	1	0	0	0	8 (7)	0
LAUREN	30 (2)	0	5	0	1	0	8	0	1	0	45 (2)	0
J LEHMANN	38	0	5	0	0	0	10	0	1	0	54	0
F LJUNGBERG	27 (3)	4	4	4	0	0	8 (1)	2	1	0	40 (4)	10
Q OWUSU-AB	0	0	0	0	1 (2)	0	0	0	0	0	1 (2)	0
R PARLOUR	16 (9)	0	2 (1)	0	3	0	4 (1)	0	1	0	26 (11)	0
M PAPADOP	0	0	0	0	0 (1)	0	0	0	0	0	0 (1)	0
R PIRES	33 (3)	14	3 (1)	1	0	0	10	4	0 (1)	0	46 (5)	19
J A REYES	7 (6)	2	2 (1)	2	1	0	2 (2)	1	0	0	12 (9)	5
F SIMEK	0	0	0	0	1	0	0	0	0	0	1	0
O SKULASON	0	0	0	0	0 (1)	0	0	0	0	0	0 (1)	0
R SMITH	0	0	0	0	0 (3)	0	0	0	0	0	0 (3)	0
J SPICER	0	0	0	0	0 (1)	0	0	0	0	0	0 (1)	0
G STACK	0	0	0	0	5	0	0	0	0	0	5	0
S TAVLARIDISO	0	0	0	3	0	0	0	0	0	3	0	
J THOMAS	0	0	0	0	1 (2)	0	0	0	0	0	1 (2)	0
K TOURE	36 (1)	1	4 (1)	2	2	0	10	0	1	0	53 (2)	3
G VAN BRON	0	0	0	0	0	0	0	0	0 (1)	0	0 (1)	0
P VIEIRA	29	3	5	0	2	0	6 (1)	0	1	0	43 (1)	3
S WILTORD	8 (4)	3	0	0	3	1	3 (1)	0	0 (1)	0	14 (6)	4

PLAYER PROFILES

Jeremie Aliadiere

Position forward **Squad number** 30
Born Rambouillet, France, 30 March 1983
Joined Arsenal as scholar in summer 1999, professional in March 2000
Senior Arsenal debut 27 November 2001 v Grimsby Town at Highbury
(Worthington Cup, as substitute)
Arsenal honours League Championship 2004
Arsenal record League: 3 (11) games, 1 goal; FA Cup: 1 game, 0 goals;
League Cup: 3 (2) games, 4 goals; Europe: 0 (1) game, 0 goals; Total: 7 (14)
games, 5 goals

David Bentley

Position forward **Squad number** 37
Born Peterborough, 27 August 1984
Joined Arsenal as scholar in summer 2000, professional in December 2001
Senior Arsenal debut 4 January 2003 v Oxford United at Highbury (FA Cup, as
substitute)
Arsenal record League: 1 game, 0 goals; FA Cup: 0 (2) games, 1 goal; League
Cup: 4 games, 0 goals; Europe: 0 (1) game, 0 goals; Total: 5 (4) games, 1 goal

Dennis Bergkamp

Position forward **Squad number** 10
Born Amsterdam, 10 May 1969
Other clubs Ajax, Internazionale
Joined Arsenal from Internazionale in June 1995
Senior Arsenal debut 20 August 1995 v Middlesbrough at Highbury (League)
Arsenal honours League Championship 1998, 2002, 2004; FA Cup 1998,
2002, 2003
Arsenal record League: 225 (37) games, 77 goals; FA Cup: 29 (5) games,
14 goals; League Cup: 15 games, 8 goals; Europe: 32 (8) games, 10 goals;
Charity/Community Shield: 3 games, 0 goals; Total: 304 (50) games, 109 goals
Holland caps 79

Sol Campbell

Position defender **Squad number** 23
Born Newham, London, 18 September 1974
Other club Tottenham Hotspur
Joined Arsenal from Tottenham Hotspur in July 2001
Senior Arsenal debut 18 August 2001 v Middlesbrough at The Riverside (League)
Arsenal honours League Championship 2002, 2004; FA Cup 2002;
Community Shield 2002
Arsenal record League: 97 (2) games, 5 goals; FA Cup: 17 games, 2 goals;
Europe: 29 games, 0 goals; Community Shield: 2 games, 0 goals; Total: 145 (2)
games, 7 goals
England caps 56

Gael Clichy

Position defender **Squad number** 22
Born Clichy, Paris, 26 July 1985
Other club Cannes
Joined Arsenal from Cannes in August 2003
Senior Arsenal debut 28 October 2003 v Rotherham United at Highbury
(League Cup)
Arsenal honours League Championship 2004
Arsenal record League: 7 (5) games, 0 goals; FA Cup: 1 (3) games, 0 goals;
League Cup: 5 games, 0 goals; Europe: 1 game, 0 goals; Total: 14 (8) games,
0 goals

Ashley Cole

Position defender **Squad number** 3
Born Stepney, London, 20 December 1980
Other club Crystal Palace on loan
Joined Arsenal as trainee in summer 1997, professional in November 1998
Senior Arsenal debut 30 November 1999 v Middlesbrough at The Riverside
(League Cup, as substitute)
Arsenal honours League Championship 2002, 2004; FA Cup 2002, 2003;
Community Shield 2003
Arsenal record League: 107 (3) games, 6 goals; FA Cup: 16 (1) games, 0
goals; League Cup: 2 (1) games, 0 goals; Europe: 32 (2) games, 1 goal;
Community Shield: 2 games, 0 goals; Total: 159 (7) games, 7 goals
England caps 24

Pascal Cygan

Position central defender **Squad number** 18
Born Lens, France, 29 April 1974
Other clubs Valenciennes, ES Wasquehal, Lille
Joined Arsenal from Lille in July 2002
Senior Arsenal debut 1 September 2002 v Chelsea at Stamford Bridge
(League, as substitute)
Arsenal honours League Championship 2004; Community Shield 2002
Arsenal record League: 26 (10) games, 1 goal; FA Cup: 2 games, 0 goals;
League Cup: 3 games, 0 goals; Europe: 11 (3) games, 0 goals; Total: 42 (13)
games, 1 goal

Edu

Position midfielder **Squad number** 17
Born Sao Paulo, Brazil, 16 May 1978
Other clubs Sao Paulo, Corinthians
Joined Arsenal from Corinthians in January 2001
Senior Arsenal debut 20 January 2001 v Leicester City at Filbert Street
(League, as substitute)
Arsenal honours League Championship 2002, 2004; FA Cup 2002;
Community Shield 2002
Arsenal record League: 35 (32) games, 5 goals; FA Cup: 13 (3) games,
3 goals; League Cup: 7 games, 2 goals; Europe: 10 (7) games, 3 goals;
Community Shield: 1 (1) games, 0 goals; Total: 66 (43) games, 13 goals
Brazil caps 1

Francesc Fabregas

Position midfielder **Squad** number 57
Born Vilessoc de Mar, Spain, 4 May 1987
Other club Barcelona
Joined Arsenal from Barcelona in July 2003
Senior Arsenal debut 28 October 2003 v Rotherham United at Highbury
(League Cup)
Arsenal record League Cup: 2 (1) games, 1 goal; Total: 2 (1) games, 1 goal

Gilberto

Position midfielder **Squad number** 19
Born Lagoa da Prata, Brazil, 7 October 1976
Other clubs America MG, Atletico Mineiro
Joined Arsenal from Atletico Mineiro in July 2002
Senior Arsenal debut 11 August 2002 at Millennium Stadium v Liverpool
(Community Shield, as substitute)
Arsenal honours League Championship 2004; FA Cup 2003; Community
Shield 2002
Arsenal record League: 61 (6) games, 4 goals; FA Cup: 4 (2) games, 0 goals;
League Cup: 1 game, 0 goals; Europe: 16 (4) games, 2 goals; Community
Shield: 1 (1) games, 1 goal; Total: 83 (13) games, 7 goals
Brazil caps 26

Thierry Henry

Position forward **Squad number** 14
Born Paris, 17 August 1977
Other clubs AS Monaco, Juventus
Joined Arsenal from Juventus in August 1999
Senior Arsenal debut 7 August 1999 v Leicester City at Highbury (League,
as substitute)
Arsenal honours League Championship 2002, 2004; FA Cup 2002, 2003;
Community Shield 2002
Arsenal record League: 158 (15) games, 112 goals; FA Cup: 14 (6) games,
6 goals; League Cup: 2 games, 1 goal; Europe: 54 (5) games, 31 goals;
Community Shield: 2 games, 1 goal; Total: 230 (26) games, 151 goals
France caps 57

Justin Hoyte

Position defender **Squad number** 45
Born Waltham Forest, 20 November 1984
Joined Arsenal as scholar in summer 2001, as professional in July 2002
Senior Arsenal debut 7 May 2003 v Southampton at Highbury (League,
as substitute)
Arsenal record League: 0 (2) games, 0 goals; League Cup: 2 games, 0 goals;
Total: 2 (2) games, 0 goals

Francis Jeffers

Position forward **Squad number** None
Born Liverpool, 25 January 1981
Other club Everton, Everton on loan
Joined Arsenal from Everton in June 2001
Senior Arsenal debut 21 August 2001 v Leeds United at Highbury (League, as substitute)
Arsenal record League: 4 (18) games, 4 goals; FA Cup: 7 (1) games, 3 goals; League Cup 1 game, 1 goal; Europe: 1 (6) games, 0 goals; Community Shield: 0 (1) game, 0 goals; Total: 13 (26) games, 8 goals
England caps 1

Kanu

Position forward **Squad number** 25
Born Owerri, Nigeria, 1 August 1976
Other clubs Federation Works, Iwuanyanwu, Ajax, Internazionale
Joined Arsenal from Internazionale in January 1999
Senior Arsenal debut 13 February 1999 v Sheffield United at Highbury (FA Cup, as substitute, match void)
Arsenal honours League Championship 2002, 2004; FA Cup 2002; Community Shield 1999
Arsenal record League: 63 (56) games, 30 goals; FA Cup: 5 (12) games, 3 goals; League Cup: 8 games, 4 goals; Europe: 27 (26) games, 6 goals; Charity Shield: 1 game, 1 goal; Total: 104 (94) games, 44 goals
Nigeria caps 44

Martin Keown

Position defender **Squad number** 5
Born Oxford, 24 July 1966
Other clubs Brighton on loan, Aston Villa, Everton
Joined Arsenal as trainee in June 1982, as professional in February 1984, from Everton in February 1993
Senior Arsenal debut 23 November 1985 v West Bromwich Albion at The Hawthorns (League)
Arsenal honours League Championship 1998, 2002, 2004; FA Cup 1998, 2002, 2003; European Cup-Winners' Cup 1994; Charity/Community Shield 1998, 1999, 2002
Arsenal record League: 304 (28) games, 4 goals; FA Cup: 37 (3) games, 0 goals; League Cup: 21 (2) games, 1 goal; Europe: 43 (7) games, 3 goals; Charity/Community Shield: 3 (1) games, 0 goals; Total: 408 (41) games, 8 goals
England caps 43

Lauren

Position defender or midfielder   **Squad number** 12
Born Londi Kribi, Cameroon, 19 January 1977
Other clubs Utrera, Seville, Levante, Real Mallorca
Joined Arsenal from Real Mallorca in May 2000
Senior Arsenal debut 19 August 2000 v Sunderland at the Stadium of Light
(League, as substitute)
Arsenal honours League Championship 2002, 2004; FA Cup 2002, 2003;
Community Shield 2002
Arsenal record League: 98 (6) games, 5 goals; FA Cup: 18 games, 2 goals;
League Cup: 1 game, 0 goals; Europe: 34 (6) games, 1 goal; Community
Shield: 2 games, 0 goals; Total: 153 (12) games, 8 goals
Cameroon caps 22

Jens Lehmann

Position goalkeeper   **Squad number** 1
Born Essen, Germany, 10 November 1969
Other clubs DJK Heisingen, Schwarz-Weiss Essen, FC Schalke, AC Milan,
Borussia Dortmund
Joined Arsenal from Borussia Dortmund in July 2003
Senior Arsenal debut 10 August 2003 v Manchester United at the Millennium
Stadium (Community Shield)
Arsenal honours League Championship 2004
Arsenal record League: 38 games, 0 goals; FA Cup: 5 games, 0 goals; Europe:
10 games, 0 goals; Community Shield: 1 game, 0 goals; Total: 54 games, 0 goals
Germany caps 17

Fredrik Ljungberg

Position midfielder   **Squad number** 8
Born Vittsjo, Sweden, 16 April 1977
Other club Halmstads
Joined Arsenal from Halmstads in September 1998
Senior Arsenal debut 20 September 1998 v Manchester United at Highbury
(League, as substitute)
Arsenal honours League Championship 2002, 2004; FA Cup 2002, 2003;
Charity Shield 1999
Arsenal record League: 127 (20) games, 35 goals; FA Cup: 20 (3) games,
8 goals; League Cup: 2 games, 0 goals; Europe: 44 (9) games, 11 goals;
Charity/Community Shield: 2 games, 0 goals; Total: 195 (32) games, 54 goals
Sweden caps 39

PLAYER PROFILES

Quincy Owusu-Abeyie
Position forward   **Squad number** 54
Joined Arsenal as scholar in September 2002
Senior Arsenal debut 28 October 2003 v Rotherham United at Highbury
(League Cup, as substitute)
Arsenal record League Cup: 1 (2) games, 0 goals

Michal Papadopulos
Position forward   **Squad number** 32
Born Ostrava, Czech Republic, 14 April 1985
Other club Banik Ostrava
Joined Arsenal summer 2003 on loan from Banik Ostrava
Senior Arsenal debut 2 December 2003 v Wolverhampton Wanderers
at Highbury (League Cup)
Arsenal record League Cup: 0 (1) game, 0 goals; Total: 0 (1) game,
0 goals

Ray Parlour
Position midfielder   **Squad number** 15
Born Romford, 7 March 1973
Joined Arsenal as trainee in summer 1989, professional in March 1991
Senior Arsenal debut 29 January 1992 v Liverpool at Anfield (League)
Arsenal honours League Championship 1998, 2002, 2004; FA Cup 1993,
1998, 2002, 2003; League Cup 1993
Arsenal record League: 282 (57) games, 22 goals; FA Cup: 40 (4) games,
4 goals; League Cup: 23 (3) games, 0 goals; Europe: 41 (12) games, 5 goals;
Charity/Community Shield: 4 games, 1 goal; Total: 390 (76) games, 32 goals
England caps 10

Jermaine Pennant

Position midfielder   **Squad number** 21
Born Nottingham, 15 January 1983
Other clubs Notts County, Watford on loan, Leeds United on loan
Joined Arsenal from Notts County as trainee in January 1999
Senior Arsenal debut 30 November 1999 v Middlesbrough at The Riverside
(League Cup, as substitute)
Arsenal record League: 1 (4) games, 3 goals; League Cup: 5 (1) games,
0 goals; Europe: 0 (3) games, 0 goals; Total: 6 (8) games, 3 goals

Robert Pires

Position midfielder   **Squad number** 7
Born Reims, France, 29 October 1973
Other clubs Stade de Reims, FC Metz, Olympique Marseille
Joined Arsenal from Olympique Marseille in July 2000
Senior Arsenal debut 19 August 2000 v Sunderland at the Stadium of Light
(League, as substitute)
Arsenal honours League Championship 2002, 2004; FA Cup 2003
Arsenal record League: 110 (13) games, 41 goals; FA Cup: 17 (4) games,
6 goals; League Cup: 1 game, 1 goal; Europe: 41 (2) games, 8 goals;
Community Shield: 0 (1) game, 0 goals; Total: 169 (20) games, 56 goals
France caps 67

José Antonio Reyes

Position forward   **Squad number** 9
Born Utrera, Spain, 1 September 1983
Other club Sevilla
Joined Arsenal from Sevilla in January 2004
Senior Arsenal debut 1 February 2004 v Manchester City at Highbury
(League, as substitute)
Arsenal honours League Championship 2004
Arsenal record League: 7 (6) games, 2 goals; FA Cup: 2 (1) games,
2 goals; League Cup: 1 game, 0 goals; Europe: 2 (2) games, 1 goal;
Total: 12 (9) games, 5 goals
Spain caps 4

Philippe Senderos

Position defender **Squad number** 20
Born Switzerland, 14 February 1985
Other club Servette
Joined Arsenal from Servette in June 2003
Arsenal record 0 games, 0 goals

Rami Shaaban

Position goalkeeper **Squad number** 24
Born Stockholm, Sweden, 30 June 1975
Other clubs Djurgaardens IF, Zamalek, Thadosman, Nacka FF
Joined Arsenal from Djurgaardens IF in August 2002
Senior Arsenal debut 12 November 2002 v PSV Eindhoven at Highbury
(Champions League)
Arsenal record League: 3 games, 0 goals; Europe: 2 games, 0 goals;
Total: 5 games, 0 goals

Frankie Simek

Position defender **Squad number** 51
Born Missouri, United States, 13 October 1984
Joined Arsenal as scholar in August 2001, as professional in summer 2002
Senior Arsenal debut 2 December 2003 v Wolverhampton Wanderers at
Highbury (League Cup)
Arsenal record League Cup: 1 game, 0 goals; Total: 1 game, 0 goals

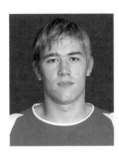

Olafur-Ingi Skulason

Position midfielder or defender **Squad number** 55
Born Reykjavik, Iceland, 1 April 1983
Other club Fylkir
Joined Arsenal summer 2001 from Fylkir
Senior Arsenal debut 2 December 2003 v Wolverhampton Wanderers
at Highbury (League Cup, as substitute)
Arsenal record League Cup: 0 (1) game, 0 goals; Total: 0 (1) game, 0 goals
Iceland caps 1

Ryan Smith

Position midfielder **Squad number** 56
Born Islington, 10 November 1986
Joined Arsenal as scholar in summer 2003
Senior Arsenal debut 28 October 2003 v Rotherham United at Highbury
(League Cup, as substitute)
Arsenal record League Cup: 0 (3) games, 0 goals; Total: 0 (3) games, 0 goals

John Spicer

Position midfielder **Squad number** 52
Born Romford, 13 September 1983
Joined Arsenal as scholar in summer 2000, as professional in summer 2001
Senior Arsenal debut 28 October 2003 v Rotherham United at Highbury
(League Cup, as substitute)
Arsenal record League Cup: 0 (1) game, 0 goals; Total: 0 (1) game, 0 goals

PLAYER PROFILES

Graham Stack

Position goalkeeper   **Squad number** 33
Born Hampstead, 26 September 1981
Other club Beveren on loan
Joined Arsenal as scholar in summer 1998, as professional in summer 2000
Senior Arsenal debut 28 October 2003 v Rotherham United at Highbury (League Cup)
Arsenal record League Cup: 5 games, 0 goals; Total: 5 games, 0 goals

IGORS STEPANOVS

Position defender   **Squad number** 26
Born Ogre, Latvia, 21 January 1976
Other clubs Skonto Riga, Beveren on loan
Joined Arsenal from Skonto Riga in September 2000
Senior Arsenal debut 1 November 2000 v Ipswich Town at Highbury (League Cup)
Arsenal record League: 17 games, 0 goals; FA Cup: 4 games, 0 goals; League Cup: 4 (1) games, 1 goal; Europe: 4 (1) games, 0 goals; Total: 29 (2) games, 1 goal
Latvia caps 57

Sebastian Svard

Position midfielder   **Squad number** 31
Born Hvidovre, Denmark, 15 January 1983
Other club FC Copenhagen, FC Copenhagen on loan, Stoke City on loan
Joined Arsenal from FC Copenhagen in November 2000
Senior Arsenal debut 27 November 2001 v Grimsby Town at Highbury (League Cup, as substitute)
Arsenal record FA Cup: 1 game, 0 goals; League Cup: 1 (1) game, 0 goals; Total: 2 (1) games, 0 goals

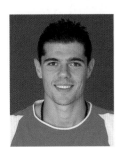

Stathis Tavlaridis

Position defender   **Squad number** 27
Born Greece, 25 January 1980
Other clubs Elpida Provata, Iraklis Saloniki, Portsmouth on loan, Lille on loan
Joined Arsenal from Iraklis in September 2001
Senior Arsenal debut 5 November 2001 v Manchester United at Highbury (League Cup)
Arsenal record League: 0 (1) game, 0 goals; League Cup: 7 games, 0 goals; Total: 7 (1) games, 0 goals

Stuart Taylor

Position goalkeeper   **Squad number** 13
Born Romford, 28 November 1980
Other clubs Bristol Rovers on loan, Crystal Palace on loan, Peterborough United on loan
Senior Arsenal debut 1 November 2000 v Ipswich Town at Highbury (League Cup)
Arsenal honours League Championship 2002; FA Cup 2003; Community Shield 2002
Arsenal record League: 16 (2) games, 0 goals; FA Cup: 3 games, 0 goals; League Cup: 4 games, 0 goals; Europe: 3 (2) games, 0 goals; Total: 26 (4) games, 0 goals

Jerome Thomas

Position midfielder   **Squad number** 53
Born Brent, 23 March 1983
Other club Queens Park Rangers on loan, Charlton Athletic (joined in January 2004)
Joined Arsenal as scholar in summer 1999, as professional in summer 2001
Senior Arsenal debut 28 October 2003 v Rotherham United at Highbury (League Cup)
Arsenal record League Cup: 1 (2) games, 0 goals

PLAYER PROFILES

Kolo Toure

Position defender **Squad number** 28
Born Ivory Coast, 19 March 1981
Other club Asec Mimosas
Joined Arsenal from Asec Mimosas in February 2002
Senior Arsenal debut 11 August 2002 v Liverpool at Millennium Stadium
(Community Shield, as substitute)
Arsenal honours League Championship 2004; FA Cup 2002; Community
Shield 2002
Arsenal record League: 45 (18) games, 3 goals; FA Cup: 7 (3) games,
2 goals; League Cup: 3 games, 0 goals; Europe: 13 (4) games, 0 goals;
Community Shield: 1 (1) games, 0 goals; Total: 69 (26) games, 5 goals
Ivory Coast caps 28

Giovanni Van Bronckhorst

Position midfielder or defender **Squad number** 16
Born Rotterdam, 5 February 1975
Other clubs Feyenoord, Waalwijk on loan, Glasgow Rangers, Barcelona on loan
Joined Arsenal from Glasgow Rangers in June 2001
Senior Arsenal debut 18 August 2001 v Middlesbrough at The Riverside
(League, as substitute)
Arsenal honours League Championship 2002
Arsenal record League: 22 (19) games, 2 goals; FA Cup: 5 (2) games, 0 goals;
League Cup: 4 games, 0 goals; Europe: 8 (3) games, 0 goals; Community
Shield: 0 (1) game, 0 goals; Total: 39 (25) games, 2 goals
Holland caps 33

Patrick Vieira

Position midfielder **Squad number** 4
Born Dakar, Senegal, 23 June 1976
Other clubs Cannes, AC Milan
Joined Arsenal from AC Milan in August 1996
Senior Arsenal debut 16 September 1996 v Sheffield Wednesday at Highbury
(League, as substitute)
Arsenal honours League Championship 1998, 2002, 2004; FA Cup 1998, 2002
Arsenal record League: 240 (7) games, 22 goals; FA Cup: 40 (2) games,
2 goals; League Cup: 7 games, 0 goals; Europe: 61 (1) games, 2 goals;
Charity/Community Shield: 4 games, 0 goals; Total: 352 (10) games, 26 goals
France caps 66

Sylvain Wiltord

Position forward **Squad number** 11
Born Neuilly sur Marne, France, 10 May 1974
Other clubs Rennes, Deportivo La Coruna, Bordeaux
Joined Arsenal from Bordeaux in August 2000
Senior Arsenal debut 6 September 2000 v Chelsea at Highbury
(League, as substitute)
Arsenal honours League Championship 2002, 2004; FA Cup 2002, 2003
Arsenal record League: 78 (28) games, 31 goals; FA Cup: 14 (6) games,
10 goals; League Cup: 7 games, 5 goals; Europe: 24 (16) games, 3 goals;
Community Shield: 1 (1) games, 0 goals; Total: 124 (51) games, 49 goals
France caps 59

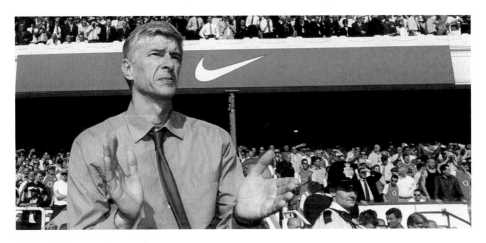

Arsène Wenger (Manager)

Born Strasbourg, France, 22 October 1949
Clubs as player Mutzig, Mulhouse, Strasbourg
Clubs as manager/coach Strasbourg (youth section), Cannes (assistant), Nancy, AS Monaco, Grampus
Eight Nagoya
Honours as manager/coach with AS Monaco French League Championship 1988, French Cup 1991,
France Manager of the Year 1988; with Grampus Eight Nagoya Emperor's Cup 1996, Japan Super Cup
1996, Japan Manager of the Year 1995; with Arsenal League Championship 1998, 2002, 2004; FA Cup
1998, 2002, 2003; Manager of the Year 1998, 2002, 2004
Joined Arsenal September 1996; First match as manager 12 October 1996
v Blackburn Rovers (a), Premier League

SENIOR OFFICIALS 2003/2004

Pat Rice (Assistant Manager)
Born Belfast, 17 March 1949.
Clubs as player Arsenal, Watford
Honours as player League Championship 1971; FA Cup
1971, 1979. Won 49 caps for Northern Ireland
Joined Arsenal as coach 1984
Honours as Arsenal coach FA Youth Cup 1988, 1994;
League Championship 1998, 2002, 2004; FA Cup 1998,
2002, 2003

Boro Primarac (First Team Coach)
Born Mostar, Yugoslavia (now Bosnia), 5 December 1954
Clubs as player Hajduk Split, Cannes, Lille. Captained
Yugoslavia, winning 18 caps
Clubs as coach Cannes, Valenciennes, Grampus Eight
Nagoya
Joined Arsenal 1997
Honours as Arsenal coach League Championship 1998,
2002, 2004; FA Cup 1998, 2002, 2003

Eddie Niedzwiecki (Reserve Team Coach)
Born Bangor, Wales, 3 May 1959
Clubs as player Wrexham, Chelsea
Honours as player Division Two Championship
with Chelsea 1984. Won 2 caps for Wales
Clubs as coach Chelsea, Reading
Joined Arsenal 2000

Gerry Peyton (Goalkeeping Coach)
Born Birmingham, 20 May 1956
Clubs as player Burnley, Fulham, Southend United
(loan), Bournemouth, Everton, Bolton Wanderers (loan),
Brentford, Chelsea (loan), West Ham United
Honours as player won 33 caps for Republic of Ireland
Clubs as coach Vissel Kobe, AIK Solna, Fulham
Joined Arsenal July 2003

Gary Lewin (Physiotherapist)
Born East Ham, London, 16 May 1964
Clubs as player Arsenal (youth), Barnet
Joined Arsenal as physio 1983
England physio since 1996

Colin Lewin (Assistant Physiotherapist)
Born Plaistow, London, 15 September 1973
Joined Arsenal 1995

Tony Colbert (Fitness Coach)
Born Paddington, London, 29 May 1963
Joined Arsenal 1998

Craig Gant (Assistant Fitness Coach/Masseur)
Born London, 27 February 1970
Joined Arsenal part-time 2000, full-time 2001

Joel Harris (Masseur)
Born Wimbledon, London, 28 August 1961
Joined Arsenal part-time 1994, full-time 1998

John Kelly (Masseur)
Born Barking, 18 March 1957
Joined Arsenal August 2002

Steve Rowley (Chief Scout)
Born Romford, 2 December 1958
Joined Arsenal 1980

Vic Akers (Kit Manager)
Born Islington, London, 24 August 1946
Clubs as player Slough Town, Cambridge United, Watford
Joined Arsenal as reserve team physio & kit manager 1986
Manager of Arsenal Ladies

Paul Akers (Assistant Kit Manager)
Born Bromley, 3 February 1976
Joined Arsenal 2001

Paul Johnson (Equipment Manager)
Born Hackney, 14 March 1961
Joined Arsenal 1981

YOUNG PROFESSIONALS

ALEX BAILEY
Position defender

ADAM BIRCHALL
Position forward

STEPHEN BRADLEY
Position midfielder

LIAM CHILVERS
Position defender

PATRICK CREGG
Position midfielder

JORDAN FOWLER
Position midfielder

RYAN GARRY
Position defender

JOHN HALLS
Position defender

INGI HOJSTED
Position midfielder

CRAIG HOLLOWAY
Position goalkeeper

JUAN
Position defender

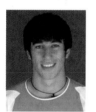

DANNY KARBASSIYOON
Position forward

SEBASTIAN LARSSON
Position midfielder

NICKY NICOLAU
Position defender

STEPHEN O'DONNELL
Position midfielder

PAULINHO
Position midfielder

ASHLEY PROBETS
Position defender

DEAN SHIELS
Position forward

These players were on Arsenal's books at the start of 2003/2004. Some may have since left the Club.

2003/2004

THIRD-YEAR SCHOLAR 2003/2004

Sam Kanu midfielder

SECOND-YEAR SCHOLARS 2003/2004

Michael Jordan goalkeeper
Neil Kilkenny midfielder
Dean McDonald forward
Sam Oji defender
Dorian Small defender
Hassan Sulaiman defender

FIRST-YEAR SCHOLARS 2003/2004

Sean Clohessy defender
Johan Djourou defender
Kerrea Gilbert defender
Matthew Hislop defender
Mark Howard goalkeeper
Issa Abdul Kadir defender
Billy Nott midfielder
Aaron Samuel forward
Daniel Spaul midfielder
Luke Webb midfielder
Chris Wright goalkeeper

These players were on Arsenal's books at the start of 2003/2004. Some may have since left the Club.

YOUTH DEVELOPMENT STAFF 2003/2004

LIAM BRADY (Head of Youth Development and Academy Director)
Born Dublin, 13 February 1956
Clubs as player Arsenal, Juventus, Sampdoria, Internazionale, Ascoli, West Ham United
Honours as player with Arsenal FA Cup 1979; with Juventus Italian Championship 1982. Won 72 caps for Republic of Ireland
Clubs as coach/manager Celtic, Brighton & Hove Albion
Joined Arsenal coaching staff 1996

DAVID COURT (Assistant Head of Youth Development and Assistant Academy Director)
Born Mitcham, 1 March 1944
Clubs as player Arsenal, Luton Town
Joined Arsenal coaching staff 1996

NEIL BANFIELD (Under-19s Coach)
Born Poplar, 20 January 1962
Clubs as player Crystal Palace, Adelaide City, Leyton Orient
Clubs as coach Charlton Athletic
Joined Arsenal 1997

STEVE BOULD (Under-17s Coach)
Born Stoke, 16 November 1962
Clubs as player Stoke City, Torquay United (loan), Arsenal, Sunderland
Honours as player with Arsenal European Cup-Winners' Cup 1994; League title 1989, 1991, 1998. Won 2 England caps
Joined Arsenal coaching staff 2001

DAVID WALES (Youth Team Physiotherapist)
Born Gateshead, 24 August 1972
Joined Arsenal 2001

JON COOKE (Youth Team Physiotherapist)
Born Colchester, 24 September 1976
Joined Arsenal September 2002 (full-time)

RESERVES

FA BARCLAYCARD PREMIERSHIP RESERVE LEAGUE (SOUTH)

Date	Opponents (Venue)	Score
Mon Aug 18	Chelsea (A)	2-3
Wed Sep 3	Ipswich Town (A)	4-1
Mon Sep 8	Tottenham Hotspur (H)	4-0
Tue Sep 16	Southampton (A)	0-2
Mon Sep 29	Charlton Athletic (A)	0-0
Tue Oct 7	Nottingham Forest (A)	3-2
Mon Oct 13	Coventry City (H)	2-2
Mon Oct 20	Fulham (H)	1-2
Mon Nov 3	Watford (H)	0-2
Tue Nov 11	Portsmouth (A)	1-1
Mon Nov 17	Wimbledon (H)	1-4
Mon Nov 24	Southampton (H)	0-1
Mon Dec 8	Charlton Athletic (H)	0-0
Tue Jan 6	Derby County (A)	0-2
Wed Jan 21	West Ham United (A)	0-2
Mon Jan 26	Chelsea (H)	2-1
Wed Feb 4	Leicester City (A)	2-2
Mon Feb 9	Ipswich Town (H)	0-2
Tue Feb 17	Coventry City (A)	2-0
Mon Feb 23	Nottingham Forest (H)	1-1
Mon Mar 1	Leicester City (H)	3-0
Tue Mar 9	Fulham (A)	3-1
Mon Mar 15	Tottenham Hotspur (A)	2-0
Mon Mar 22	Derby County (H)	4-0
Wed Apr 7	Watford (A)	0-0
Tue Apr 13	Portsmouth (H)	1-0
Wed Apr 21	Wimbledon (A)	0-0
Mon Apr 26	West Ham United (H)	3-5

APPEARANCES (SUBS IN BRACKETS) AND GOALS

Player	App	Gls	Player	App	Gls
JEREMIE ALIADIERE	7	8	DANNY KARBASSIYOON	8 (2)	0
ALEX BAILEY	17 (2)	0	SEBASTIAN LARSSON	2 (3)	0
DAVID BENTLEY	14	3	DEAN McDONALD	0 (2)	0
DENNIS BERGKAMP	1	0	NICKY NICOLAU	16 (3)	0
ADAM BIRCHALL	6 (12)	3	SAM OJI	4	0
STEPHEN BRADLEY	22 (2)	2	QUINCY OWUSU-ABEYIE	7 (3)	1
LIAM CHILVERS	1	0	MICHAL PAPADOPULOS	12	4
GAEL CLICHY	8	0	RAY PARLOUR	2	0
PATRICK CREGG	3 (3)	0	PAULINHO	8 (4)	1
PASCAL CYGAN	1	0	ASHLEY PROBETS	0 (4)	0
JOHAN DJOUROU	0 (2)	0	PHILIPPE SENDEROS	3	1
EDU	1	1	RAMI SHAABAN	8	0
FRANCESC FABREGAS	13	3	DEAN SHIELS	1 (2)	0
JORDAN FOWLER	6 (4)	0	FRANKIE SIMEK	18 (1)	0
RYAN GARRY	1	0	OLAFUR-INGI SKULASON	19 (2)	1
KERREA GILBERT	1	0	DORIAN SMALL	0 (1)	0
JOHN HALLS	4 (1)	1	RYAN SMITH	7 (6)	0
CRAIG HOLLOWAY	5	0	JOHN SPICER	23 (2)	3
MARK HOWARD	1	0	GRAHAM STACK	8	0
JUSTIN HOYTE	16	3	ANTHONY STOKES	0 (3)	0
JUAN	7	1	STATHIS TAVLARIDIS	11 (1)	1
KANU	1	0	STUART TAYLOR	6	0
MARTIN KEOWN	1	0	JEROME THOMAS	8	4

FA BARCLAYCARD PREMIER RESERVE LEAGUE SOUTH
FINAL TABLE

	P	W	D	L	F	A	Pts
Charlton Athletic	28	17	6	5	46	19	56
Derby County	28	13	10	5	46	31	49
Southampton	28	14	6	8	43	28	48
West Ham United	28	12	8	8	37	35	43
Tottenham Hotspur	28	11	9	8	42	35	42
ARSENAL	28	10	9	9	41	35	39
Chelsea	28	11	6	11	37	33	39
Leicester City	28	9	11	8	34	40	38
Coventry City	28	9	10	9	38	40	37
Wimbledon	28	9	5	14	35	47	32
Watford	28	6	12	10	32	40	30
Portsmouth	28	6	11	11	36	39	29
Nottingham Forest	28	6	11	11	33	41	29
Ipswich Town	28	8	4	16	34	44	28
Fulham	28	6	8	14	27	54	26

YOUTH TEAMS

FA ACADEMY LEAGUE UNDER-19

Date	Opponents (Venue)	Score
Sat Aug 23	Manchester United (H)	0-4
Sat Aug 30	Derby County (A)	0-0
Sat Sep 6	Millwall (H)	3-2
Sat Sep 13	Tottenham Hotspur (A)	5-3
Sat Sep 20	Southampton (H)	1-1
Sat Sep 27	Wimbledon (A)	1-2
Sat Oct 4	Chelsea (H)	4-0
Sat Oct 11	Watford (H)	3-0
Sat Oct 25	Leicester City (A)	2-0
Sat Nov 1	Bristol City (H)	3-0
Sat Nov 8	Aston Villa (A)	2-0
Sat Nov 15	Birmingham City (H)	1-1
Sat Nov 22	Fulham (A)	1-0
Sat Dec 6	Reading (A)	4-1
Sat Dec 13	Leicester City (H)	5-1
Sat Jan 10	Bristol City (H)	3-0
Sat Jan 17	Aston Villa (H)	1-2
Sat Jan 24	Birmingham City (A)	1-2
Sat Feb 7	Fulham (H)	4-1
Sat Feb 14	Reading (H)	4-2
Sat Feb 21	Chelsea (A)	1-3
Sat Feb 28	Watford (A)	2-1
Sat Mar 13	West Ham United (H)	3-1
Sat Mar 20	Norwich City (A)	0-0
Fri Mar 26	Charlton Athletic (H)	4-1
Sat Apr 3	Crystal Palace (A)	0-1

FA ACADEMY LEAGUE UNDER-17

Date	Opponents (Venue)	Score
Sat Aug 23	Manchester United (H)	2-3
Sat Aug 30	Derby County (A)	0-0
Sat Sep 6	Southampton (A)	1-1
Sat Sep 13	Charlton Athletic (H)	4-3
Sat Sep 20	Wimbledon (H)	1-0
Sat Sep 27	Millwall (H)	1-4
Sat Oct 4	West Ham United (A)	1-0
Sat Oct 11	Tottenham Hotspur (A)	0-2
Sat Oct 18	Reading (H)	2-0
Sat Oct 25	Coventry City (A)	0-3
Sat Nov 1	Aston Villa (A)	0-0
Sat Nov 8	Bristol City (H)	2-1
Sat Nov 15	Birmingham City (A)	0-1
Sat Nov 22	Watford (H)	1-3
Sat Dec 6	Leicester City (H)	3-0
Sat Dec 13	Fulham (A)	2-2
Sat Jan 10	Aston Villa (H)	0-5
Sat Jan 17	Bristol City (A)	5-3
Sat Jan 24	Birmingham City (H)	1-1
Sat Feb 14	Leicester City (A)	3-2
Sat Feb 17	Watford (A)	2-1
Sat Feb 21	Fulham (H)	2-1
Sat Mar 6	Millwall (A)	1-2
Sat Mar 13	Charlton Athletic (A)	1-1
Sat Mar 20	Crystal Palace (H)	1-0
Sat Mar 27	Coventry City (H)	3-1

FA ACADEMY LEAGUE UNDER-19 PLAY-OFFS

Date	Opponents (round)	Score
Sat Apr 24	Southampton (SF)	1-2

FA YOUTH CUP

Date	Opponents (venue)	Score
Fri Nov 28	Crawley Town (A)	9-0
Thu Jan 15	Southampton (H)	0-2

FA ACADEMY LEAGUE UNDER-19 GROUP C FINAL TABLE

	P	W	D	L	F	A	Pts
ARSENAL	26	16	4	6	58	29	52
Chelsea	26	12	3	11	40	33	39
Aston Villa	26	12	2	12	54	48	38
Birmingham City	26	10	7	9	30	24	37
Watford	26	10	5	11	38	51	35
Leicester City	26	10	4	12	40	44	34
Reading	26	9	4	13	36	40	31
Fulham	26	4	7	15	22	52	19
Bristol City	26	3	5	18	37	64	14

FA ACADEMY LEAGUE UNDER-17 GROUP C FINAL TABLE

	P	W	D	L	F	A	Pts
Aston Villa	26	16	5	5	90	41	53
Leicester City	26	14	5	7	59	54	47
Coventry City	26	12	6	8	55	46	42
ARSENAL	26	16	4	6	58	29	52
Birmingham City	26	11	7	8	52	47	40
Bristol City	26	9	3	14	55	62	30
Fulham	26	7	6	13	37	56	27
Watford	26	5	5	16	38	71	20

ARSENAL LADIES

Arsenal Ladies celebrate winning the double, making six League wins and six FA Cup triumphs in total

SEASON REVIEW

Arsenal Ladies completed another fabulously successful season by clinching the League and FA Cup double in dramatic style. Having already lifted the knockout trophy by beating Charlton Athletic, thanks to a magnificent hat-trick by Julie Fleeting, they pipped the Addicks to the Championship by a single point.

As they faced Fulham in the last match of the campaign, the title was on a knife-edge. If Arsenal won, they would take the crown, but the same applied to Fulham. To add to this, if the game ended in a draw, then Charlton would be

Champions. In the event, Vic Akers' side ran out deserved 3-1 winners, courtesy of strikes by Julie Fleeting, Lianne Sanderson and Ellen Maggs. The occasion was rendered all the more momentous as the game was played at Highbury, only a few hours after the men's team had been presented with the Premiership trophy.

To Vic, who operates in the dual roles of Arsenal Ladies manager and kit manager for their male counterparts, it meant a great deal that Arsène Wenger stayed on to watch part of the game, as did some of his players, including Patrick Vieira.

'It was marvellous to have them there, and I was delighted during the celebrations the following day when Thierry Henry made a point of shaking the hand of each member of the Ladies team and wishing them good luck. In fact, all the boys joined in the congratulations, which was a wonderful

Jayne Ludlow, the Nationwide Women's Players' Player of the Year, manager Vic Akers and Ladies captain Faye White with the League trophy after their last-day triumph over Fulham at Highbury.

demonstration of the spirit and togetherness we have at this Club.'

Vic's side suffered only two defeats all season, both to Charlton, the first at the Valley in October and the second in the League Cup semi-finals in December.

'I changed things round at Christmas, bringing in Julie Fleeting, a top goalscorer whose progress I had been monitoring ever since I first saw her playing for Scotland against England at the age of 16. Now she has played 70-odd times for her country, averaging around a goal a game, which is a phenomenal record, and she made a huge difference to us.

'We ended the season very strongly and gave ourselves a chance of the title by beating the League leaders Charlton in mid April. Eventually it all came down to the last match. What a fantastic finish. You couldn't make it up.'

It was the team's sixth League Championship, to go with their six FA Cup triumphs, and a hat-trick of honours was completed by Jayne Ludlow's selection as players' player of the year for the third time.

One of the busiest men at Highbury, Vic relishes both his jobs, somehow managing to balance the two, no matter how hectic life becomes. When there is an occasional clash of interests, he concedes that the men's team takes priority, but he continues to derive enormous satisfaction from his central involvement with Arsenal Ladies, which he set up 18 years ago.

As to the future, despite being hampered by knee problems in the spring, Vic has every intention of continuing his work with both teams. A former professional full-back who played more than 150 times for Cambridge United and Watford during the 1970s, he enjoys coaching, having learned plenty from managers ranging from Ron Atkinson at the Abbey Stadium to Arsène Wenger at Highbury.

'I've got ambitions to develop some of the young players whose parents have been bringing them to the club since they were nine and who are now knocking on the door for senior recognition.

'I believe the women's game has improved dramatically in recent years, and I hope it continues to grow in popularity.'

You can't keep a good side down: Vic Akers' side
suffered just two defeats in the 2003/04 season

FIRST-TEAM FIXTURES

(FA Women's National Premier League except where indicated)

Date	Opponents (Venue)	Score
Sun Aug 17	Tranmere Rovers (A)	9-2
Sun Aug 24	Everton (H)	0-0
Sun Aug 31	Aston Villa (A)	7-1
Sun Sep 7	Doncaster Belles (A)	2-0
Sun Sep 14	Ipswich Town (H, League Cup R1)	4-0
Sun Oct 5	Doncaster Belles (H)	7-0
Sun Oct 12	Sunderland (H, League Cup R2)	4-2
Thu Oct 16	Charlton Athletic (A)	1-2
Sun Oct 26	Fulham (A)	1-1
Sun Nov 2	Doncaster Belles (H, League Cup QF)	4-0
Sun Nov 23	Bristol Rovers (A)	3-0
Sun Dec 7	Tranmere Rovers (H)	6-0
Sun Dec 14	Charlton Athletic (A, League Cup SF)	1-2
Sun Jan 4	Stockport County (H, FA Cup R4)	3-0
Sun Jan 18	Millwall (H, London County Cup QF)	4-0
Sun Jan 25	Middlesbrough (A, FA Cup R5)	6-1
Sun Feb 8	Cardiff City (H, FA Cup QF)	11-1
Sun Feb 15	Wimbledon (A, London County Cup SF)	9-0
Sun Feb 22	Bristol Rovers (H)	3-1
Thu Mar 4	Birmingham City (A)	3-0
Sun Mar 7	Leeds United (A)	2-1
Sun Mar 14	Bristol Rovers (A, FA Cup SF)	2-0
Sun Mar 21	Leeds United (H)	4-0
Sun Mar 28	Birmingham City (H)	2-1
Sun Apr 4	Everton (A)	3-1
Wed Apr 7	Fulham (London County Cup Final)	4-0
Thu Apr 15	Charlton Athletic (H)	1-0
Sun Apr 18	Aston Villa (H)	8-0
Mon May 3	Charlton Athletic (FA Cup Final)	3-0
Sun May 16	Fulham (H)	3-1

ARSENAL LADIES OFFICIALS

VIC AKERS General Manager

CLARE WHEATLEY Development Manager

CIARA GRANT Assistant Development Officer

FAYE WHITE Assistant Development Officer

JAYNE LUDLOW Medical Officer

FRED DONNELLY Academy Director

SIAN WILLIAMS Assistant Academy Director

Ciara Grant, Clare Wheatley and Lianne Sanderson lead the celebrations after a season that saw the Ladies win both the FA Cup and the League Championship.

APPEARANCES (SUBS IN BRACKETS) AND GOALS

Player	League App	League Gls	League Cup App	League Cup Gls	FA Cup App	FA Cup Gls	London County Cup App	London County Cup Gls	Totals App	Totals Gls
ANITA ASANTE	7(6)	0	2	0	2	0	1	0	12(6)	0
EMMA BYRNE	18	0	4	0	5	0	2	0	29	0
LEANNE CHAMP	13	0	4	0	4	3	1	0	22	3
ELERI EARNSHAW	0(1)	0	0	0	1	0	0	0	1(1)	0
JULIE FLEETING	6	7	0	0	4	9	0	0	10	16
JULIE FLETCHER	0	0	1	0	0	0	0	0	1	0
CIARA GRANT	18	10	3	4	5	0	2	0	28	14
CAROL HARWOOD	0(1)	0	0	0	0	0	0	0	0(1)	0
MIHOKO ISHIDA	0(3)	0	1	0	0	0	0	0	1(3)	0
HAYLEY KEMP	2(2)	0	3(1)	1	0(1)	0	0(1)	0	5(5)	1
JUSTINE LORTON	7(3)	1	2(2)	2	0(4)	2	0(1)	0	9(10)	5
JAYNE LUDLOW	18	18	3(1)	4	5	1	2	6	28(1)	29
ELLEN MAGGS	18	9	3	0	5	2	1(1)	1	27(1)	12
KIRSTY PEALLING	18	3	3	0	3(1)	0	2	1	26(1)	4
VERONICA PHEWA	0(1)	0	0	0	0	0	0	0	0(1)	0
JO POTTER	6(10)	2	1(2)	1	3(2)	3	2	3	12(14)	8
LIANNE SANDERSON	11(4)	6	3(1)	1	3	2	2	1	19(5)	10
ALEX SCOTT	9(5)	5	2(1)	0	0(5)	0	1(1)	1	12(12)	6
EMMA THOMAS	0	0	1(1)	1	0	0	0	0	1(1)	1
YVONNE TRACY	10	1	4	0	3	1	2	0	19	2
CLARE WHEATLEY	16(1)	0	1	0	4	0	2	0	23(1)	0
FAYE WHITE	13	0	3	0	5	2	1	0	22	2
SIAN WILLIAMS	7(1)	0	0	0	1	0	1	0	9(1)	0

FA WOMEN'S NATIONAL PREMIER LEAGUE FINAL TABLE

	P	W	D	L	F	A	Pts
ARSENAL	18	15	2	1	65	11	47
Charlton Athletic	18	15	1	2	52	17	46
Fulham	18	14	2	2	60	20	44
Leeds United	18	8	4	6	32	28	28
Doncaster Belles	18	8	3	7	41	40	27
Everton	18	6	2	10	21	36	20
Birmingham City	18	4	5	9	17	31	17
Bristol Rovers	18	3	3	12	27	37	12
Aston Villa	18	1	4	13	18	63	7
Tranmere Rovers	18	1	4	13	13	63	7

ASTON VILLA

Villa Park, Trinity Road, Birmingham,
B6 6HE
Tel: 0121 327 2299
Tickets: 0121 327 5353
Website: www.avfc.co.uk

TRAVEL INFO
By Road
From the M1 take the M6. Leave the M6 at junction 6 and bear right, following signs for A38NE (not A38M). At the traffic island follow signs for city centre (A5127). After that there are signs to the stadium.
Car parking most of the street parking around Villa Park is restricted to permit holders only. The two main car parks are located at the Aston Villa Leisure Centre on Aston Hall Road, and the Brookvale Road car park, at the junction with Tame Road.

By Rail
At Birmingham New Street Station, change for Witton or Aston. This is a local service and takes about five minutes to reach Aston. From there the ground is about a ten-minute walk. A further three minutes along the line is Witton, which is closer to Villa Park. However, not all trains travel to Witton.

By Bus
The number 7 goes closest to Villa Park and can be caught outside McDonalds in High Street in the city centre, a five-minute walk from the train station. Bus stops at Trinity Road or Witton Island. You can also catch numbers 102 or 104, which stop on Lichfield Road about ten minutes away from the ground.

League position 2003/2004 6th

BIRMINGHAM CITY

St Andrews, Birmingham, B9 4NH
Tel: 0121 772 0101
Tickets: 0121 202 5333
Website: www.bcfc.com

TRAVEL INFO
By Road
Leave the M6 at junction 6, follow signs for city centre (A38M). Leave the A38M at the second exit, turning left onto the ring road A450. Continue on the ring road until you reach the fourth traffic island. Turn left into Coventry Road and soon you will see the stadium.
Car parking limited street parking available, there are also large pay car parks near stadium.

By Rail
The stations are Birmingham New Street or Birmingham Moor Street, a 20-minute walk from the ground.

By Bus
Numbers 15, 15A and 17 run from Birmingham New Street station along Coventry Road. Numbers 96 and 97 run from Carrs Lane (behind High Street) to Garrison Lane.

League position 2003/2004 10th

BLACKBURN ROVERS

Ewood Park, Blackburn, BB2 4JF
Tel: 08701 113 232
Tickets: 08701 123 456
Website: www.rovers.co.uk

TRAVEL INFO
By Road

Exit the M6 at junction 31, or take the A59/A677, following signs for Blackburn, then the A666. After 1.5 miles turn left into Kidder Street. From the east, use the A679 or A667 and follow the signs for Bolton Road, then follow directions as above.

Car parking there are extensive secure private parks adjacent to the stadium, allowing for up to 800 vehicles, but only if pre-booked. There is street parking within a short walking distance of Ewood Park and there are a few car parks off the A666 Bolton Road.

By Rail

The nearest railway stations are at Blackburn (1.5 miles) and Mill Hill (1 mile).

By Bus

Use any bus from the Blackburn town centre heading for Darwen and it will drop you off two minutes from the ground.

League position 2003/2004 15th

BOLTON WANDERERS

Reebok Stadium, Burnden Way,
Lostock, Bolton, BL6 6JW
Tel: 01204 673673
Tickets: 0871 871 2932
Website: www.bwfc.co.uk

TRAVEL INFO
By Road

Exit the M61 at junction 6, and take the first exit off the slip road roundabout onto the A6027 Mansell Way. Go straight over the roundabout and take the slip road for the car parks.

Car parking there are 2,000 spaces at the ground, including an away area (section A). There are few roads to park in around the stadium because of its out-of-town location.

By Rail

Horwich Parkway is immediately outside the stadium.

By Bus

Bus station at Trinity Street. Football specials run from Bolton city centre to the stadium, otherwise catch the number 11 from outside the court house in Black Horse Street.

League position 2003/2004 8th

TRAVELLING WITH ARSENAL

CHARLTON ATHLETIC

The Valley, Floyd Road, Charlton,
London, SE7 8BL
Tel: 020 8333 4000
Tickets: 020 8333 4010
Website: www.cafc.co.uk

TRAVEL INFO
By Road
Leave the M25 at junction 2, stay on that road until it becomes the A102(M). Continue along the A102(M) until you reach the exit sign for Woolwich Ferry. Turn right onto the A206 Woolwich Road. At the first set of traffic lights turn right and Floyd Road is the second turning on the left.
Car parking there is a large car park at the Valley behind the West Stand, plus plenty of street parking in the area.

By Rail
Charlton train station is one minute's walk from the Valley. Exit the station to Charlton Church Lane, and across the road you will see a row of shops to your right; turn down the road to the left of them, and the visitors' stand is down a turning on the right.

By Bus
The following buses stop at or near the Valley: 161, 177, 180, 380 and 472.

League position 2003/2004 7th

CHELSEA

Stamford Bridge, London, SW6 1HS
Tel: 020 7385 5545
Tickets: 0906 600 7760
Website: www.chelseafc.co.uk

TRAVEL INFO
By Road
From the north, west and east: go to junction 15 of the M25, and turn onto the M4 towards London. Follow it until it becomes the A4, staying on it over the Hammersmith Flyover and for a further 1.5 miles before turning off for Earls Court. Go past Earls Court station and round the one-way system until you hit Fulham Road, then turn right at the traffic lights. Go straight on for 600 yards and the ground is on your right.
From the south head for Wandsworth Bridge to cross the river, then head straight up Wandsworth Bridge Road. At the junction with New Kings Road turn right and then immediately left. This will take you up to Fulham Broadway; turn right onto Fulham Road and the ground is 400 yards on your left.
Car parking very limited. It's advisable to park away from the ground and travel by Tube.

By Tube
Fulham Broadway and West Brompton stations are within easy walking distance.

By Bus
Plenty of buses to the ground from central London.

League position 2003/2004 2nd

CRYSTAL PALACE

Selhurst Park, London, SE25 6PU
Tel: 020 8768 6000
Tickets: 020 8771 8841
Website: www.cpfc.co.uk

TRAVEL INFO
By Road
From the east M25 then A20 signposted London. After 4 miles, turn left onto the A224, signposted St Mary Cray. After 3 miles, turn onto the A232 spur road and follow this until you see Shirley Park Golf Club, then turn right onto the A215 Shirley Road. Turn right at the top of this road, then first left into the A215 Spring Road. After 1.5 miles, turn left onto the B266 and the ground is a quarter of a mile on the left.
From the north and west M1 to A406 North Circular Road heading west to Chiswick roundabout. Take the third exit at the roundabout onto Chiswick High Road, then first left onto the A205 signposted Kew. After 2 miles, take a left at the T-junction signposted Putney. Continue until the road merges with the A3, then a mile later turn right onto the A214 signposted Tooting and Streatham. When in Streatham, turn right onto the A23 Streatham High Road and after one mile, turn left into the B273 Green Lane which becomes Parchmore Road. At the bottom of the road, turn left into the High Street, go straight over the crossroads and the ground is on the right.

By Rail
Norwood Junction, Selhurst and Thornton Heath stations all close to ground (10 to 15-minute walk).

League position 2003/2004 6th in Division One, promoted via play-offs.

EVERTON

Goodison Park, Liverpool, L4 4EL
Tel: 0151 330 2200
Tickets: 09068 121 599
Website: www.evertonfc.com

TRAVEL INFO
By Road
From the M6 join the M58 at junction 26. Continue until the end of the M58. At the gyratory, go left to join the M57 at junction 7. Exit the M57 at junction 4 to turn right into the A580 East Lancashire Road. Follow the road across Queens Drive into Walton Lane. Goodison Road is less than a mile long and the ground is on the right.
Car parking the Stanley Park car park next to the ground has 1,000 spaces.

By Rail
Liverpool Lime Street station is about two miles from Goodison Park. Kirkdale Station is a ten-minute walk from the ground.

By Bus
Numbers 17 or 217 from stand L outside Lime Street station.

League position 2003/2004 17th

FULHAM

Craven Cottage, Stevenage Road,
Fulham, London, SW6 6HH
(Fulham are currently ground-sharing
with Queens Park Rangers at Loftus Road
South Africa Road, London, W12 7PA but may
return to Craven Cottage for the new season)
Tel: 020 7893 8383   Tickets: 0870 442 1234
Website: www.fulhamfc.co.uk

TRAVEL INFO
By Road
From the south follow A3 signs for Hammersmith,
take A219 to Shepherds Bush. Head towards the White
City and Wood Lane, turn left into South Africa Road.
From the north take the M1 onto A406 West, then A40
at Hanger Lane to Cent. London. Turn off to White City,
right into Wood Lane, then right into Sth Africa Road.
From the east take the A40(M) Westway, turn off to
White City, left into Wood Lane, then right into
South Africa Road.
From the west take the M4 to Chiswick, A315 and
A402 to Shepherds Bush, then head towards White
City and Wood Lane, turn left into South Africa Road.
Car parking spaces available in the BBC car park
on match days.

By Rail
Acton Central station is the closest to the ground,
bus or taxi then needed.

By Bus
Number 283 to Bloemfontein Road; numbers 72,
95, 220 to White City station.

By Tube
Loftus road is a five-minute walk from White City
station (Central Line). Alternatively go to Shepherds
Bush on the Hammersmith & City Line, the ground
is a ten-minute walk from there.

League position 2003/2004 9th

LIVERPOOL

Anfield Road, Liverpool, L4 0TH
Tel: 0151 263 2361
Tickets: 0870 444 4949
Website: www.liverpoolfc.tv

TRAVEL INFO
By Road
Take the M6 then M62 until the end of motorway.
Then turn right at signs for the A5058 into Queens
Drive. After 3 miles, turn left into Utting Avenue.
Then turn right into Anfield Road for the ground.
Car parking it's residents-only parking near the
ground so try a little further out or use the car parks
at Stanley Park, Anfield Comprehensive on Priory
Road or at Goodison off Bullens Road.

By Rail
Liverpool Lime Street is about 3 miles away from the
ground. An alternative is to park at one of the stations
on the Merseylink Northern Line – Ormskirk, Kirkby,
Southport, Bootle – and get the train to Sandhills, just
over a mile from the ground.

By Bus
Catch numbers 17, 17C, 17D, or 217 from Queen's Sq.
by Liverpool Lime Street station. Numbers 26 and 27
run from Paradise Street.

League position 2003/2004 4th

MANCHESTER CITY

City of Manchester Stadium,
Rowsley Street, Eastlands,
Manchester, M11 3FF
Tel: 0161 231 3200
Tickets: 0161 226 2224
Website: www.mcfc.co.uk

TRAVEL INFO
By Road
Leave the M6 at junction 19, follow the signs for the M56, then join the M60. Head anti-clockwise and leave the M60 at junction 23. Turn right onto Ashton Road (A662) and you can see the stadium from there. *Car parking* at the Velodrome, next to Asda.

By Rail
Manchester Piccadilly is 20 minutes' walk from the City of Manchester Stadium. A smaller station, Ashburys, is situated on Alan Turing Way and is 15 minutes' walk to the stadium.

By Bus
There are plenty of buses from the city centre and from Ashton-under-Lyne. Direct services include numbers 53, 54, 185, 186, 216, 217, 230, 231, 232, 233, 234, 235, 236, 237, X36 and X37.

League position 2003/2004 16th

MANCHESTER UNITED

Sir Matt Busby Way, Old Trafford,
Manchester, M16 0RA
Tel: 0161 868 8000
Tickets: 0870 757 1968
Website: www.manutd.com

TRAVEL INFO
By Road
Leave the M6 at junction 19, follow signs for the M56, then join the M60. Go clockwise on the M60, leave at junction 9 and join Parkway (A5081) heading towards Trafford Park. At the first traffic island take third exit on to Village Way and remain on this road until the next island (controlled by traffic lights). Here take the second exit and join Wharfside Way, from which Old Trafford is visible. *Car parking* use official secure car parks, identified by brown location signs on all approaches to the stadium.

By Rail
The overland train from Piccadilly and Manchester Oxford Road stop at the ground itself, though large groups of fans may not be allowed on. The Old Trafford Metrolink station is half a mile away from the ground. To walk it, come out of station into Warwick Road. Go straight over the lights and straight over the crossroads by the Old Trafford pub into Sir Matt Busby Way.

By Bus
Numbers 252, 253, 254, 525, 256, 257, 17, 114 and 236 run from Manchester Piccadilly to Old Trafford.

League position 2003/2004 3rd

MIDDLESBROUGH

Riverside Stadium, Middlesbrough,
TS3 6RS
Tel: 01642 877 700
Tickets: 01642 877 809
Website: www.mfc.co.uk

TRAVEL INFO
By Road
Take the A19 all the way to Middlesbrough, until the junction with the A66, south of the River Tees. Turn right onto the northern route and follow for two miles. Exit the A66 when you see the sign for St Hilda's and take the first left off the roundabout. Follow through to the traffic lights into Dockside Road. The stadium is on the right.

Car parking: none at the ground. There's a pay-and-display at Sainsburys on Denmark Street (not just for customers); also the Bretnall car park – take second exit from A66, after roundabout turn right, then go straight over at the lights and turn left at the next lights. Also there is plenty of street parking if you are prepared to walk.

By Rail
Middlesbrough station is less than a mile from the ground. To walk it, come down the steps and turn left, avoiding the ticket office. Turn right, and go straight at the crossroads towards the Bridge pub in Bridge Street East. Turn right into Windward Way and you will see the ground.

By Bus
Numbers 36, 37 and 38 run from the bus station to North Ormesby. Take the underpass from there to the ground.

League position 2003/2004 11th

NEWCASTLE UNITED

St James' Park,
Newcastle-upon-Tyne, NE1 4ST
Tel: 0191 201 8400
Tickets: 0191 261 1571
Website: www.nufc.co.uk

TRAVEL INFO
By Road
From the A1(M), after Washington Services and junction 65, the motorway divides. Keep left, following signs for the A1. Take the centre or right-hand lane and continue following signs for Newcastle and air-port. Pass the Angel of the North on the right and continue for a further 3 miles before turning left onto the A184, signposted Gateshead/Newcastle centre. Continue for 1.5 miles, then take the right-hand lane signposted A189 to Newcastle. This takes you over the Redheugh Bridge, which leads into St James' Boulevard. After half a mile turn left at Gallowgate roundabout and the stadium is on the right.
Car parking parks near the ground include the St James' and Corporation Street. There is a multi-storey Greenmarket car park signposted from Corporation Street.

By Rail
Newcastle Central is half a mile from the ground. To walk it, cross the road towards the Bakers Oven and turn right down Central Street. Turn left into Grainger Street and left again into Westgate Road. Turn right into Bath Lane and the ground is on your right. The Metro station is next to the stadium, though if you are taking the Metro it may be quicker to walk from Monument station instead.

By Bus
There are plenty of buses which head for the ground. Get off at Gallowgate.

League position 2003/2004 5th

NORWICH CITY

Carrow Road, Norwich, NR1 1JE
Tel: 01603 760 760
Tickets: 0870 444 1902
Website: www.canaries.co.uk

TRAVEL INFO
By Road
Take the M11, then the A11. Turn right onto the A47, skirting Norwich to the south. Leave the A47 at the Trowse Newton junction, and Carrow Road is sign-posted from there.

Car parking there is a large car park at the ground, but this is for season ticket holders only. The closest pay-and-display is located in Rouen Road, and holds about 500 cars. The town centre is a 15-minute walk from the ground.

By Rail
The ground is a ten-minute walk from Norwich station. Walk along Riverside Road and into Carrow Road.

League position 2003/2004 1st in Division One

PORTSMOUTH

Fratton Park, Frogmore Road,
Portsmouth, PO4 8RA
Tel: 023 9273 1204
Tickets: 023 9261 8777
Website: www.pompeyfc.co.uk

TRAVEL INFO
By Road
From the north and west: take M27 and M275 to the end, then take the second exit at the roundabout. After a quarter of a mile turn right at the T-junction into London Road (A2047). After another mile or so cross the railway bridge and turn left into Goldsmith Avenue. Turn left into Frogmore Road half a mile later.

From the east take A27 following Southsea signs (A2030). Turn left at the roundabout (3 miles) onto A288, then right into Priory Crescent and next right into Carisbrooke Road.

Car parking look for street parking, or use the park at the Bridge Centre in Fratton Road.

By Rail
Portsmouth mainline train station is a half-an-hour's walk from Fratton Park. Most trains to Portsmouth also stop at Fratton station, and this is only a ten-minute walk from the ground. Walk over the bridge and turn left into Goldsmith Avenue. Carry on until you reach Apsley Road and the visiting supporters' turnstiles are directly ahead.

By Bus
Number 13 from Commercial Road South, Fratton Bridge, Goldsmith Avenue, White House, Furze Lane; numbers 17 or 18 from the Hard Interchange, Commercial Road, Victoria Road North/Elm Grove, Highland Road Post Office, White House, Goldsmith Avenue, Fratton Bridge, Commercial Road. Other services which stop close to the ground include numbers 3, 13, 16, 16A, 24 and 27 (all Fratton Bridge), 4, 4A and 6 (all Milton Road).

League position 2003/2004 13th

SOUTHAMPTON

The Friends Provident
St Mary's Stadium, Britannia Road,
Southampton, SO14 5FP
Tel: 0870 2200 000   Tickets: 0870 220 0150
Website: www.saintsfc.co.uk

TRAVEL INFO
By Road
It is not advisable to drive to the ground on a match day unless you have a pass for one of the nearby car parks. Surrounding roads are subject to police road closures.

However, if you do go by car, here are directions. Drive to the end of the M3 southbound and get onto the M27 eastbound. Leave M27 at junction 4 (first junction you approach) and follow signs to A33 into Southampton. Continue to the end of this road (The Avenue). The road merges into Dorset Street. Continue until you reach roundabout, then take second exit (Six Dials); on the dual carriageway stay in the right-hand lane and go through traffic lights; continue into Kingsway (following A33 on road signs). Drive approximately a quarter of a mile and take the fourth left into St Mary's Street. Follow bend to right into Chapel Road and continue to end of road. Turn left into Marine Parade and stadium is approx 600 metres on the left.

Car parking extremely limited so the club has set up numerous alternatives. Spaces can be booked, via the ticket line, for car parks and also for the park-and-ride schemes operated by the club.

By Rail
From the Southampton Central station to the ground is a 25-minute walk. There is also a free shuttle bus service running to the stadium from the station, operating from the Blechynden Terrace bus stop. Fans using this service will be required to show the bus driver their match or season ticket.

There are several local line stations that are within 15 minutes of the ground. These include Bitterne, Woolston and St Denys.

By Bus
All season and matchday tickets include free matchday travel vouchers for use before and after the game in the central Southampton area bounded by Totton, Bassett Roundabout, Hamble, Portsmouth Road (Veals), Bursledon Road (Botley Road) and Calmore. Vouchers are valid on both Solent Blue Line and First Bus services and are not transferable. They must be detached from the match ticket in the presence of the driver. Extra buses will be laid on for matchday travel.

The following services pass by the stadium on Northam Road: numbers 3/3A, 5/5A and 8A (First Southampton); 18/19 (Solent Blue Line). The following services operate via Itchen Bridge which is within sight of the stadium and only a short walk away: numbers 8, 10/10A, 11/11A, 16 and 17/17A (First Southampton).

On Foot
The stadium is a signposted ten-minute walk from the city centre.

League position 2003/2004 12th

TOTTENHAM HOTSPUR

White Hart Lane, Bill Nicholson Way,
748 High Road, Tottenham,
London, N17 OAP
Tel: 020 8365 5000
Tickets: 0870 420 5000
Website: www.spurs.co.uk

TRAVEL INFO
By Road
Take A406 North Circular to Edmonton and at traffic lights follow signs for Tottenham (A1010 – High Road) to the ground.
Car parking there is limited car parking in surrounding streets. Probably best to park at a train station north of ground.

By Rail
Use White Hart Lane, Northumberland Park or Seven Sisters stations.

By Tube
Use Seven Sisters (Victoria Line) or Manor House (Piccadilly Line).

By Bus
The following bus services frequently pass the ground: number 149 Ponders End Garage to Liverpool Street Station; number 259 Edmonton Green to King's Cross; number 279 Waltham Cross to Holloway.

League position 2003/2004 14th

WEST BROMWICH ALBION

The Hawthorns, West Bromwich,
West Midlands, B71 4LF
Tel: 0121 525 8888 (all departments)
Website: www.wba.co.uk

TRAVEL INFO
By Road
Leave the M6 at junction 8, continue south on the M5 for 1.5 miles. Exit the M5 at junction 1. The stadium is half a mile along the A41.
Car parking there is ample off-street parking and pay parks near the ground.

By Rail
The Hawthorns railway station is situated on Halfords Lane, 250 metres south of the stadium itself. There is also a Metro tram link which services the main route from Birmingham to Wolverhampton. Otherwise, from New Street, head for Smethwick Rolfe Street (ten-minute walk).

By Bus
Numbers 74, 77, 79 and 450 all pass the ground.

League position 2003/2004 2nd in Division One

ARSENAL'S NEW STADIUM

Arsenal will kick off the 2006/2007 season in front of 60,000 fans packed inside a new state-of-the-art stadium which will be quarter of a mile away from Highbury. The announcement in February 2004 that funding for the new stadium had been secured was greeted as the most significant statement in the modern history of the Club. It followed four and a half years of intense discussion, negotiation and speculation, and enabled construction work to forge ahead untrammelled by uncertainty.

The creation of the Gunners' new home, which will enable the Club to compete at the highest level for the foreseeable future, involved one of the most complicated redevelopment programmes London has ever known, including thousands of legal agreements. Among the major aspects of the scheme is the relocation of the North London Waste Authority's waste transfer unit and Islington Council's vehicle maintenance depot, currently operating from the site but destined for a new start at Lough Road, near the Caledonian Road Tube station.

Although the move from Highbury was unavoidable, the Club is keen to preserve its heritage and fans have been encouraged to contribute ideas for a time capsule which will be sunk deep under the new stadium. The response has been massive and the most popular ideas to date include a list of every man to play for Arsenal, Tony Adams' captain's armband, a piece of Highbury turf, all the Gunners' home shirts, a replica model of Highbury and some marble from the famous marble

The projected finish for the new stadium is August 2006 and as of June 2004, much of the foundation work at the construction site was already completed. The outer shell of the stadium is beginning to take shape, with four cores (pictured) giving an idea as to the stadium's size. It is hoped that by the end of the 2004/2005 season three of the four stands will have been constructed.

The pedestrian bridge to the north of the site has been raised and 'launched' over the railway line with the southern bridge expected to be lowered over Drayton Park station in August 2004.

For all the up-to-date news on the new stadium site and the latest pictures visit www.arsenal.com/thestadium.